Woody and his Women

Woody and his Women

TIM CARROLL

WARNER BOOKS

A *Warner* Book

Published in Great Britain by Little, Brown and Company in 1993

This edition published by Warner in 1994

Copyright © 1993 by Tim Carroll

The moral right of the author has been asserted

A CIP catalogue record for this book
is available from the British Library

ISBN 0 7515 0493 9

Typeset by Solidus (Bristol) Limited
Printed and bound in Great Britain by
Clays Ltd, St. Ives plc

Warner Books
A Division of
Little, Brown and Company (UK)
Brettenham House,
Lancaster Place
London WC2E 7EN

Contents

Acknowledgements

Many thanks to Jack Victor for many pleasurable hours discussing Woody's youth, and for checking the first chapters of the book. Thanks too, to Woody's second wife, Louise Lasser, for her insights into the years of his life which have not received the scrutiny they deserve, and also for checking the chapters she contributed to.

Woody's high school friend Bryna Goldstein, her brother Paul and mother Sadie provided invaluable help, as did Alan Lapidus. Woody's other childhood friends Elliott Mills and Mickey Rose supplied valuable insights into his work and childhood.

With appreciation to: Douglas Brode, Kathleen Carroll, Susan Crimp, Paul Francis, Wendy Leigh, Stella and Arnold Levy, Marsha Leis, Harvey Meltzer, Zachary Meltzer, Richard Mineards, Arnold Marx, Tony Schwartz, Linda Swidenbank, Vicky Tiel and Simon Winder.

Thanks to those who do not wish to be identified. Most of all, thanks to my editor Hilary Foakes for originally suggesting the idea and patiently nursing it to fruition with her colleague Martin Bryant.

Prologue

'I've always felt more sanguine about women than about men … They're more mature, less bellicose, more gentle. They're closer to what life's supposed to be about. They bring up kids. Men are stiffer, don't cry, die of heart attacks. Women are just more into nature. They know what sex should be. They never disassociate sex with love.'

Woody Allen[1]

Women are the centre of Woody Allen's world. His movies deal almost exclusively with that complex web which binds the sexes during their brief, sometimes sad and often comical odyssey through life. Uniquely among contemporary movie makers, almost all Allen's films reflect his *own* tortuous grappling with the meaning of life in a seemingly senseless universe, amidst a series of passionate and emotionally perplexing interludes with women.

His romantic comedies have touched the hearts of millions. Since the enchanting love story of *Annie Hall* and a string of bitter-sweet tales from *Manhattan* to *Broadway Danny Rose*, and *Hannah and Her Sisters*, this prolific film maker has tapped a rich vein of melancholy which provokes tears as well as laughter, joy as well as pain. His Oscar-winning work, which features so many easily identifiable characters and memorable scenes, prompted excited speculation about his own love life and the desires and motivations behind America's greatest cinema 'auteur'.

Here we find Mia Farrow, the wide-eyed flower child who won and lost Hollywood's hard living 'rat-packer'

Frank Sinatra, the waif-like actress who lured composer André Previn into her arms, the compulsive mother who bore bachelor Woody his only child and directed him into fatherhood. Here also is one of the greatest friendships in his life – Diane Keaton, who started as a misfit actress but turned into a major movie star. This is the woman who poured intense adoration on Woody only to desert him for the brooding Al Pacino and ladykiller Warren Beatty.

Woody Allen's life has been the source of intense speculation since his early days as a stand-up comic when he appeared to begin laying bare his inner neuroses for the world to see. His gags referred to real people, and for years fans assumed that his films were an ongoing cinematic portrayal of his own progress through life. *Annie Hall* bore so much resemblance to his relationship with Diane Keaton, that it was hard to credit his disclaimers to the contrary. It was difficult to accept that *Hannah and Her Sisters* was not Mia Farrow and her family. The movie was shot in Mia's home, it included her mother and her children, yet Woody insisted the story was 'fiction'.

Rumour ran riot as each new film appeared to chart a new twist to the tangled web that he spun around the loves of his life. He was said to have fallen for Mariel Hemingway, his beautiful teenage lover on screen in *Manhattan*. It was reported once that cast and crew were convinced that he had become close to *Hannah and Her Sisters* screen wife Dianne Wiest, a claim that both parties denied. The Australian actress Judy Davis laughed off implications that she had fallen for the diminutive director. Woody was said to be annoyed that Warren Beatty had 'stolen' Diane Keaton, and wreaked light-hearted revenge with a withering portrayal of his alleged rival in two of his movies.

But it was not until last year, when he walked unwittingly into a headline hitting story which could have been one of his own scripts, that the real nature of his work was

2

revealed and the true nature of his links with the women of his world were exposed. Ironically, Woody had built an international career by transforming his petty problems and minor worries into some of the greatest cinematic comedy of his generation. Now the biggest tragedy of his life was turning into a worldwide spectacle attracting a bigger audience than he had ever called for. They were watching a script of his own making, but unlike those movie favourites which had won him a loyal audience in every corner of the globe, this drama had never been intended for celluloid.

Nevertheless, on a suitably grey and bleakly Allen-esque day which would have done for the settings of one of his own New York stories, the television cameras were there to record him acknowledging the news which had knocked Fergie and Princess Diana off the front pages, and was to turn the reclusive man into a tabloid star as the protective shroud of secrecy surrounding his world was ripped apart. The 56-year-old film maker acknowledged he had fallen in love with the adopted daughter of his long-time love Mia Farrow, Soon-Yi Previn, and that he was suing for custody of three of their children. He categorically denied accusations of molesting Mia's seven-year-old child Dylan.

'My first lines in years and all straight,' he quipped, leaving the hastily prepared Plaza Hotel press conference held to quell the avalanche of increasingly sensational headlines following his bust-up with Mia Farrow. The man who had jealously guarded his privacy for decades became the subject of frenzied speculation, unfaltering adoration and intense hatred.

On hearing the news André Previn announced that he would have 'hoped for better' for his adopted daughter, while Frank Sinatra was less circumspect and it was even suggested later, privately offered to break Woody's legs.[2] Mia Farrow's mother, Maureen O'Sullivan, the veteran actress who had appeared in *Hannah and Her Sisters*, and once known best as Jane to Johnny Weissmuller's Tarzan, condemned her daughter's ex-lover as an 'evil, evil man'.[3] Mia's sister Tisa joined in the tirade, and even her adopted son Moses – who, it was said, once idolised Allen – appeared on CNN to berate the man he had adored.

Characteristically for those who knew him, Woody's father, Martin Konigsberg, appeared unmoved by the scandal and indifferent to the implications for his son. Brushing questions aside, he said Mia was a 'sweet girl' but he had never had any time for the showbiz community and the things they get up to.[4] Even so, he offered a crumb of comfort to Woody by casting doubt on the veracity of the allegations. Privately, friends knew that Martin and his wife Nellie were devastated by the crisis. Meanwhile old lines of Allen's surfaced to haunt him and a gleeful press lost no time in reprinting them with painful regularity.

> 'You're a kid, and I never want you to forget that, I mean, you're gonna meet a lot of terrific men in your life and, you know, I want you to enjoy me, my wry sense of humour and astonishing sexual technique ... As long as the cops don't burst in we're, you know, I think we're gonna break a couple of records.'
>
> Isaac to Tracy in *Manhattan*

> 'Child molestation is a touchy subject ... Read the papers! Half the country's doing it!'
>
> *Hannah and Her Sisters*

> 'I'm dating a girl who does homework.'
>
> *Manhattan*

> In another film, a wise man advises that the secret of life is a steady diet of 'two blonde 12-year-old girls whenever possible'.
>
> *Love and Death*

His pal Tony Roberts in *Annie Hall* speculates on the mathematical possibilities of his romp with 16-year-old twins.

From a short story published in 1980: 'I am in love with two women, not a terribly uncommon problem. That they happen to be mother and child? All the more challenging!'

Side Effects

Husbands and Wives opened as the world was beginning to learn about the ageing director's affair with Soon-Yi. 'Why is it I keep hearing 50,000 dollars worth of psychotherapy trying to dial 911?', he asks as the ageing English professor, Gabe Roth, furiously trying to dampen his passion for a precocious and pouting 19-year-old student, Juliette Lewis, a line that won more laughs than he had originally intended it to.

Mia and Woody drafted in legal heavyweights to fight their corner. His were to portray Mia as the classic spurned woman, with an unbalanced mind and bitter about his new girlfriend. Woody's lawyers went to great lengths to justify the claim that he had never had a father-daughter relationship with Soon-Yi. Mia meanwhile hired celebrity lawyer Alan Dershowitz to cast doubt on Woody's already tarnished reputation, to question his perplexing views of morality and to challenge his adequacy as a father.

It was a Nineties variation of the child sex scandals which brought down one of Woody's own heroes, Charlie Chaplin, and the more recent scandal that saw Mia's movie mentor Roman Polanski knocked off his perch. Starlet loving Chaplin had been exiled to Switzerland after being labelled 'abnormal' and 'degenerate' in the face of a paternity suit. Polanski fled the country when he was caught making love to an underage girl in Jack Nicholson's house. But the Woody and Mia bust-up went one better, for the uncrowned king and queen of Manhattan stood captured in the constant glare of a relentless media. The two unlikely protagonists faced one another across the same Central Park over which they used to blow kisses but now exchanged vitriolic volleys of accusations and counter charges.

The accusations were serious and involved the emotional and physical security of young children and a girl of tender age. But as befits a move maker who could make people smile when they should have been crying, the audience of his private woes wallowed in the humour rather than the tragedy of the director's personal predicament. Reporters could hardly stifle their giggles at the familiar startled look of Woody's eyes behind those owlish glasses, as he confronted yet another outlandish allegation from his angelic and wide-eyed ex-lover, dressed in her Catholic convent girl clothes and leading her children around like a badge of maternal honour.

We learnt that after Mia discovered her daughter was sleeping with Woody, the actress would phone the director on the other side of the Park in his Fifth Avenue apartment, in the early hours and threaten mayhem. But it was hard *not* to laugh at the image of an alarmed Woody cringing beneath the bedsheets in the dead of the night as a telephone rings in the distance, which was too much like a scene from one of his films – the perpetually harassed Kleinman of *Shadows and Fog* who is roused from his sleep by vigilantes on the look out for a killer.

It was claimed that Mia even joked about poisoning his wine, and a nervous Woody had responded by bringing supplies of his own food whenever he had to stay over at her Connecticut farm. As an extra precaution he would remove sharp pointed gardening tools from the outhouse in case Mia should be gripped by unbridled hostile passions in the middle of the night. Woody had never been happy in the countryside apparently, because of an irrational and inexplicable fear of deer.

Mia told how Woody had rolled around on the floor complaining of a stomach ache when she started to tell André Previn of the affair with Soon-Yi. 'Don't tell André! Don't tell André!' wailed Woody.[5]

It was not difficult to imagine him wearing that familiar look of anguish, pacing backwards and forwards in his book-lined living room high above Manhattan, wringing his hands at the impossible imbroglio he had found himself in. The donnish movie maestro who refused to talk about anything but his work was transformed into a living parody of his own neurotic screen persona, sitting on the analyst's couch with reporters from *Newsweek* and *Time*.

'We'd chat when I came over to Mia's house,' he confessed to *Time*'s Walter Isaacson. 'It started to become hotter and heavier late last year, very late. We had a number of conversations, saw a couple of movies, and you know it just – well, I can't say there was a cataclysmic moment. My flair for drama. What can I say?'[6]

Woody Allen could say more but has jealously guarded his private life with the help of a loyal cadre of friends and associates who have shored up the carefully constructed wall of secrecy around his world.

But here, for the first time, is the authentic story of Woody Allen and his women. It's the story that he would not want to come out, if only to perpetuate the image of the quiet and guileless New York intellectual which had become so endearing to his army of fans who related to their idol more strongly than any other cinema clique. The truth is not particularly shocking in film circles where audience acclaim and financial success bring their own unique rewards. But it's a truth which will surprise those fans who associate his screen image as a hapless loser with the real person. This is the true story of an unlikely Casanova, a maestro of the movies who in one instant can seduce and charm women and in another, make them shake with fear.

Woody is a wealthy film star and movie mogul in his own right, and like the Lotharios of Hollywood legend, he is used to having his every whim catered for, albeit in his Manhattan penthouse rather than by a fabled Beverly Hills poolside. He has long displayed the foibles and fantasies of the jet set, relishing his Rolls Royce and front stage seats at the best restaurants.

Once on a movie set, Woody lived up to the most degrading traditions of Tinseltown by 'winning' in a bet a young costume designer whom he ordered to strip off and join him in bed.[7] And although he has never been known to deploy the notorious casting couch, he has demonstrated a penchant for hiring beautiful actresses, from John F. Kennedy's girlfriend, Daryl Hannah and *Basic Instinct*'s sultry star, Sharon Stone, to the blooming delights of *Wish You Were Here* starlet, Emily Lloyd and *Cape Fear* sensation, Juliette Lewis.

Woody has been praised as one of the few male directors to be sensitive to women's needs and aspirations. He claims to see most of himself *not* in the stereotypical hypochondriacs of his *Hannah and Her Sisters* persona, Mickey Sachs, or *Annie Hall*'s Alvy Singer, but in the contemplative women he created for his more serious works of *Interiors* and *Another Woman*. His closest friends are female, from his sister Letty to the small circle of women who work with him and enjoy his company at Elaine's.

But his two marriages were failures. The first ended bitterly; his wife later threatened to sue him for holding her up to ridicule and scorn. After his second marriage to comedienne Louise Lasser he was never to marry again, and only lived with another woman briefly when Diane Keaton came into his life. Woody has been the victim of women preying on his success, but he's also demonstrated a liking for easily impressed girls who fall readily for his charm.

He is known to display a rare capacity for platonic friendship with women – from his best friend, the enigmatic producer Jean Doumanian, and his colleague Jane Read Martin who accompany him on holidays, to ex-love Diane Keaton and former wife Louise Lasser. Woody engenders an intense loyalty in these women and many others from way back in his past. Not least is his mother Nettie, with whom he has had a loving but combative relationship, and with whom he is – literally – obsessed.

Woody has great intellectual pretensions and his works are littered with references to Kafka, Sartre and Kierkegaard. Yet at school, he was, in his own words a 'classic low-brow' who preferred to read comics and crime stories, than learn about literature and philosophy. When he did immerse himself in education, it was for one thing – to seduce the clever girls he had become obsessed with, and who were not impressed by someone who read Mickey Spillane novels.

This is the story of a Woody Allen who has been fixated with sex since his earliest living memory, and who has made it the subject of practically every thing he's ever written. But it is an affectionate picture, a portrait of a troubled boy overwhelmed with irrational fears about his world, and struck with incomprehensible feelings towards others, not least towards his over-bearing mother whom he would taunt as a child, and who haunted him as a man. This is also the story of that other Woody, the perennial adolescent hoping for romance but never having courage or confidence in himself. The story of a grown man approaching 60 who can hardly use a telephone because it reminds him of those torturous teenage days when, as Allan Stewart Konigsberg, he would suffer from chronic stomach pains and roll around on the floor, at the thought of having to phone a girl and ask her out.

It is the story of a small man who has achieved great things against overwhelming odds; a modern day fable of a little Brooklyn boy ignored by girls who later grew to be labelled one of 'the 10 sexiest men on earth'. It charts his years of futile struggle to stay in long-term relationships, and his grappling with the moral dilemma posed by his sometimes perverse but always passionate emotions. Revealed is the story of the devils that danced in young Allan Stewart Konigsberg's mind, and his lifelong fight to exorcise them as he progressed from stand-up comic and Bob Hope gag writer, to famous film maker. *Woody and his Women* is the most intimate look yet at the man for whom life really does imitate art, a man overwhelmed by deep longings for happiness but ultimately crippled by the pessimistic belief that everlasting love will always elude him.

Mother Was Groucho Marx

'I never forgot that New Year's Eve when Aunt Bea awakened me to watch 1944 come in. And I've never forgotten any of those people, or any of the voices we used to hear on the radio, although the truth is, with the passing of each New Year's Eve, those voices do seem to grow dimmer and dimmer.'

Joe, *Radio Days*

The memories may have grown dimmer and dimmer, but Woody Allen's 1987 film foray into his childhood revived many of them for those who grew up with him and recognise *Radio Days* as a startling and authentic recreation of their Brooklyn youth in the Thirties and Forties.

'The scene is Rockaway, the time is my childhood. It's my old neighbourhood, and forgive me if I tend to romanticise the past ... but that's how I remember it.'

This most overtly autobiographical of Woody Allen's movies does paint a romantic portrait of the era, managing to omit along the way one or two unsavoury elements which cast a shadow over its golden hue, but otherwise presenting a homage to a happy youth.

Brimming with nostalgia, *Radio Days* is a tribute to his childhood; the story of Joe, the scrawny red-head growing up in a bustling household full of cousins, aunts, uncles, and bickering next door neighbours raging against one another as well as the rest of the world. Ever present amid the din is the radio, with its quiz shows, emotive sports' commentaries and snippets of celebrity success.

11

It is an innocent era when the worst things bad little boys did was to pinch pennies meant for the new Jewish homeland in Palestine, or dye their mothers' fur coats with solutions from their chemistry sets. In *Radio Days* boys idolised heroic figures like the fictional 'Masked Avenger', and fantasised about a glamorous world they heard about over the airwaves to the tunes of Benny Goodman, Glenn Miller and Tommy Dorsey. It was a time when over-crowded but happy households were bursting at the seams with aunts and uncles living under the same roof as grandmothers and grandfathers. It was a time when neighbours actually talked to one another, and their arguments could be heard over the garden fence – or on the telephone party line which adjoining homes would share.

It was not a prosperous time for most people, but even the badly off had plenty of food on the table, and *Radio Days* is populated with women dressed in fur coats and the men are rarely decked out in anything less than tailored three piece suits. German submarines *really* could be spotted in the chilly depths off Long Island, and there *were* an uncommon number of maiden aunts on the perpetual look-out for romance with the few bachelors not in uniform.

It was Woody Allen's age.

Or rather the age of Allan Stewart Konigsberg, the redheaded Brooklyn boy who was to become Woody Allen, the movie giant. In an unprecedented way Woody Allen has turned his own progress through life into an ongoing cinematic exploration of his world, an invariably grim but sometimes sweet odyssey of love and death.

'*Radio Days* was our childhood,' says Woody's boyhood friend Jack Victor. 'In a way it was frightening to watch it, and to see how accurately he'd recreated a time that many of us had forgotten about.'

'It was like watching my childhood complete with my maiden aunt Rose,' says Alan Lapidus, another contem-

porary. 'Those incidents were so real it was uncomfortable watching them. Woody's genius is in his ability to see
those moments, remember them, capture and distil them,
altering them just enough so that when you see it it's fresh
and wonderful.'

And although Woody persistently, and dubiously,
claims his work is no more autobiographical than any
other artist's, he's always been happy to confess that
Radio Days does indeed closely resemble his youth. As his
manager and friend, Charles Joffe, said, 'Woody denies a
lot of truths in his life. *Radio Days* was easy to admit
because he was six in it.'[1]

Woody Allen was born Allan [sic] Stewart Konigsberg
on December 1, 1935 in the Bronx, where his constantly
moving parents, Nettie and Martin Konigsberg, were
temporarily living, before returning to Brooklyn where
he spent most of his childhood in a bewildering variety of
houses and apartments. They never actually lived in
Rockaway where *Radio Days* was set, although they did
spend a summer at nearby Long Beach which has a
similar New York seaside atmosphere – and happy
memories for the young Allan.

While he was growing up Nettie and Martin were to
change homes (by one calculation) as much as 12 times, a
novelty that initially proved amusing for their only boy,
but later became trying as he had to adapt to new schools
and new friends. It was also not unusual for the family to
share accommodation with his maternal aunt and uncle,
Ceil and Abe Cohen (both of whom were characterised
hilariously in *Radio Days*) and their daughters Jane and
Marjorie who were younger than Allan. At times the
Konigsbergs also lived with Nettie's sister Sadie and her
husband Joe Wishnick, whose daughter Rita had to share
a bedroom with Woody once. Grandparents were never
far away. It was a state of permanent upheaval which
Woody later thought caused his nervousness.

'It was hectic,' he said. 'Partly because of economic

circumstances, partly because of wartime apartment shortage. My family was always getting billeted with relations. There were always uncles and cousins running in and out of rooms, and we were always moving.'[2] And again: 'Relatives were always running in and out of rooms. It was like living in the middle of a Marx Brothers movie.'[3] It was not only relatives, as Allan, and later his younger sister Letty, grew older and acquired friends, they often invited them around for dinner. Letty recalled that she and Woody would often arrive home with friends to stay for a meal. At one stage the Konigsbergs had a cleaning lady whose duties sometimes came to resemble a restaurant receptionist, taking phone calls from people intending to come around for the night.

The problem, inexplicably, was money. Inexplicably, because Mr and Mrs Konigsberg appeared to be able to afford minor luxuries like the cleaning lady and nannies, and were never without good food or any of the finer necessities of life. But somehow or other things always seemed to be in state of financial flux thus creating the manic insecurity that was to afflict their son. This may have been due to the fact that many of their contemporaries in the neighbourhood came from solid professional backgrounds and were conspicuously secure in comparison to them. Martin Konigsberg's family had been quite wealthy once but suffered a number of setbacks during the Depression forcing them into a more humble lifestyle. Their son was thrown unprepared, with no profession to speak of, into a harsh world in which he worked at a variety of jobs, sometimes juggling two or more at once. His main job was as a jewellery engraver, and he once worked for a relative making badges for the New York City Police Department. But he also took jobs as a taxi driver and waiter at the popular Manhattan club, Sammy's Bowery Follies.

To make ends meet Nettie, unusually for the time, found work of her own – as a book-keeper in a florist shop. The two of them struggled in Brooklyn's bustling economy of second generation families who, like the rest of Americans, were only just emerging from the deprivations of the last unhappy decade to face the uncertainties of the next.

Their neighbourhood, the Flatbush area of Midwood, was a predominantly Jewish area which owed more to the Old World than the New, with the craggy faces of its people, their exotic names and traditions, betraying roots in central and eastern Europe. Nettie (whose maiden name was Cherry) and Martin were both born in Manhattan's Lower East Side in New York's great Jewish ghetto, across the East River from Brooklyn. But their parents came from Vienna and Russia respectively and their lifestyles betrayed that background. As was common in that era and milieu, they would often share their homes with other members of the extended family, and all of them would move from place to place in a desire to stay physically close to their relatives.

These were the children of the great Jewish exodus from Europe, a hardy race of battered but proud people making their way in a strange culture, where the curse of anti-Semitism was not only limited to Europe. This was a people whose overriding and simple ethics were work and worry: work to survive, work to live and prosper in the New World. Worry about everything – and nothing in particular. Nettie was a born worrier, and this too would have a big impact on her son. Like the other ethnic groups in America, the Jews did not 'melt' into the vast and sprawling 'pot' of the new land; if anything they became a more isolated culture and reacted to their surroundings with the justified anxiety of a persecuted race.

Brooklyn at this time would launch a myriad of major talent on to the international stage, especially entertainers like Danny Kaye and Barbra Streisand, and the film editor Woody was later to hire for his own movies, Ralph

Rosenblum. Rosenblum's own account of his childhood home a few years previously reads thus:

> 'Its lessons and ways were those of impoverished immigrants hanging on desperately to the niche they had made for themselves. Thrift, self-improvement and a thudding practicality ruled everything, a heavy spirited regime that was moulded into permanence by the weight of the Depression. Ten years later when Woody Allen was growing up in the same milieu, its values and oppressive conformity would still prevail.'[4]

But Woody's childhood, and their lives, were not as hard as it may appear in the telling. Nor was it the gruesome one, either financially or emotionally, he often later depicted or implied in stand-up comic routines. This can be confusing since fact and fiction are mixed in his work. In *Crimes and Misdemeanors* Cliff says:

> 'Where I grew up, in Brooklyn, nobody committed suicide, ya' know? Everyone was too unhappy.'

Woody Allen would claim the family was so poor that one of his father's jobs was as a caddie on a miniature golf course. Another time, he said: 'My grandfather was a very insignificant man. At his funeral his hearse followed the other cars.'

In reality Woody has said, 'I really wasn't a scared and lonely child at all. I played all sorts of games and was good at quite a lot of them. I wasn't poor, or hungry, or neglected. We were a well-fed middle class family. We wore good clothes and lived in a comfortable house.'[5] Jack Victor, a childhood friend, says, 'Woody makes his childhood sound much worse than it really was. He had an unusual family background, but no more so than many kids in Brooklyn at that time, and I certainly don't remember those days as hard times for Woody by any stretch of the imagination.

'In fact Woody always had a greater allowance than me and his father was incredibly generous. I remember Martin taking him to a clothes' store once and buying him six suits.'

Woody benefited from an indulgent Martin who has always had a very close relationship with his son. It was Martin who bought Woody the chemistry set which *really did* end up dyeing his mother's coat. And the preponderance of so many relatives meant he was always being given little gifts of candy and more pocket money than was good for him.

Midwood was a lower to middle class neighbourhood with sprawling homes surrounded by lawns, lining the avenues. More modest houses, often of the 'two family' type occupied the narrower streets, and apartment blocks stood on the corners. The neighbourhood was intersected by the B.M.T. 'subway' on its elevated railway lines that took commuters into downtown Brooklyn and across the river to Manhattan. The shopping streets were colourful and thriving districts with kosher butcher shops, appetising stores, coffee shops and candy stores, and the ever present food emporiums like the popular Embassy Tea Room.

At home there was always food on the table. Struggling as Nettie and Martin Konigsberg were, they were doing well enough not only to hire household helps, but to take their children to expensive Manhattan doctors. It was a mixed community and the Konigsbergs were neither at the bottom nor at the top. Woody's friends included Jack Victor whose parents were one of the few in their circle to be immigrants rather than second generation Americans, and Jerry Epstein, who came from a family of well-to-do judges and had a father who was an attorney. Alan Lapidus's father was the architect who distinguished himself by designing the world famous Fontainebleau Hotel in Florida. For several years the Konigsbergs' next door neighbours were what Woody viewed as a combative and endlessly complaining family, who would constantly flout Hebrew laws and pamphleteer in a bid for 'workers of the world to unite', just as Woody would portray them in *Radio Days*.

As both his parents worked, Woody was often left at home with one of his grandparents, aunts or uncles to take care of him – which was good because they spoiled him with candy and gifts of nickels and dimes. Or, alternatively, left him in the charge of a nanny, which was not so good because they did not spoil him at all. Indeed, Woody was later to recall that they would often turn up with their 'seedy' boyfriends and at least one threatened to suffocate her three-year-old charge. How he can possibly remember this at such an early age is a mystery. Nevertheless it's quite understandable that he would often cry when his mother left for work.

What is less comprehensible is the relationship that gradually developed over the years with Nettie. From an early age it was a strained one, and the pair have never 'got on'. He also admits to a 'genetic dissatisfaction' with everything;[6] she says something turned him morose early on. He has no idea what this was, but has said, 'Early in life I was visited by the bluebird of anxiety, being terrified of death, being kidnapped, of being on boats and especially of the dark.'[7] A problem he still has today.

But Nettie took good care of her difficult and precocious boy, and when he eventually made a fortune, he provided for her generously – eventually buying Nettie and Martin an apartment in Manhattan a few blocks from his own, and a condominium in the Florida sun where she likes to spend much of her time today. His sister Letty, who was to arrive when he was eight, is great friends with her mother but says she understands why Woody never got on with her.

In the heat of the Mia Farrow scandal many years later, somewhat absurdly, *Vanity Fair* magazine was to hint that there was more to this strained mother-son relationship than met the eye, darkly suggesting that this conflict could cast more light on the allegations of child abuse. The magazine reported that Woody, 'who seemed to have intense negative feelings for his mother', once said to his little girl about Nettie, 'She's the Wicked Witch of the West, Dylan. Twist her nose off.'[8]

Woody acknowledged that there is a rift, and tackled it recently in the form of a documentary he made when still on talking terms with Mia Farrow's family. He filmed Nettie and Mia's mother, who is the actress Maureen O'Sullivan, who was most famous as 'Jane' to Johnny Weissmuller's 'Tarzan' but also achieved some acclaim as Hannah's flirtatious mother in *Hannah and Her Sisters*. What was to have been a documentary film entitled *Two Mothers*, never got further than his cutting room according to Mia. The project seemed to have never got off the ground – and not necessarily because of the spectacular bust-up between Woody and Mia. The motivation behind Woody's making of the documentary will remain a mystery. Perhaps he was trying to explore for real, those dark and distant corners of his past life which he has so successfully explored in his fiction. And perhaps his failure to complete the quest is partly because those areas are too difficult or painful to confront.

But in his biography of Woody, Eric Lax, who is a close friend going back some 20 years, reports that part of an exchange between Woody and Nettie concerned the director's apparent annoyance that his mother had hit him 'every day' when he was a child. An apologetic Nettie explained that as a child he had just been too hard to handle.

But Woody's second wife, Louise Lasser, said that whatever was at the bottom of the dislike there was never any hatred. 'He didn't like her, but she was a good mother who always put food on the table, and he and Letty would eat up and get out of the house. He's set them both [Nettie and Martin] up for life financially, and there's nothing they both can't have.

'That's an entirely different background to Mia. She came from a flamboyant showbiz family. Her parents were both high-flying jet setters, and she had a very lonely childhood.'

In fact there was more comedy than tragedy in this mutually antagonistic relationship – not just with Nettie but with Martin too. *Zelig* features a character who is locked in a closet by his parents when he misbehaves, and when he's been particularly bad, they lock themselves in with him. One of Woody's routines recalls the time he was 'kidnapped' as a boy:

'They ... send a ransom note to my parents. And my father has bad reading habits. He gets into bed at night with the ransom note and he reads half of it and gets drowsy and falls asleep ... Meanwhile , they take me to New Jersey, bound and gagged, and my parents finally realise that I'm kidnapped and snap into action immediately. They rent out my room. The ransom note says for my father to leave $1,000 in a hollow tree in New Jersey. He has no trouble raising the $1,000, but he gets a hernia carrying the hollow tree.'

It was an archetypal squabbling Jewish household with Nettie as a comic character in the centre, more like the nagging Jewish mother played by Mae Questel in Woody's hilarious vignette *Oedipus Wrecks*, than the Wicked Witch of the West. 'I'm obsessed by the fact that my mother genuinely resembles Groucho Marx,' he later said. In *Take the Money and Run* the quasi-documentary style movie about bank robber Virgil Starkwell, the ill-fated crooks' parents adopt Groucho Marx disguises for the camera because they are so ashamed of their son.

In *Oedipus Wrecks* the overbearing Jewish mother disappears in a magician's act and returns to haunt her long-suffering son Sheldon from the sky, much to the entertainment of his incredulous Manhattan neighbours. It's an affectionate portrait of a mother, not the embittered recollection of an abusive childhood.

'She wasn't nefarious,' says Jack Victor. 'She's what we'd call in Yiddish, a "nudge" – a nag. Nag, nag, nag – much more than usual. She was constantly nagging him. But she wasn't horrible. We were far more afraid of other mothers than Woody's. Long after he became famous, I was interviewed by a writer for *Look* magazine who was trying to get some insights into Woody. She'd already interviewed his mother, but didn't have anything for her story because Nettie didn't seem to be pleased with her son at all. She would say things like, "What can I do? I tried to get the boy to go to school. I did my best for him. We tried to teach him the right way. But this is how he repays us! This is the way he's turned out! It's a tragedy for any parent."'

Nobody could understand how his mother and father could ever have married each other. Not only did they appear to be in an almost constant state of contention with one another as Woody later admitted, but they were also completely different people to begin with. He was a relaxed and gregarious charmer, a Damon Runyon character who carried a gun licence because of the jewellery business; she was an anxiety-prone, stereotypical Jewish mother with an incomprehensible child on her hands.

A friend says that: 'She was always complaining about him, because the poor woman didn't know what to do with him. Even when he began to enjoy some success, she was never really satisfied with him. She wanted him to be a pharmacist and this show business concept held no appeal for Nettie at all.

'He was out of control most of the time, and she just couldn't cope because like every working mother, she had a million other things to do at once. So who could blame her? He deliberately provoked her into arguments and enjoyed seeing her get angrier and angrier. The angrier she would get, the funnier she would be although she didn't realise it.'

Jack Victor says: 'It was astonishing to me how he would talk back to her. I had a rather meek mother, but I wouldn't say half the things he said to her. Once, she had an operation for a cataract and she was wearing an eyepatch over one eye which made her look like Popeye. She was nagging Woody as she always did and he said, "Shut up Ma, or I'll blind you in the other one." It was hilarious but shocking, I didn't know whether to laugh or get out of there.'

Elliott Mills has similar fond memories: 'All our parents were crazy, but Woody's mother was like a cartoon character. She was on the verge of hysteria most of the time. She was always in absolute panic – I mean the house was in a constant state of panic, and Woody used to drive her into even greater fits of hysteria. She didn't know how to cope with him. He was beyond her, always answering back, always up to no good.

'Beyond any shadow of a doubt it was a strange family situation with this marriage which inexplicably survived and all these relatives coming in and out of the household. But I think he paints the family situation darker than it is. I never got the impression that he was unhappy. It was an incredibly funny household. His mother was unconsciously funny, his father was naturally a very funny man, and his sister Letty was just as funny as Woody – in exactly the same way. Considering how young she was, it was amazing how quick, witty and hilarious she could be.

'That's why his comedy touched people so much in the early days. Many of the childhood themes he's explored aren't just drawn on autobiographical knowledge, they are actually the re-telling of specific incidents that actually happened.'

Woody once said of his parents: 'They're all silly people in a grotesque way. Nerve-rackingly silly. They're preposterous. And they can't do anything right. My father is a comical gnome who looks like Fernandel and has always been preoccupied with silly business schemes. My mother is Groucho. She is. She looks like Groucho Marx and she talks like him.'[9]

Mickey Rose, another friend, who went on to write scripts with Woody, said, 'The mother was a typical nagging kind of mother, a stereotypical Shirley MacLaine character, critical without knowing why they're critical. They're not happy or relaxed people. They're unhappy because they're too busy nagging and worrying about things – although they don't know what they're worrying about.

'He would say she looked like Groucho Marx and then instead of being insulted or taking umbrage she would say: "Well, So what? He's a handsome man!" And so Woody would say, "But Ma, you're a woman," and we would fall about but she didn't have a clue what we were laughing at.

'Woody's dad was a cross between George Raft and Fernandel. His father was funny, changing clothes three times a day for no apparent reason. We would come into the house on a few different occasions during the day and he'd be wearing a different suit on each occasion. Always very elegant suits too. I don't think there was any decision process going on, I think he just did it, and we never did ask him why he kept changing his suits.'

One of Woody's closest childhood friends says that the picture of a Jewish household in *Radio Days* was exactly what Woody's household was like. 'Nettie was hilarious without knowing it. She'd come out with one-liners. She was just terrifically funny and when we laughed she couldn't understand why we were laughing. He would provoke her and she would get angrier and as she got angrier she got funnier and would say things that were really, really incredible and she had no idea why people were laughing. It wasn't just Nettie he provoked, it was everyone, friends, relatives, neighbours. They were always moving because of financial difficulties of one sort or another and he lived in that house with all those people he would argue with because he provoked them all the time. And next door across the alleyway was the communist family who were always protesting and distributing leaflets. It was comical. It was just like *Radio Days*.

'There was a terrific background split. His mother was orthodox from an orthodox family and tried to be observant but his father came from a totally atheistic direction. The mother tried very hard to push him in that direction and of course he built up a caricature in his mind about Judaism. But I think his father was the domineering influence so when it came to something like a very important Jewish holiday like Yom Kippur, the mother would go up the synagogue but the father would be home eating Chinese food and watching westerns on the television.'

Woody said: 'I never ate dinner with my family. I'd eat in the cellar or my bedroom, read my comic books, lock myself in my room and practice the clarinet and my card and coin tricks. It would drive my mother crazy.'[10]

Perhaps Woody's movies speak more eloquently about his mother. In *Oedipus Wrecks* the Woody character, Sheldon Miles, starts dating blonde *shiksa* goddess Lisa, played by Mia Farrow. But his mother Sadie rebels against her son's alliance and continually berates him from the sky until he sees sense and finally finds true love with the good old Jewish girl played by Julie Kavner. Interestingly, Lisa abandons Sheldon after Sadie calls her a 'korva' (whore). The message appears to be that his mother was right in the end. Arguably, if his parents are full of superstition and perhaps said stupid things, they did well in bringing him up in the end.

***

Nettie has defined a huge part of Woody's life, but there were other women too from the very beginning, who explain what he is and how he is today. He said once: 'With the exception of roles written for myself, I feel more comfortable writing female characters. It would be because I was brought up mostly by women. My father's alive and all that, but otherwise I was the only male in the family. My mother had seven sisters, and all of those sisters had only daughters. I was constantly being ministered by aunts and female cousins. I would always be playing with girls. So I have a lot of sympathy for them. There are many women in my work situation even now. My editor is a woman, two assistants are women, and our foreign representative is a woman. The people I work with most closely are women.'[11]

It's interesting that although fans tend to associate the 'real Woody' most with Alvy Singer from *Annie Hall*, Isaac Davis from *Manhattan*, or Cliff Stern from *Crimes and Misdemeanors*, he has always insisted the characters he most closely resembles are female ones – Eve (*Interiors*), Cecilia (*Purple Rose of Cairo*) and Marion (*Another Woman*).

Women are Woody's enduring influence and interest. He was surrounded by them then, and prefers their company now, enjoying closer friendships with them than many people have within their own sex. He has taken Mia Farrow and Diane Keaton out to dinner together, and has often had holidays with close women friends like Jean Doumanian.

He has been described as the most woman friendly director in the business. His friend Jack Kroll said: 'Woody agrees with Camus that women are all we know of paradise on earth.'[12] And Louise Lasser says that Woody was desperate for her to have little girls when they were married, and when Letty had a baby son, Woody told Lyn Tornabene, 'I like little girls overwhelmingly better than little boys'.[13]

Nettie was the first woman in his world, followed by aunts and cousins who were always so kind to him. Then there was Rita Wishnick, the cousin with whom he shared a passion for the cinema, and for many years, a bedroom, when the two families lived in the same house. She would tell him about film stars whose pictures she would cut from movie magazines and hang on the walls. When they were not living in the same house, they lived near each other and were constantly in one another's company.

There was a five year age difference: Rita was approaching the dating age and Woody was at the start of his adolescent youth. Given the circumstances of that time, there was nothing particularly unusual in the sleeping arrangements, and Rita was such a close cousin that there were no raised eyebrows in the Konigsberg family household or elsewhere in the neighbourhood. Jack Victor tells a different story: 'She was very beautiful and Woody had a crush on her. He would talk quite explicitly about his sexual appetite in relation to the opposite sex. But then at that age you tend to be ravenous about girls so there wasn't much wrong or unusual with that. I think we all had crushes on our cousins then!'

In one of the many scenes cut from the original *Annie Hall*, the young Alvy had a voluptuous cousin 'Doris'. To avoid school Alvy faked a fever by putting a thermometer over the radiator, and Doris nurses Alvy back to health by reading comics to him. Half way through she notes, 'Alvy you're drooling'.

Another female entered his world when he was eight years old, a little girl who was to become a lifelong companion and soul mate, his sister Letty. The arrival of a sibling for an only child often causes disruption and jealousy. But since the day that Letty arrived he and Letty have got on like a house on fire. It's a relationship Louise Lasser described as 'very special' and continues to this day. Now Letty Aronson, she lives on Park Avenue only a few blocks away from her big brother, and they talk practically every day on the phone. Like the many other women he knows and respects, Woody often bounces film ideas off Letty.

Louise Lasser says: 'From the moment she arrived they've never really been apart. He took her to the movies when she was young, and to museums, art galleries and shows later in life. He's been a huge influence on her life.'

Female sensitivity is a trait that many actors have and in no way diminishes their masculinity. Far from it. Women generally fall head over heels for the sort of men who understand their needs and desires, men who don't fall for peer pressure to pretend otherwise. Gerard Depardieu, that most male and womanising of actors, openly boasts that actors *must* have 'feminine' traits. What Woody Allen invariably disparages in his work is the boastful, strutting pseudo macho guise which is often passed off as masculinity by the sort of Neanderthal popular culture he despises.

It's noticeable that that cheapest form of 'macho' bravado – the frequent use of blatant obscenity – is rarely heard in Woody's movies. Significantly, until *Husbands and Wives*, he has only ever used the word 'fuck' in two movies, *The Front* and *Scenes From a Mall*, neither of which he directed. Privately, he's rarely been known to swear, but the last film in which he was to star with Mia Farrow, *Husbands and Wives*, contained much gratuitous foul language.

The Australian actress Judy Davis said: 'Many men find it difficult to write female characters, as if they don't recognise that we're the same animal – the mysterious feminine! But Woody likes women and finds them fascinating. He's written some fantastic roles; it's extraordinary that a man wrote *Another Woman* with such empathy.'[14] The writer Ron Rosenbaum said: 'The great thing Woody Allen has done for the image of intelligent and creative women is to reverse the Hollywood stereotype and portray women as highly erotic too.'[15]

In 1941, at the tender age of five, Woody fell in love for the first time when he arrived in the city that his life would later revolve around. Gripping on to Martin's hand, the five-year-old boy emerged from the Time Square subway, on 42nd Street, in the heart of Manhattan. He had never been in the city before, and he was staggered at what he saw, the rows of cinemas stretching as far as the eye could see, along Broadway and across 42nd Street. Today he still marvels at that first sight, and the way Manhattan once was. He agrees that New York was a metaphor for the decay of civilisation but it was a world, perhaps a fictitious one, which he was instantly at home in with its delicatessens, magic shops and variety of life.

He says: I think of it often as it used to be. When I was growing up and could ride the subways with impunity at age 10 ... it was coming to the end of the really golden age. My guess is that in the Twenties and Thirties there was probably nothing to equal Manhattan ever in the history of the world. When you know that there would be a hundred plays at once, you just can't get your mind around that. And the movie houses and nightclubs and speakeasies.

'I speak to people that were in Broadway shows, older actresses, and I was speaking to one woman who was saying to me she and her girlfriend would do a show and then the curtain would come down at 11:15, and they would get dressed and go out for dinner in Time Square – two girls, about 19 years old, totally unescorted – and then go to a movie house on 42nd Street after dinner and see a Katharine Hepburn or Spencer Tracy picture. And then walk home through Central Park. I wish I could have lived in New York in a different period.'[16]

To Allan Konigsberg in 1941, it was a vision, a dream come true. Manhattan would become the first lady of his life, the one he never had any doubts about, and the one he would recreate time and again on the big screen.

Rita first, and later Letty, were to share with Woody and many of the other kids from the neighbourhood, his passion for the movies. Midwood boasted almost a dozen cinemas, and like all the other kids in his neighbourhood, he was a motion picture fan from very early on, often going to the pictures with Rita, an avid celebrity buff whose bedroom walls were plastered with posters of the stars. Jack Victor was also a regular companion on these jaunts into this glowing new world.

From a very early age, while other children's parents would shove their children outside or off to the beach to get some exercise and enjoy themselves, Woody would amble off to the dark confines of the cinema to get his daily 'fix'. (Alvy in *Annie Hall*: Sun is bad for you. Everything our parents said was good is bad. Sun, red meat, milk, college ...) The cinemas became a sanctuary from reality, the fantasies they peddled making more sense to the young Woody than the puzzling world outside, like Cecilia in *The Purple Rose of Cairo*, the inveterate cinema goer who falls for one of the stars of a popular caper. For Woody it was an innocent and a glamorous world. In those days the movies and songs were happy and upbeat, all about people having fun and enjoying themselves, dressing 'up to the nines' in tuxedos and tails, and going to glitzy night clubs to drink champagne and dance through the night. Dates were spent at outdoor skating rinks with the rolling Atlantic surf framed in the background by fairy lights while courting couples dined on oysters and beer.

Favourite movies for Woody were those of the Marx Brothers or the classy comedies of Preston Sturges. In his youth there were no 'Terminators', 'Rambos', or 'Universal Soldiers'. Even the popular cult heroes who did attract huge followings, like 'Batman' and Woody's fictitious 'Masked Avenger' from *Radio Days*, were comically noble creatures, not cynical killers. In the movie, when we see little Joe arriving at Manhattan's fabulous Radio City music hall to watch *The Philadelphia Story*, we hear the strains of Frank Sinatra singing 'If You are but a Dream', and the huge art deco foyer takes on a celestial appearance, bathed in rich golds and royal red. 'It was like entering heaven,' says Joe. And it was.

Douglas Brode comments on the movies of this era that: 'Essentially Cecilia symbolises the American public of the 1930s, people whose lives were so drab that they gladly grew hooked on the glamorous, glittery alternate world … in a way no other generation has; it's not for nothing the best-loved, most warmly remembered American movies were made during the troubled Thirties. That was the era when, as a people, we needed movies most and appreciated them best.'[17]

Woody would attend as many movies as possible and loved going to matinées, sitting there for hour after hour submerged in a dream world, eating chocolate and raisins. Often he would be alone, and sometimes he would be with friends. Many times he would be with his parents. Martin liked westerns and Nettie loved romances, so over the years young Woody was to see many of both. At the age of three, Nettie took him to his first ever film, *Snow White and the Seven Dwarfs* which so surprised him when its image first flickered on the screen, that he thought it was real and ran out to touch the characters causing Nettie to pull him back. 'I was shy but at the movies I used to yell out at things on the screen.'[18]

His love of the movies developed during these years. After watching Tyrone Power in the swashbuckling pirate tale *The Black Swan*, he began to realise that he could tell a story for the screen even if he did not have the requisite good looks or confidence to act it out. On another occasion, walking home from the Midwood cinema, he found some clipped up film of Phil Silvers and Carmen Miranda and began to understand something of the mechanics of film making.

He was hugely influenced by English comedians. Not just those who had made their living in Hollywood like Stan Laurel and Charlie Chaplin, but others like Alec Guinness, Alistair Sim, Ian Carmichael and Terry Thomas. 'He loved *Private's Progress* with Terry Thomas,' says Jack Victor, 'and we must have seen *The Belles of St Trinians* a dozen times. We especially loved the opening sequence where the schoolgirls riddle the signpost with machine-gun bullets. A great combination of comedy and rebellion! Joyce Grenfell was a great favourite, and we loved the early Alec Guinness movies like *The Lavender Hill Mob* and *Kind Hearts and Coronets*.'

Later in life, he began to admire comics like Peter Sellers and Peter Cook and comic teams like 'The Goons', which when he was young he could occasionally pick up on the wireless. *Beyond the Fringe* and *Monty Python's Flying Circus* would be great favourites, along with *Doctor in the House*.

It was another English born comic who was to be the biggest ever influence on Woody, a comedian he saw for the first time at the age of seven when Nettie took him to watch *Road to Morocco* with Bing Crosby and London born Bob Hope, whose swaggering yet cowardly heroic pose he immediately fell in love with. Woody Allen's character has often been described as a *schlemiel*, the Yiddish phrase for a loser, a small guy endlessly being picked on. Bob Hope was a Gentile version of the *schlemiel*, a hopeless bumbling fool who was also a winner and successful womaniser. From that moment on, he was to tell friends he knew exactly what he wanted to do with the rest of his life.

But knowing what you want to be and being unable to accomplish it immediately is a burden many people have had to put up with. Even a budding genius like him was no exception; for the time being, he was a prisoner of fortune.

* * *

He may have exaggerated some of the deprivations of his childhood, but whatever traumas, imagined or otherwise, beset the young red-headed Woody, his first taste of the public school system (which in America means the state school system) proved to have the most impact.

Brooklyn's Public School 99 is one of his most enduring hatreds, an experience he was later to describe as like 'rat poison'. He has not missed an opportunity to disparage his old alma mater in interviews and in many scenes in his movies teachers are invariably portrayed as backward and barbarian. ('I went to a school for emotionally disturbed teachers.') Ironically, he was to immortalise his hated school principal Eudora Fletcher in *Zelig* as the psychiatrist played by Mia Farrow who ends up loving Zelig, the human chameleon. But Woody does not have any fond memories of the real Eudora.

> 'So while we wait for a cab I'll give you your lesson for today. Your lesson is this: Don't listen to what your school-teachers tell you, you know? Don't pay any attention to that. Just see what they look like and that's how you'll know what life is really gonna be like.'
>
> Cliff to his niece in *Crimes and Misdemeanors*

Eudora Fletcher is not here to defend herself but Woody's memory is of a stern woman with hard features. She presided over a strict school staffed mostly by Irish teachers intent on venting whatever pent-up frustrations they had on the young girls and boys under their control – particularly the Jewish ones.

Today Woody lapses into hyperbole at the slightest recollection of those days, labelling the teachers 'nasty' and 'unpleasant', and the school 'humourless, joyless and educationless'.[19] It was a daily experience he put off for as long as possible, often taking a longer route than absolutely necessary to the intimidating red-brick block of a building some 15 minutes away. He said later: 'There were natural things that kids would not like: sitting still, being disciplined, not being able to talk and not being able to have fun. It was a loathsome thing. The teachers were backward and anti-Semitic ... They were stupid and mean. They were unpleasant people, and one never wanted to go to school.

'... and I used to write things that they thought were dirty ... they were dirty by the backward, ignorant standards of my teachers. My mother was called so often because of that and other problems. She was called to school so frequently that into her sixties, when my mother was still in the old neighbourhood, kids who went to school with me would recognise her and say "hello" because she was such a familiar figure.'[20]

More often than not Woody was quiet at school and never said anything, and Jack Victor remembers that he was far from being the most troublesome boy in class as is sometimes portrayed. He would get into trouble occasionally, but no more than others. His big get-out scam was pretending to be sick, which was particularly easy in the sort of Jewish neighbourhood he came from where mothers were constantly worried about their sons' health and the potential burden of medical bills.

Not only was it a 'spectacular treat' to be sick, it was a relatively simple task to feign illness, something that he and his friends would do with carefree abandon. 'We all used to leave the thermometer on the radiator and claim to have a temperature!' recalls Alan Lapidus. 'It worked every time because our mothers were so nervous about us.' The slightest suspicion of a fever would have Nettie confining the young Woody to bed, and consequently the thermometer was frequently being placed on top of the radiator in the Konigsberg household.

Some students – like Woody's later girlfriend Bryna Goldstein – confess to having no bad memories of Brooklyn's Public School 99, but the general consensus is that Woody was right. Says Jack Victor: 'By and large the teachers were extremely strict, bordered on the sadistic and many were probably somewhat anti-Semitic. Most of them were Irish – a fact that was reflected in the school colours of Kelly green and white.'

'We were entering P.S. [Public School] 99 when World War Two was in full bloom,' says Alan Lapidus, 'and here was Eudora Fletcher, this very Germanic caricature of a principal who terrified everyone. We all knew she was an S.S. bitch. And the assistant principal was Miss Read, who was Irish and we all knew whose side the Irish were on. The teachers were mainly stupid and Irish and hated us precocious little Jewish kids trying to prove how smart they were. We were a small Jewish enclave surrounded by working class Italians.'

He remembers that one of the girls, Shelly Greenberg, was so tall it upset the teachers' senses of equilibrium. 'If they could subtly crush you they certainly did. Shelly was so tall she towered over the girls, so they made her stand with the boys. Ironically, she still towered over us.'

Elliott Mills is more forgiving. 'It wasn't a bad school, it was alright. The teachers were old – they were the tail end of some of the teachers our parents had when they were our age.'

To add to Woody's misery Nettie also insisted that he attended Hebrew school after regular classes, which he did, for eight years. Another point of conflict was that he scored very highly in an IQ test, and there had been an opportunity to enrol in a special programme for bright students at Hunter College Elementary in Manhattan. This was an option Nettie and Martin rejected because of the impracticality of taking the subway there and back every day. Woody later seemed to begrudge his parents this but as Jack Victor pointed out, he had difficulty enough coping at P.S. 99, so why he should think a tougher school would be any different is not clear. Jack also remarked that school systems are geared to the average child and since he was never the average child nothing would have worked for him.

Alan Lapidus points out that it was not all darkness and despair: 'There were a few Jewish teachers and we clung to them like sticking gum. Mr Needleman was one. (It was Mr Needleman in *Radio Days* who was driven crazy and ran riot with a meat cleaver.) We worshipped them because they were open to inquiry and they could empathise with us.'

School had its bright moments – like the substitute teacher, the memory of whom has also been committed to celluloid in *Radio Days* where Joe and his friends ogle through binoculars at a window through which they can spot her naked and voluptuous form. 'I'm damned sure I know who she was,' says Alan Lapidus. 'I remember we were sitting there with our little eight-year-old tongues hanging out because she was a curvaceous, busty blonde, and we were used to these dowdy old Irish spinsters. One day this dish came in and it was all we could do to wait until recess and say "Wow! Wow! Wow!"' Jack Victor remembers a teacher called Miss Chast who inevitably became known as "Miss Chest". 'One of the guys pretended to fall over once so he could grab her bosom – or "cop a feel" as we said.' To 'cop a feel' would crop up years later in the medieval sketch of *Everything You Always Wanted to Know About Sex, But Were Afraid to Ask*.

With school came the inevitable bouts of bullying, particularly for a small boy whose unusual red-headed looks attracted the sobriquet 'Red' from his detractors, a nickname he despised. Woody was a loner who would often walk to school via back streets rather than mix with other boys and girls. In 1987 Woody Allen was named one of the world's 'top 10 sexiest men' but at school he was a *schlemiel* – the weedy little boy with odd looks in a world that admired physical strength and beauty. The comic Len Maxwell, who became a great friend, once said: 'Woody Allen hasn't changed in the 10 years I've known him. He's still a scared little rabbit. He's the only person who ever brought the mother out in me.'[21]

Woody constantly denies he was ever a *schlemiel* but if there is any misapprehension it's fuelled by his own gags and screen persona.

One writer said: 'He was truly bullied as a kid; from these experiences comes the story of a vacation at the interfaith camp, where "I was sadistically beaten by boys of all races and creeds". He was once mugged, and that led to a routine about his carrying a sword, which, "in case of attack changes to a cane so I can get sympathy".'

And Nora Ephron once noted: 'To this day he seems to wear the scars so frequently earned by myopic, short sixth-graders at the hands of larger, all-seeing boys. "They were the sockers," he used to say, "I was the sockee".'[22]

But amateur psychoanalysts may be reading too much into the sort of sporadic school-yard bullying that every boy falls foul of at one stage or another. A friend of Woody's says that he never once recalled Allen being bullied. 'I met him when he was 12 and certainly from that day on bullying was not a consideration. There were some pretty tough Italian gangs but we kept our distance from them. Woody was never bullied.' And among his own tight group of friends, Woody was in charge, although he did get bullied once or twice. And Elliott used to impose his views on Jack [Victor] until he got bigger than him, for not supporting the Brooklyn Dodgers.[23]

Really, Woody and his friends were far from the serious street violence that could affect some American urban areas even then, but nevertheless, its presence was *felt* and the aura of crime and violence would ultimately be another great influence in the director's work. The Second World War era was a time of great juvenile delinquency in New York, and huge numbers of – mainly Italian – gangs had infiltrated Brooklyn, some of them active in the high schools even in Midwood. The gangs were juvenile but quasi-criminal with tentative links to the Mob.

Woody loved crime movies and TV serials, and adored the classic crook actors like James Cagney and Edward G. Robinson. Legs Diamond had been killed in his neighbourhood. And he could even claim a tentative family link with the Mob after one of his distant cousins was the victim of a Mafia hit. Arnold Schuster, a distant cousin, had the misfortune to share a train to Brooklyn with the notorious bank robber Willie Sutton who had just escaped from jail. Schuster fingered him and the police apprehended Sutton. Within a few weeks Schuster was gunned down in Brooklyn by members of Albert Anastasia's crime family.

Martin Konigsberg came into occasional contact with an unsavoury element working at Sammy Bowery's Follies. Besides which, Martin used to make badges for the New York Police who were an endless source of gripping tales about the underworld. Woody's father always had a great sympathy for the criminal classes. There is a scene in *Annie Hall* where Alvy's bickering mum and dad are arguing about the black cleaning lady. Mrs Singer sacks her for stealing.

'She's a coloured woman, from Harlem! She has no money! She's got a right to steal from us! After all, who is she gonna steal from if not us?'

Woody's friend, Jerry Epstein came from a family of attorneys and the cases of his father's clients would become normal dinnertime conversation. It was an atmosphere that engendered an interest in crime and legal issues for both of the youths, although friends say that Woody's later claims that he was interested in joining the F.B.I. were exaggerated. He did however send away for the F.B.I. brochure which showed how to count the ridges on fingerprints. His first unadulterated Woody Allen movie, *Take the Money and Run*, was the story, said Woody, of how he would end up if he ever turned to a life of crime.

One of his friends recalls: 'He always had a tremendous interest in crime, and he was fascinated by criminals, criminology and the Mafia. Certain friends from childhood were marginally, peripherally connected to quasi-criminal activities. There was one guy from high school who became a petty criminal, and he was calling Woody and bothering him for years after he became famous. The epigraph of *Take the Money and Run* is "Crime Lives".'

It was an interest that was to be one of his greatest influences later in life. Crime crops up in practically every movie Woody made, from *Take the Money and Run*, which was overtly about a failed criminal, through *Broadway Danny Rose*, to Danny Aiello's hit man character in *Radio Days* and the contract kill in *Crime and Misdemeanors*. His current movie, *Manhattan Murder Mystery*, is the unadulterated murder mystery he's always wanted to do. Woody says he always wanted to write a murder mystery but considered it a 'lesser art form'. (Perhaps after his disastrously boring experimentations with 'greater' art forms in *Interiors*, *September* and *Another Woman* he changed his mind.)

But the crime that affected Woody Allen most was the biggest crime of the century: the Holocaust. His childhood was a time of great anti-Semitism. Slogans like 'Kill the Rosenbergs' and 'Kill the Jews' were daubed over subway station walls. Jewish children were beaten up simply because of their race. Jack Victor was a victim. 'I was beaten up several times because I was Jewish, and I remember my sister coming home in tears because some people had told her the Jews killed Christ. My father's brother was killed in Europe along with half my mother's family.'

It was an unnerving time for Jews in America, with their compatriots by no means solidly unified against the Nazi menace in Europe. There were many Americans like the influential Ambassador to England, Joe Kennedy, who did not want the United States in the war.

Woody Allen has often spoken about fascism and the Holocaust, yet his movie references to them are subtle and often amusing.

> 'If the Gestapo would take away your Bloomingdale's charge card, you'd tell them everything.'
>
> Alvy to Annie, *Annie Hall*

That scene came after Alvy had taken Annie to see his favourite documentary, *The Sorrow and the Pity*, the film chronicle of a French town during the Occupation. In *Radio Days*, that sinister threat which did so much to mould Woody's view of human nature, is reduced to a whimsical near dream scene when Joe spots a German submarine through the lenses of his binoculars. For Joe and his friends, the Germans were little more than yet another entertaining distraction. The idea of a Nazi submarine surfacing off Rockaway is presented as a fantastical, almost magical experience. Yet the German navy *was* active off the United States' coast, and Long Island was riddled with advance warning towers and anti-shipping guns which were obviously a delight to children.

The original version of *Annie Hall* had much more Nazi references in it than any other Woody Allen film, most of which were cut out. Besides Doris bringing the bedridden Alvy comics about Germans, there is one scene in the S.S. headquarters where Woody is a Resistance fighter being interrogated. He refuses to answer their questions prompting them to pull out a gun and threaten to shoot him on the spot. Woody pulls a puppet from his pocket and says: 'Because of my moral convictions I cannot name names. But he can.' The puppet starts talking.

But Alan Lapidus, who was a year younger than Woody, remembers that the Second World War and its outcome was not the casual joke that Woody presents it as: 'Everything in that movie was so real it was painful. There really were submarines off Long Island and we would go down to where the Verrazano Bridge is now, to try and see them, although I can never remember seeing anything but the smoke from torpedo tankers. For a nickel you could take the Coney Island trolley down to the beach, so we would all go down there and sit on the boardwalk looking intently for Nazi subs. The blackouts in *Radio Days* were because of ships in the straits which would be silhouetted by New York's lights.

'And we were all issued with spotter cards so that we could identify enemy aircraft, and we'd always be quizzing one another – "What's the difference between a P51 and an ME 109?" Of course, it transpired later that there was never the slightest chance any enemy aircraft would ever actually reach the U.S.

'But I'm surprised at how Woody has down-played the impact of Nazism on our youth. We were all acutely conscious of it, and at the onset of the war it looked likely Germany would win. You could sense that people were looking at us as if we were the losers. And we were bullied – not just because of the normal course of school-yard bullying, but because we were Jewish. I remember being tackled by some boys who demanded to know my name, and I just couldn't think quickly enough of a Gentile one. So they beat me. It was an awful time.

'And we were constantly being subjected to violence. Fine, the movies had these glamorous society capers which everyone enjoyed. But they also had non-stop propaganda films and war movies with the constant sound of martial music in the background. The big thing to be then was a pilot because the films were all about aviators taking on the Hun! But the pilots were never Jewish. The Jews were always reduced to some laughable, comic role.'

Jack Victor and Jerry Epstein were to be annoyed with Woody later in life when he signed a pro-Palestinian petition. 'We felt so strongly about anything that was anti-Jewish even if we could understand his reasoning and sympathise to an extent with what the Palestinians were saying. To say nothing about the injustices against Jews and then to be strong in condemning Israel was not exactly even-handed. Woody always had an internal wrestling match with his Jewishness. So much of the way he is now is accounted for by it, yet he never really was involved in those Jewish things.'

In New York there is what verges on a cottage industry of intellectuals endlessly speculating on the motivations of Jews who try to assimilate themselves into the American mainstream. For these people, Woody Allen's movies are almost a casebook for evidence of this process: the persecuted Jewish boy attempting to understand the WASP world and gradually ingratiating himself into its culture. These people invoke his romantic odyssey as vivid proof of their theory, charting a course from neighbourhood Jewish girl to blonde *shiksa* goddess. But how much this has to do with assimilation, and how much it has to do with straightforward romantic adventure is anyone's guess. Jack Victor is not one of those Jews that is interested in this never-ending debate and does not view his own culture as being any more outside the American mainstream than that of Catholics or Hispanics. But there is a New York Jewish community which is obsessed with the notion and Woody Allen has at least contributed to that community. In *Annie Hall*:

Alvy: 'You know, I was having lunch with some guys from NBC, so I said, "Did you eat or what?" and Tom Christie said, "No, didchoo?" ... Not, not did you eat but jew eat. Jew. You get it? Jew eat?'
Rob: 'You see conspiracies in everything.'
Alvy: 'No, I don't! You know, I was in a record store – so there's this big tall blond crew-cutted guy and he's looking at me in a funny way and smiling and he's

saying, "We have a sale this week of Wagner". Wagner, Max, Wagner – so I know what he's really trying to tell me ...'

(In this famous sequence Woody also reveals that other peculiar side of his character; the desire to remain anonymous, yet to blatantly seek publicity. In private, he often referred to himself as 'Max' when booking restaurant reservations and the like. Often as a joke, his friends would call each other 'Max'. By revealing this in *Annie Hall*, fans became familiar with this name.)

Woody told Frank Rich in 1977: 'Life is a concentration camp. You're stuck here and there's no way out, and you can only rage impotently against your persecutors. The concentration camp is the real test. There are those who chose to make terrible moral decisions and betray their best friends and do horrible things, and there are others who behave with unbelievable courage. That's exactly what happens in life – some respond terribly and some beautifully.

'I've never been tested and I have the greatest fears and doubts about how I'd respond under real pressure. If you're a person who thinks about these things, you're always anticipating the worst or having dreams of glory, but it never gets confirmed.

'The fundamental thing behind all motivation and all activity is the constant struggle against annihilation and against death. It's absolutely stupefying in terror, and it renders anyone's accomplishments meaningless.'[24]

My Schoolmates Were Idiots

'I would my life take for a bare bodkin. If only I could see the Queen's bare bodkin – or anybody's bare bodkin for that matter ... or a bodkin with a little clothes on even. I'm so melancholy ...'

The Fool, *Everything You Always Wanted to Know About Sex, But Were Afraid to Ask*

Like adolescent boys from time immemorial, Allan Konigsberg's high school days were overshadowed by one overriding thought – and it was not the curriculum. 'I've thought about sex since my first intimation of consciousness,'[1] he said years later, claiming it was the one autobiographical element of his movies he would acknowledge.

'We spent a lot of time scheming to get women, mostly unsuccessfully,' says Jack Victor. 'The problem was that Woody always went for the most popular girls in the class. I would only look for somebody who was realistically obtainable, but he would select the most voluptuous object of desire – and pursue her remorselessly! But we all had problems. It was nerve-racking and anxiety provoking.'

Elliott Mills says: 'Woody was lustful but girls just wouldn't go out with him. He was a small red-head.'

Woody's friend Mickey Rose was the exact opposite of his diminutive companion: tall, handsome, and confident. Rose was in many respects his real life alter ego personified by Tony Roberts and Michael Murphy for the screen in *Annie Hall* and *Manhattan*. Today, Mickey Rose says, 'Woody was the "King of Turndowns", but it was a terrible period for all of us. Washing hair was the biggest activity of our girls on Saturday night. Whenever we called they would be washing their hair. We would be in a tremendous panic on say, Wednesday, when we'd first call, and they would say,"Maybe". We'd be on tenter-hooks for the rest of the week, and then on Saturday – always – they were washing their hair. We used to wonder why they always had to do it on the night we were supposed to take them out.

'We used to get Jerry [Epstein] to make calls for us because he was thought to have more "elan", but I remember him making a call on Woody's behalf and still being turned down.

'Woody had the hardest time because of his appearance. Years later when he was in Vegas performing, Woody would still look the same as he did at high school. And women who had been at high school with him would come up and say: "Hi, I'm a great fan", and they would maybe be 35 by now, but Woody would think they were their mothers. They had changed but he looked the same.'

Jack Victor was shy and quite puritanical about girls, preoccupied, but not obsessed like Woody. Yet he went to quite entrepreneurial lengths to get women – he would pick out a girl on a bus and follow her home and get the name off the mail box and call her up. Jack would talk to girls in the street and ask them out. He picked one girl out on the street and was knocked out by her.[2] With Woody, Jack cooked up a scheme to get over their chronic shyness.

Jack Victor remembers: 'He would always be getting us to make calls, and would rarely do it himself. It was hair-raising and I would be shaking like a leaf, so much so that sometimes I literally couldn't bring myself to speak. Woody made a pre-recorded tape saying he was another student (a boy whose name we frequently used in crank calls.) The tape was done in Bob Hope-style humour extolling the caller's own virtues. At the end of the routine Woody says "Don't just sit there, say something!"'

'There was a girl at the time called Charlotte who was among the many to turn me down, so we decided to play the prank on her. I dialled Charlotte's number and when the other end picked up, the tape began recording.

'The romantic dialogue went ahead as planned and Charlotte seemed to be intently listening so Woody and I were getting quite excited at the prospects of success – although we regretted giving the credit to someone else. But when it got to the stage where the recording says, "Don't just sit there, say something!" she did, she said, "Goodbye." … It was Charlotte's mother.'

Another childhood friend says, 'He was a complete failure with girls. Absolutely. What held him back was the shyness. He would literally get physiological symptoms in the abdomen whenever he tried to call a girl. He would pick up the phone but his stomach would be in knots and he just couldn't do it.

'He bloomed later and became more confident in his relationships, but at the time the knowledge that he just wasn't physically attractive enough gave him great inhibitions in making an approach. But he wasn't the only one who got knots in his stomach when he tried to call a girl, we all had that kind of problem, although I took the initiative more often than him.'

Unlike Jack who confesses to being interested but not obsessed with girls at this stage, Woody was overly conscious of the opposite sex. Years later he would claim, 'I feel I discovered Marilyn Monroe. When I was a kid, thirteen or less, and she was totally unheard of, I paid 60 cents for an introductory subscription to a short-lived magazine for college students called *Varsity*. In the back pages of the first issue there was this tiny picture of this girl – just filler really – and it was Monroe. I was dumbstruck by her sexuality. It absolutely destroyed me. I thought she was the sexiest thing I'd ever seen in my life

– and I saved the book, and then, a few years later, she began to emerge, with the calendar and all that.'[3]

Adolescence is a torturous time for most boys, but at least for Woody Allen it was a time of sexual trials and tribulations that he would eventually capitalise on by making it into some of the most memorable comedy of his generation. While others would be dejected at social disasters or embarrassing situations, Woody managed to transform them into humour, even at that early age displaying a resilience to emotional hurt.

'We were all bumbling idiots at school, not just Allan,' says Jack Victor. 'What distinguished him was that he was always aware of the reality of the situation, and while making a fool of himself would be able to look at the situation objectively and realise how ridiculously funny it was. That was his genius, and the fact that he has the wonderful ability to look back and recreate it, whereas the rest of us shut it away in the closet for twenty years before admitting it.

'The rest of us were quite illusory in our analysis of what was happening, but he was sharp. He'd write gags while the rest of us would hook ourselves to great ideals and delude ourselves that we were going to write great literature. In fact he came the closest because he knew the reality of the world before any of us tumbled it.'

'He had a date at high school, and was wearing white buckskin shoes which were the rage at the time,' says Mickey Rose. 'Some of the local toughs came by and made fun of the shoes and they would scuff one, so Woody would scuff the other.' In *Take the Money and Run* Virgil ended up breaking his own glasses to save his bullying tormentors the trouble. In fact, Woody didn't wear glasses at Midwood.

He was the target for neighbourhood thugs and school bullies who needed someone to pick on. 'Of course they were nice thugs in those days, nothing like you have today,' says Mickey. 'Woody would get a little local harassment because he wasn't part of the crowd and he didn't join in things. When we were playing ball they would link up and throw all their balls at the same time. But there was never anything major, I don't think we had any scraps, and what dust-ups we did have he could always see the funny side of things.

'I had a pen and pencil set once, and all of a sudden I found my pen was missing and I suspected this guy of taking it. Woody and I ran into him, he was a bigger guy, and he had this pen in his pocket so I said, "Hey! That's my pen", and he said, "Yeh. So what?" in the threatening kind of way that means "beat it!" So Woody gave him the rest of the set joking, "Hey, well, you may as well have the pencils too because it would be a shame to break up the set." It was a perfect Bob Hope joke.

'There was another time when I was reading in the library and a huge encyclopedia came flying over my head landing with a huge thump on the table in front of me. It was this guy's way of challenging me to a meeting outside. Typically, Woody persuaded me not to because, he said, I would probably make mincemeat of him, but knowing what those Italian guys were like, he would probably get his friends to beat me up.'

Woody may have been picked on a little more than the rest of them because he was physically small. Strangely though, he did not wear glasses until after he had left school, but the image they lend him is so firmly engrained, many old friends recall him as wearing them all the time. The fact that he later went to clarinet lessons made him an easy target, partly because your average low-brow thug finds something inexorably amusing about people who carry musical instruments around, and partly because the very musical instrument rendered its owner vulnerable. Woody also learnt at an early age that confronting bravely an overwhelming enemy is not necessarily the wisest course. On a double date with Elliott Mills and two girls once, he spotted a bunch of neighbourhood toughs approaching from the other end of the street. Without a moment's hesitation Woody hailed a cab, jumped in and left his friend and their dates to their fate.

In graduating from P.S. 99 Woody finally escaped the dreaded clutches of Eudora Fletcher, with her iniquitous regime indelibly etched on his memory. But as far as he was concerned, it was out of the frying pan into the fire, as he was thrown into what he saw as yet another repressive academic institution. Like most of his friends, in the autumn of 1949 he entered Midwood High, a huge school with some of the most talented teachers in New York and an enviable quota of extremely clever students. Midwood High was something of a social experiment having been created by Franklin D. Roosevelt's administration to create jobs during the Depression. The principal had been given the pick of the best teachers in the city school system, and the results were impressive.

Far from being the lone genius surrounded by crass fools, as some portrayals of his past seem to imply, Allan Konigsberg was in one of the best public schools in the United States. Contemporaries included Erich Segal, the brilliant philosophy professor who wrote *Love Story*, and the composer John Corigliano. Years later Mia Farrow would be amazed at the number of successful people she met, who had been taught at Midwood.

The school measured its grade averages to a remarkably exacting four decimal points, and Alan Lapidus ruefully observes that although he graduated with an 86 per cent average, he was still in the lower third of the class. (When Woody graduated his overall percentage was in the 70s).

'That says a great deal about what Midwood was like,' says Lapidus. 'You had 4,000 kids of whom easily half had an enormously high IQ, and they inherited the ambition to succeed from their parents who had all been through

48

the Depression and didn't want their kids to suffer the same.

'None of us knew whether we were poor or not. It's a situation I call "Jewish poverty" – you'll never drive a Cadillac but a Buick will do. Money was never an issue and none of us knew whether we were middle class or lower middle class. Clothes weren't an issue – we all wore schleppy clothing – a pair of pants and a shirt. Among the girls, the only mark of status was whether you had a lambswool sweater or a cashmere sweater set – and they all wore poodle skirts. Fashion, objects or travel weren't important. The only thing that mattered was intellectual and creative achievement. There was an absolutely amazing drive to achieve.'

Elliott Mills says: 'The atmosphere and the environment of the time was unique. Education was important, people were intellectual and there was a tremendous push for *achievement*. That's why all these people eventually became a success in one way or another. We were the first people with a chance to go to college and so we were expected to do something, to become doctors and lawyers, to be great writers or to be university professors. We were expected to aim for the top.'

There was something else about the atmosphere of Midwood that goes a long way to explaining later events in Woody's life. The older students at the school, which would include Woody and his friends, were in the vanguard of that Sixties movement that challenged authority. They were being brought up in a world where everything had been black and white. The Nazis had been evil, and Franklin Roosevelt was a god. But as they matured, they began to realise there were shades of grey which their teachers did not encourage them to explore. These grey areas attracted their interest.

The students just below them were also starting on a mission of uncharted territory. These students, like Bryna Goldstein and Alan Lapidus, began to explore sexual and other social taboos. 'We were a highly sexed group of people, extraordinarily so,' says Alan Lapidus. 'We were growing up in the Fifties when it was total repression time and we were being fed a lot of nonsense at school particularly about sexuality where the simple rule was "You shouldn't do that". But we were an extraordinarily bright group of students who were extremely inquisitive and into breaking taboos. This was the first generation that was into grass and the psychedelic, and it was all people of my age who were to go on and lead the hippie movement and Woodstock.

'We were the first because of that combination of too much intelligence and too much passivity on the home front where our immigrant and first generation parents were only interested in making their way in America and not exerting a tremendous amount of control over us. So there was much experimentation with heavy breathing and so on and so forth, but very damn few of us actually did a thing about it.

'This high IQ and talent combined with repression was very destructive, and it's seen more than its fair share of catastrophic lives. A shocking amount of people from Midwood at that time are dead or dysfunctional. Some have actually physically destroyed themselves, and others have done things that some people may think bizarre: I wouldn't because I understand the background. We all have these wild destructive things that come out which is why none of us were at all surprised about Woody's affair with Mia's daughter. I don't know anyone who's found themselves in the exact same situation but I know of several parallel cases which would shock some people.

'We were the group that grew up thinking we were the Brave New World with the idea that it's okay to make up our own rules because the old ones were so obviously wrong.'

Jack Victor says that it was the group immediately after Woody's which got into dope and the Jack Kerouac traditions who eventually became Greenwich Village beatniks. Woody's first wife Harlene Rosen was one of them, a natural bohemian who orientated towards art and the artistic. Jack says: 'One of our closest girl friends smoked a lot of grass but when she tried to show off to her even younger sister, it was clear that the younger one knew how to roll it better than the elder.

'But we were the outside group and we often saw comedy in the way other people behaved in situations, what their reactions were. We spent a great deal of time psychoanalysing our own behaviour and the behaviour of others. It's no surprise that my degree is in psychology, another friend is a psychiatrist and Woody's the best psychologist of us all.'

They would psychoanalyse one another and the reactions of girls, their motivations and rationale. Wryly observant of the fact that they were not the Adonis-like heroes girls like Nancy Kreissman, Pearl Besserman, Shelly Greenberg, Bryna and Linda Goldstein wanted, Woody and Jack would work out what it was that motivated them. Years later when Woody was a success and living on Fifth Avenue, a fan was allowed into his apartment and noting the fabulously elegant furnishings and paintings, said, 'the person that owns them ought to be Cary Grant'. Which was exactly Woody's problem when he was a kid and wanted all the girls who didn't want him. By the time he was a big star, they all did want him – but it was too late for either party to get any satisfaction. 'All we were interested in at the time was six foot tall boys – who we thought of as men – with square chins and fabulous physiques,' says Bryna Goldstein.

Iain Johnstone recalled an earlier incident, writing in *The Sunday Times* about *Husbands and Wives*, the picture which was being shot while he and Mia were in the middle of their domestic tribulations: 'Some years ago, I pointed out to Allen that the theme of men being sexually voracious and women not really liking sex runs through nearly all his work. His reply was entirely candid: "That was unquestionably the experience of my early life. I was born in 1935 and for the first 20 years of my life that was the tone of sexual relations here in the United States. Men wanted sex all the time – I know I did – and women were always on the reluctant end. That was the general structure of the sexual contract: men were always pursuing women with sexual appetites and women were constantly saying: 'Later ... not now ... I have a headache', or variations on that."'

'With greater candour, he went on: "There are times when one is in the mood for a fast sexual experience: you're driving down the street, you see someone, you'd like to get them in, slam the car door, do it, and then let them out. I've had that feeling." Now, many men might harbour such desires but few would choose to articulate them.'[4]

It was a sexually and intellectually charged atmosphere that may have been rubbing off on him, but at the time, he appeared to be unconscious of it and was no more enamoured with Midwood than he was with the earlier elementary school of P.S. 99. His IQ was high – up in the 150s – but he scored average grades. Soon Nettie and Martin were to become as familiar sights at Midwood as their son. They were summoned regularly to talk to the principal about their offspring who would skip school or include daring esoteric sexual references in his essay compositions.

'Even now my parents would feel much better if I had lived up to their dream and been a pharmacist. There's tremendous pressure where I come from – a middle class Jewish neighbourhood – to be an optometrist or a dentist or a lawyer, and that's what my friends have become. They exhibited at an early age an ability to get along at summer camp.'[5]

'My teachers all loathed me. I never did homework – I mean I never ever did homework. I'm amazed to this day that they really expected me to go home and work on those sleazy projects that they had outlined.'[6]

'I loathed it. I went at the very last minute in the morning and left the minute the bell rang. I didn't have one extra-curricular activity. I avoided everybody. I was not popular, and I was not funny.'[7]

Which was partly true. Jack Victor has the 1953 graduation book record for Midwood showing the solemn fresh faced students, and proudly listing their scholarly achievements and extra-curricular activities. Next to Allan Konigsberg is nothing. Not a word. 'He didn't take part in anything,' laughs Jack. 'But he *was* terribly funny and his close circle of friends knew it.'

By now Woody's group of friends were an inseparable coalition united in what they saw as the pursuit of intellectual integrity and achievement, something that would set them apart from the crowd which they so assiduously avoided. They were, in Jack's words, a cadre of close friends with whom caring, warm and mutually respectful relationships developed. Their intellectual aspirations may have been a little pretentious, as they would be the first to admit, but it was nevertheless a genuine bond of friendship which sought to seek out 'the truth', whatever it might be. 'Soul mate' was a popular phrase at the time, and this is exactly what Jack, Jerry, Mickey, Elliott and Woody were – soul mates.

They were dedicated to their private ball games and would go to baseball matches. They would get together as often as possible to listen to jazz music, dabbling with magic and going to the movies. The friends would hang out at the regular pizza joints, especially the Capri on Coney Island Avenue, and the Joy Fong Chinese Restaurant. Although Woody may have been seen as a *schlemiel* by the in-crowd at school, he was the leader among Jack, Elliott, Jerry and Mickey.

'Woody was the most popular one of our group at the time, no doubt about it. We'd go to one another's places and have a glass of milk and a tuna sandwich,' says Mickey Rose who, as time went by, would increasingly join Woody in skipping school. They would watch a film or travel to Manhattan and head for the Magic Circle shop on Broadway and Irving Tannen's Circle Magic Shop in midtown where both were regular visitors and where Woody once met the comedian Milton Berle. He tried to impress Berle with a trick which failed miserably, but the experience of meeting his idol was worth it. 'Woody always taught us that it was sleight of hand that mattered more than anything else,' says Jack. 'You can buy tricks and they're fine, but it's the visual and mental manipulation that really does the trick. He used to manipulate cards and coins with great adroitness and could force you to choose the card he wanted you to.'

Woody first became interested in magic at age 10 when someone bought him a magic set. His interest was revived on his 13th birthday when he got as a gift a book on magic. By now fans are familiar with his obsession which he has featured in several movies, notably *Oedipus Wrecks* where his mother disappears, and *Alice*, where Alice discovers mystical potions that give her new life. But at first, in his early teens, magic was just an ideal pastime for a lonely child who enjoyed experimenting with the various, and often intricate, tricks which he would spend his generous allowance on. While school was boring, and even intimidating, magic was endlessly fascinating. While he could not comprehend what his teachers wanted out of him at school, with magic he could create his own puzzles and answers to the riddles.

Like everything he turned his hand to though, magic, illusion and trickery soon became skills to be expertly mastered. The basic children's trickery he quickly mastered and he would soon be demonstrating more complex ones to his friends. The next step was mind-reading and illusion, which he and his friends tried to turn to their pecuniary advantage when they mastered a con-trick aimed at predicting the winners of basketball matches, but which, fortuitously, they failed to put into effect.

The aspiring showman also tried to get a magical act on to children's television a couple of times, once with his next-door neighbour Jack Freed as a side-kick. Unfortunately, neither bid got through the audition stage, but at age 15, Woody was at least learning invaluable lessons about the world of entertainment.

A year later, after hearing that there was a demand for performers at one of the many summer camps in upstate New York, he persuaded Nettie to take him there for a short holiday. Hard-pressed for money, Nettie nevertheless agreed to go to a less expensive holiday camp nearby with Letty and Woody who performed with another young girl there called Marion Drayson. Years later Marion realised that the Woody Allen she had grown to know and love was the very same Allan Konigsberg she had met in that Catskill mountain retreat.[8]

Woody had fantastic sleight of hand and his mind-reading tricks became legendary. He remorselessly practised with playing cards, coins, and matches to improve his skills, explaining to Jack that they were the most precious attributes of a magician and illusionist. Magic tricks could be bought in shops, but skill had to be learnt. He became so well-regarded for mind-reading that one friend began to look upon him as having been granted almost supernatural powers.

'There was one guy who was persuaded that Woody had the power of "Looking Up",' says Jack Victor. 'We called this power "The Look" and at the time believed this power was held by only a few people in the world. The others, Woody would tell us, were magicians like Ruda Bucks or Blackstone. I would be granted secondary status in this deception as if I was the "Messenger of the Gods" or the "Mercury of Looking Up".'

'Our friend fell for this to such an extent that for a five

year period he was virtually incapable of making decisions without Woody's advice. It got so bad that one day in a record store he couldn't decide which record to buy without Woody there to guide as to whether he was making the right move. Because he couldn't make his mind up the manager threw him out of the store.'[9]

Later in his adult years Woody would perform Extra Sensory Perception with another friend. Woody's E.S.P. powers were to become a bone of contention with this particular man when the two friends became older, a deception which may account for their coldness toward one another nowadays.

On the other hand one of his friends is convinced to this day that Woody Allen has psychic abilities. 'Woody took "Looking Up" very seriously. I know some people laugh in your face when you say that, but Woody didn't let everyone in on it, he only shared it with a few people. He used to do experiments in E.S.P. and when we were in our early twenties he wanted to hire himself out to a national psychic research society. I think I have strong intuitive abilities, but he very definitely had psychic powers.'

The all-consuming obsession of Jack, Elliott and Woody was music, and in particular – jazz. Their high school years were dominated by the sounds of Louis Armstrong, Sidney Bechet and George Lewis. Woody was quite influenced by a French jazz player who was convinced that only black musicians could play jazz well. Later the group came to appreciate Charlie Parker, Duke Ellington and Dizzy Gillespie. The boys would spend many hours in each other's basements or bedrooms developing a taste for New Orleans, Traditional and Dixieland-style jazz music. They would make trips to a Manhattan children's music club called the Child's Paramount, and would spend their pocket money on records in Brooklyn stores.

Woody became so fascinated halfway through high school that he bought a clarinet and later would take up the saxophone. He still plays the clarinet almost every Monday night with his own band, the New Orleans Funeral and Ragtime Orchestra, in Michael's Pub, not far from his home in Manhattan. 'He was always full of jazz and always respectful of those who play, yet he was incredibly shy and would only practise behind the closed shades in the morning. I never thought he would reach the point where he would play in front of people,' says Bryna Goldstein for whom Woody harboured undisguised romantic intentions. Bryna had a younger sister, Linda who was also beautiful, to such an extent that Jerry and Woody would both vie for their attention

Jack Victor, Elliott Mills, Mickey Rose and Jerry Epstein all threw themselves into each of these fascinations with vigour, but what was unique about Woody was the extent to which he worked on his hobbies. Elliott Mills thinks that: 'We would always have these fantasies about doing something but he would do it. He didn't leave any stone unturned and always pursued it with the idea of being the best in the world ... Undoubtedly, the fact that he was small and red-headed gave him this tremendous drive to excel, but what was unusual was that he would devote an endless amount of time to these things. He's an extraordinarily good musician and he worked very hard at it. He would latch on to other things and would work enormously hard at them. It wasn't clear what he was going to do, but it was clear he was going to be successful at whatever he chose.'

'We all knew Woody was going to be famous one day,' says Jack Victor. 'There was never any question about it. The only question was how would his genius be expressed in life?'

One interest he did not excel at was sport, despite later attempts to portray himself as something of an athlete. It is also a puzzle to many of his friends why he is such a big fan of the New York Knicks now because he rarely displayed any interest in basketball then. He loved watching baseball but, characteristically, provoked arguments and rancour by deliberately choosing to support the New York Giants instead of the traditional Brooklyn Dodgers. Jack Victor joined in the perversity by supporting the New York Yankees, a decision that provoked arguments with ardent Dodgers' loyalist Elliott Mills.

He was good at the short sprint, and not bad at throwing a ball, but Woody's field and sport activities were very much minor league within a minor league. He was a competent, fast, and good athlete, and even expressed an interest once in entering the local 'Golden Gloves' boxing tournament, an ambition destined to be ruined after Nettie refused to allow him. Jack however, thinks that the 'Golden Gloves' episode was more bravado than anything else. 'I think Woody was utterly relieved to be saved from that particular competition.'

Woody's rosier recollections of his high school sporting prowess undoubtedly could owe much to his frustration with critics dissecting his work and attributing every single twist and turn in his career to the fact that he was a little lad who was bullied at school. In view of the number of times this theory is cited, it must be tempting for him to impose a more rational look at history in a bid to rid himself of the image in the hope that it might go away once and for all.

'The *schlemiel* image never did describe me. I've never been that. It's an appellation for the unimaginative to hang on me. The things I did on nightclub stages were fantasies or exaggerations from my own life – school, women, parents – which I set out in an amusing way. But you look up after a year and the press has created you, "Well, he's a small man at odds with mechanical objects who can't cope with his relationships with women." But all I was doing was what was funny: there's no conscious design to anything.'[10]

'I've had a certain amount of successes and failures in

every aspect of life. My life where I grew up in Brooklyn and in Long Beach was completely average. I was a perfectly good school-yard athlete. And I had friends and dated some girls and was rejected by others.'[11]

But that was not apparent at all outside the little group they formed at Midwood High, who were virtual nonentities in the hyper-competitive Midwood environment. As Mickey Rose has said, Woody was the most popular of their group, and Jack Victor has no doubts he was the leader. But the rest of the school regarded Allan Konigsberg as a nobody.

'Those guys stayed completely apart and joined in absolutely nothing which was most unusual because this was a school where students loved to excel, take part and do something. They were precocious but on the whole invisible to the rest of us. Those that did notice Konigsberg noticed him as a *schlemiel*. None of us were raving beauties at that age but Allan was withdrawn and never really part of the school. He was the character he plays in his movies,' says Alan Lapidus.

'I came from the other end of the spectrum in the mainstream of the school, the one who wrote plays and worked on the school newspapers and magazines. I was the one elected class writer. Everyone knew I was going to be a great writer, and I knew I was going to write the next Great American Novel!

'The only reason I knew Konigsberg was through Bryna Goldstein who was a mutual friend and [who] said one day, "You two ought to get together because you're both writers". It was news to me because he was just a little *schlemiel* who hung out with strange people. But we got together, and talking to him was like talking to someone on a different level. He was so very fast. I was making jokes but he was looking right into life and hitting it on the bullseye.

'I realised immediately he had great talent, and I knew that my talent might single me out as a great school newspaper editor, but that was about it.'

It was something Allan Konigsberg had been aware of for some time. With the gang he would visit the neighbourhood Flatbush Theatre where they would play everything from movies to vaudeville acts. He would copy down some of the stand-up comic routines to repeat them in front of his friends later. They all knew he was funny. But how exactly he could win wider recognition for his talents was the big question.

On the advice of his mother who was pushing him to aim for the very best, he wrote some jokes for a cousin who worked in a Manhattan public relations firm. The cousin suggested that he submit them to one of New York's eight newspapers, all of which had some sort of celebrity column which often relied on short witticisms to liven up the daily diet of trivia.

For Allan Konigsberg the idea was tantamount to entering a world he had only ever dreamed of, and so in the spring of 1952, partly out of uncertainty and embarrassment at such flagrant self-promotion, partly out of respect for the age old tradition of aspiring entertainers, he changed his name. Woody Allen was born.

The name Woody Allen has disputed origins and over the years has been attributed to everything from a fondness for Woody Woodpecker, or even the US president, Woodrow Wilson, to a shortening of the area he was brought up in, Midwood. Confusingly, when he first hit the big time, journalists writing profiles about the up-and-coming new star often identified him as Heyward Allen or Haywood Allen, and he didn't correct them. As a kid he liked to be called 'Al'.

Martin Konigsberg said: 'The kids on the block named him "Woody" because he was always the one to bring the stick out for the stickball game.'[12] But the man himself claims that he simply liked the name 'Allan' but decided to use the more commonly spelled 'Allen', and chose 'Woody' for completely arbitrary reasons because it sounded somewhat comical. He considered first names like 'Mel' and 'Max' which he was eventually to use in any case as a not very secret pseudonym. (He insists that he gets away without being recognised by using 'Max' but since he revealed the ploy in *Annie Hall* this is questionable.)

A different story about the origins of the name 'Woody' told by his boyhood friends rings true, and foreshadows Allen's habit of immortalising moments and people from his past. 'Woody was the name of the pet dog of a girl he was enamoured with,' says one friend. 'Her name was Nancy Kreissman and Woody was absolutely struck by her. I think he may have gone out with her once, but nothing ever came of it. You get different versions of this story because I guess he thinks the idea of being named after a dog is a degrading image. Why would he want anyone to know that? He would certainly press his father to say something else.'

Jack Victor tells a more likely story: 'He named himself after Nancy Kreissman's little brother who was called Heywood.'

It was not until the Sixties that Allan Konigsberg legally became Woody Allen, a name he was by then universally known as, although friends like Bryna and Alan Lapidus continue to call him Allan today. It was a transformation he later had reason to regret. 'He told me that he wished he hadn't changed it because the name Allan Konigsberg was actually quite well suited to being a director,' says Mickey Rose. But it really did not make much difference because it was not as if Woody was leaving his past behind – in fact he was taking it with him to greater heights than those students at Midwood who thought of him as a *schlemiel* could ever have imagined.

While the rest of Midwood was competing for Westing-house science scholarships and the handful of highly-prized places at Harvard, Yale and Princeton, and while most of the other students had their eyes firmly fixed on professional careers as doctors, dentists, psychiatrists and optometrists, 16-year-old Allan Konigsberg was dashing off one-liners for the likes of celebrated gossip Walter Winchell whose *Daily Mirror* column was the most widely read in New York. He would post a handful of jokes every day, tailoring the individual pieces to the style of a particular column in all of the eight newspapers, signing each one 'Woody Allen'. Rapidly his gags began to appear, first as anonymous 'fillers' in the midst of rambling gossip items, and then – victoriously! – with his new name attached in the *New York Post* in Earl Wilson's column towards the end of 1952: 'Woody Allen figured out what OPS prices are – Over People's Salaries.' (A contribution Woody admits is not very funny today but then was a topical reference to the post World War Two's Office of Price Regulation's efforts to keep costs down.)

Woody once said: 'There it was, my name in Earl Wilson's column, a column that I had read a million times before with news and gossip of people whose lives I couldn't imagine I would ever touch. But there it was. It was all I could think about.' It was the first of many 'Woody Allen' snippets that were to begin appearing all over Wilson's columns but also in the pages of other New York newspapers. 'I'd write jokes and mail them to the newspapers and a week later there was my name. I couldn't believe it.'[13] Soon it seemed that the whole of the joke business was asking: 'Who's Woody Allen?' until one press agent in particular posed the question – and decided to give the unknown Brooklyn school kid a job.

Almost exactly a year after Woody changed his name, he was jumping on the train after school and riding into the heart of Manhattan to crank out up to fifty jokes a session for the well-known publicity firm of David O. Alber on Fifth Avenue opposite Central Park. The jokes would be put in the mouths of Alber's celebrity clients like Guy Lombardo, Sammy Kaye and Arthur Murray, to make them look witty and to publicise their latest movies. Unlike his previous year's labour which had been unpaid, Woody was getting 25 dollars a week for his services, a sum that was to rise to 40 dollars before long. Not bad for a 17-year-old in 1953. More importantly, he finally seemed to have found what he'd been looking for.

He was thrilled, and he has said many times since that he was finally in the heart of the showbusiness world he had dreamed of. 'It was marvellous. At the time the minimum wage you got for working for a tailor or something was 75 cents an hour. I'd give them 50 jokes a day. There was nothing to it. I'd get out of school, get on the B.M.T. subway and start listing jokes. Always five to a page, ten pages.'[14]

David Alber and his team loved the newcomer who, despite his growing success and glowing reputation, continued to be the shy and unobtrusive character he had always been. His hero, Bob Hope, saw some of his work and a tentative meeting was arranged, although it never came off. He was the apple of everybody's eye, and familiar elements of his later style began to emerge.

A trait that would characterise his later work emerged now. He was rarely topical in his jokes, insisting that a good joke is a good joke, period. And when one of his superiors told him to be more topical Woody insisted that it was unnecessary. One of the few topical gags he ever made was a comment in the Sixties that he was working on a factual version of the Warren Commission Report into Kennedy's death. And during Kennedy's office, one commentator noted how Woody was one of the few stand-up comedians who did not do imitations of the young president.

Undoubtedly, Woody really does believe that that sort of political satire was ultimately pointless. He has in any case tried to avoid overt political activity, disappointing Jack and Jerry for not taking part in anti-Vietnam War demonstrations. 'I hate politics,' he would say' ... Political thinking throughout history has never worked. As long as it's a question of is it going to be a Democrat or a Republican, Communist or whatever, as long as people delude themselves into thinking if they can solve these issues they'd be happy, nothing's going to happen. The real problem is human nature. I think that if there were only two people in the world and they were identical twins, one would find something wrong with the other somehow.'[15]

His most overtly political movie, *The Front* – about censorship in Hollywood during the McCarthy period and directed by Martin Ritt – elicits a similar lacklustre response to politics. 'I don't think *The Front* is an angry movie. It is not a devastating indictment of the blacklist. I believe it is meant to be an entertaining reminder that these things went on in this country in 1953, that people were losing jobs, committing suicide, and other people were behaving, choosing to behave, in terrible ways. What would have been truly courageous would have been to make the film in 1953 ... Now it's an utterly, utterly safe project, conceivably one that studios see a buck in from the entertainment point of view.'[16]

Yet there is a paradox to this apoliticalness: he was the first star to sign up for George McGovern's 1972 campaign, and he openly campaigned for Lyndon Johnson. He also supported liberals Eugene McCarthy and John Lindsay, and was later to openly criticise Ronald Reagan. His *Who's Who* entry says 'Democrat'.

There were good, practical reasons for avoiding trouble if it was at all possible. Jack Victor thinks that Woody simply did not think political satire was worthwhile but if he did avoid controversy it was for the very good reason that it could affect his career. 'I was heavily involved in the anti-war movement, had eggs thrown at me, got involved in scuffles,' Jack says. 'And some of us thought that Woody should have done more. But in retrospect I think Woody realised at an early age that there was no mileage in topical humour. He was more interested in the psychoanalytical, and I've always said he's the best psychologist around.' William K Zinsser watching Woody's stand-up routine at an early age said, 'What he does is sock his listeners with jokes and, at the same time, cater to their emotional needs. As therapy, this is hard to beat – it is psychiatry made entertaining.'[17]

America is a country where politics and showbiz are intricately intertwined, and making a political statement, particularly in those days, amounted to making a career choice. Interestingly, shortly after he appeared in *The Front*, Woody's recently purchased Fifth Avenue apartment was raided by the F.B.I. This was the era of Nixon, of whom Woody had already made a critical programme which was pulled by the networks. The F.B.I. records are open only to him, but the raid did not seem to worry him. He told an interviewer: 'They seemed to know their way around the apartment.'[18]

In a very telling interview years later, Woody explained why he had never gone for direct action, expanding on the theme of guilt that the Holocaust seems to have left him with. 'An actor thinks that if he does some benefit for something or marches with Martin Luther King, he's taking a stand – but that's not what it is. A real test is if someone has your wife and kids at a train station and is going to shoot them if you don't give him a piece of information.'[19]

Overall, although Woody once described himself as a probable non-violent revolutionary, he's been sceptical of social and political organisation, relying much more on the honesty and integrity of personal relationships. Which is fortunate, because as he grew in confidence at work, relationships began to develop for him in a far more satisfying way and girls became less of the awe-inspiring obstacle that they once were. He was still Allan Konigsberg to his friends, and although gag writing was glamorous to him, most Midwood scholars thought it was something to be looked down upon. So it was not as if Allan Konigsberg was seeing any romantic kick-back from the growing fame of Woody Allen. But he was becoming more at home with girls, and on one or two occasions dated Bryna Goldstein for whom he had developed great affection.

Bryna was the one girl accepted by their whole group. After a game of stickball, Woody, Jerry, Elliott and Mickey would gather across the street at Bryna's house on Avenue K between 9th Street and 10th Street. Jack was rarely there because he had started an after school job. Bryna and her younger sister Linda were both beautiful girls, and both were touched by how Jerry and Woody were to vie for their attentions. Jack says: 'We were outside the regular school group so a lot of our conversations were about trying to understand the motivations and thoughts and those who hung out with the popular crowd, including Linda and Bryna.'

Bryna said: 'Those guys would play stickball and afterwards they'd drop by our house regardless if I was there or not. There was always my brother Paul or mother to talk to.

'We jumped school a lot and would go to the matinées – and I remember once stealing the cardboard paper cut out of Marlon Brando from outside one cinema. We'd have parties at the White Castle where hamburgers cost a dime.

'He [Woody] was very loyal. If you were his friend and if he said he had a commitment to you then you were his friend 24 hours a day. It was a lifetime commitment. He would write you every day or call you every day and I believe that's why he has such a good reputation with the people he knows.

'Woody would sometimes be around at my house until two in the morning, and my mother would have to kick him out. He later incorporated it into a gag about the chenille bathrobe coming down the staircase.'

Bryna's mother Sadie, has vivid memories of the boy who was chasing her daughter: 'He was around at our house all the time and they used to hang out in the basement where they could have some fun. They regularly used to talk until two in the morning and I was wondering what the hell was going on there.

'The one scene I remember distinctly was Bryna had some party going in the basement. She was a grown up 14-year-old but my husband and I played chaperone, getting up from the living room every so often and going down to the basement to see how things are going.

'And one time I got down there and there was a pair of heavy corduroy trousers on the stairs with nobody in them which I thought was distinctly suspicious. I knew exactly who they must belong to and I wondered, "What the heck are his pants doing on the stairs." After I inquired, it turned out that Woody said it was cold that day and he had extra pants that day and he left one of those there.

'He was dating her and they had been to some function and afterwards tried to get rice pudding from various diners, none of which seemed to have any. The next day a huge package arrived – at least six feet tall, and the package took us hours to unravel one wrapping after the other. And way at the bottom was a dish of rice pudding.

'He was one of the ugliest kids you ever saw, red hair, skinny, as well and big glasses. That's all you saw, the red hair and big glasses. But he was a delight and I knew when I opened the door to the house and heard laughs that he'd be there because he was always up to something funny. He was a sweet guy.'

There is one problem with Sadie's recollections: Woody never wore glasses when he visited her house – and the corduroys belonged to another boy. Bryna finds the rosier tint to her mother's view of Woody typical. 'My mother threw Woody out of the house every night of the week for four years. He was the last person on earth she wanted me to be with. Years later when he was a big name with his Broadway plays, then my mother wanted me to go out to dinner with him (which I did) and drive up to Connecticut and get married (which I didn't). This was Woody's big problem and it's no wonder he's sceptical of women's behaviour and motivations.'

This sense of how time and fame can change people's perceptions pervades Woody's work. A scene cut from *Annie Hall* had Alvy Singer revisiting his old neighbourhood and intervening in a brawl between a bully and a small man. Alvy manages to save the little man – but only because the bully recognised him from TV. It was different when Woody Allen really was a kid.

Bryna was more of a 'friend' than a girlfriend to Woody, much to his frustration. Years later he would regale his second wife Louise Lasser with stories of their time together, so much so that Louise always presumed Bryna was the first love of his life. To Louise, he even spoke of Bryna more than he did of Harlene, his first wife. In the early Forties though, it seemed that Bryna was keen on any boy but Allan Konigsberg. She was seeking the archetypal six footer with a promising career in dentistry, not some small red-head. One summer in particular, Woody would religiously go out to Long Beach where Bryna's family had a house. He would sit waiting for her for hours to the exasperation of her mother Sadie, who would demand, 'What are you waiting for? Bryna's not coming.' He would reply, 'I'm waiting for Bryna, she said she'd be here.'

She had probably said she would be there, but had forgotten. 'I had my head in the air,' says Bryna. 'I probably wasn't listening to a word he said. How I must have hurt him. I just wasn't thinking of Woody. I suppose that means he was right in the end about people's motivations. I'm not surprised the way he is with women now.'

One night she was out on a date with a hunk at

Columbia University where they went to a dance. He was so drunk he dropped Bryna, crushing her foot which had to be put in a plaster for six weeks. Throughout her convalescence Woody steadfastly took care of her every need, bringing books around to the Goldstein house, writing the occasional letter and phoning practically every day.

Finally the big day arrived when her foot could be taken out of the cast, and characteristically, Woody sent a tribute to the beauty of her legs, comparing them to those of Marlene Dietrich. These were the days when a mock front page of one of the New York newspapers could be bought in Times Square. Woody bought one and had it sent around to Bryna's house. The headline read: Bryna Goldstein, Cast Removed, Dietrich Faints.

Woody continued to work at Alber's office after his undistinguished graduation from Midwood in June 1953, but the following autumn he signed up for a course in motion picture production at New York University. The move was meant to please his parents who were unimpressed by his high school performance and newly-found gag writing career. But Woody managed to miss even more university classes than he did at school, displaying exactly the same disregard for the more academic courses and devoting his time to watching the films they required him to study.

Achieving persistently poor results in practically every field, Woody was told he could not continue unless he improved, and one dean advised him to seek psychiatric help if he expected to find gainful employment. According to Eric Lax, when Woody explained that he was already working quite profitably in show business, the dean replied: 'Well, if you're around other crazy people, maybe you won't stand out.'[20] Later, in his stand-up routine, Woody insisted that he was expelled for cheating in his metaphysics exam by looking into the soul of the boy who sat next to him. Flunking New York University,

Woody signed up on another motion picture production course, this time with New York's City College which proved to be even more disastrous than the first one.

He did not give a damn. 'My life began being special when I was 16 and got a job writing comedy. But even then I went to school in the daytime. I had lower than average marks and only went to N.Y.U. [New York University] for a very short time to please my parents. I was dropped by N.Y.U. because of bad marks. I was a film major at N.Y.U. but couldn't even pass my major. I took what was called the limited programme (which I failed) and I couldn't care less, because I'd ride the train to N.Y.U. from Brooklyn and I'd think to myself, "Don't get off here. Keep going." And I'd go right up to 42nd Street, cutting school and go to the movies, hang out at the automat, buy the newspapers and go to the Paramount – and then go into work in the afternoon.'

By the time he was 18-years-old, and by now convinced that showbiz was the only future he wanted, Woody put years of wasted academic life behind him. He found an agent in the form of Harvey Meltzer, a nearby neighbour, and the elder brother of one of Woody's classmates, Zachary. The relationship proved to be a short lived and unhappy one when, after five years, Woody failed to renew his contract with Harvey in favour of Charles Joffe and Jack Rollins, who represent him to this day. But Harvey did win Woody one of his biggest breakthroughs in comedy writing – and Woody immortalised his old manager – affectionately most people think – in the form of Danny Rose, the good natured theatrical manager who would champion lost causes and was a friend to all his woeful acts.

In the meantime his love life had taken a distinct turn for the better. Back in Brooklyn, life for him and his friends went on much the same as it always had, devoted to dating, watching the movies and hanging out at fast food joints like the White Castle. The East Midwood

Jewish Centre was one of their regular haunts, a place to be entertained and to entertain, since members of the audience joined in with their own contributions. Woody had already performed some magic acts there and did his first stand-up comic routine which had gone down well.

The group of friends formed a band, and although they always talked about playing at several venues around Brooklyn, they were too scared. Jack played the kazoo (comb and newspaper), Elliott and Mickey played the drums and Woody was on the clarinet. One night Elliott asked Woody to join him in a trio with a pianist, Harlene Rosen. He had never met her before but she was to become his first serious girlfriend. She was, recalls Alan Lapidus, a dark, pretty and very sexy young girl.

Bryna Goldstein was still a close friend. 'The years I shared with him most deeply were the years he spent with Harlene. He used to bring her to my house to see my drawings, and he was always supportive of my work. Every time I did some new drawings or got back from college with some drawings he used to bring Harlene up and go over them all.

'He used to say: "If I could draw I wouldn't bother doing anything else because everything I do dissolves but drawings stay there".' His relationship with Harlene was to be a case in point. The two would soon be married, but the union dissolved into ruins.

My Wife Was An Animal

'It was my wife's birthday ... so I bought her ... an electric chair. Told her it was a hairdryer.'

Woody Allen, Vol 2

Woody did not really try to electrocute his first wife but he certainly tried to 'bury' her in the figurative sense. Harlene Rosen is a woman Woody would rather forget, and indeed to all intents and purposes, he has wiped her out of his life. There are no affectionate references to Harlene in his movies. He has even managed to obliterate her semi-officially: of all his *Who's Who* entries since 1979, none of them includes a mention of the Brooklyn sweetheart he was married to for almost seven years. They only mention Louise Lasser, the beautiful blonde he fell for in the final throes of his marriage to Harlene, and before he hit the big time. Yet it was Harlene who was with him before the big time began, it was she who married him before he was a well-known name.

Woody has not seen Harlene in almost 26 years, and the last time they talked to one another was in the wake of a messy 1967 wrangle in which a lawyer representing her threatened to sue him and NBC – where he was writing for *The Tonight Show* – to the tune of one million dollars for 'holding her up to scorn and ridicule'. Harlene was devastated by his comic routines which mercilessly lambasted her long after their marriage was over. To be fair to Woody, he lambasted everyone and everything, not least himself, but most of his friends found it amusing and the women in his world came from the same sort of theatrical background which thrived on self-parody. Harlene was no show-girl.

He has since tried to play down the bust-up, portraying it as little more than a parting of the ways. But one of their closest friends at the time remembers differently: 'Harlene left on very, very acrimonious terms. In his act he would show a picture to the audience and say this is a picture of my ex-wife standing in front of my house. She's the one that has the shingles.'

In her action – which resulted in a judge slapping a temporary gag order on Woody and *The Tonight Show* host Johnny Carson – Harlene complained that he had referred to her as 'Quasimodo', a well-known hunchback of literature. Woody's other comic claim – that he once choked on the bone in a chocolate pudding – was refuted by her lawyer who pointed out that Harlene never made chocolate puddings.

Other gems from his act and written work include:

'The Museum of Natural History found her shoe and, based on measurements, they reconstructed a dinosaur.'

From *Private Life* on *Woody Allen* Vol 2

'I want to discuss my marriage … or as it was known, "The Ox Bow Incident".'

From *My Marriage* on *Woody Allen* Vol 2

'I kid my ex-wife all the time, but she was animal … She was not technically animal officially. Officially, she was reptile.'

From *What's New, Pussycat?* on *Woody Allen* Vol 2

The problem with his first marriage, Woody would say, was his attitude toward his wife – he 'placed her under a pedestal.' And also that … their deep philosophical discussions always ended with her proving that he did not exist. And she was very immature: whenever he took a bath, she would walk in and sink his boats.

Woody and Harlene were married on March 15, 1956 after a brief engagement. They parted company in 1961 and were divorced a year later. The threat of legal action surfaced some years later and was to leave a sour taste. But in public Woody has, despite his cruel comic routines, never said anything uncomplimentary about Harlene.

The legal action went on for some time during which Woody may have been forbidden to refer to it specifically, but managed to get in the odd joke about tipping the process server who came to his apartment with the writ. It was strange for an artist who makes such persistent claims about privacy, to launder so publicly his own dirty linen. Ultimately the action was settled privately in an out-of-court agreement, the details of which remain secret, but it's unlikely Harlene ever saw anything near the one million dollars, which even for litigation-happy America, was a ridiculous sum in the late Sixties. Woody blames the action on a lawyer he feels persuaded Harlene to take an action she would not otherwise have contemplated. The pair had been estranged since 1961 and divorced in 1962, yet to some it appeared that Harlene had not complained about the gags until almost five years later.

But even Woody's friends have their doubts about that explanation. 'My recollection is that Harlene was upset immediately,' says Jack Victor. 'There was something particularly vicious about Woody's jibes at Harlene and she was personally upset by his references to her. They were disturbing. I don't know what happened. But I don't think she sued him just because of some lawyer out to make a quick buck. I think she was genuinely upset by it and I think he hurt her. I remember watching Woody doing one of his anti-wife routines at The Blue Angel. One of the members of the audience was a rather inebriated banker who reacted to the hostility of the routine, and Woody was extremely unpleasant about him. "Who keeps you warm at night?" he asked.'

As far as the unhappy union goes, Louise Lasser says that Woody and Harlene were never a good match, even perhaps in the happiest stages of their marriage. She cannot remember Woody ever having a good word for his first wife – in stark contrast to the effusive way in which he would talk to her about Bryna Goldstein, a girl he had never even 'dated' in the accepted sense of the word. According to Lasser, the couple only got married as a way of getting out of their parents' homes, which was not such an unusual thing in those days. It cannot have helped having to spend the first few months of their marriage in a hotel in Los Angeles where Woody had landed a brief writing job, and where Harlene's mother was soon to join them.

Woody and Harlene met in the East Midwood Jewish Centre where he had performed his magic tricks as a student, and later tried out a stand-up routine when he was working for David Alber. She was a student two years his junior from nearby James Madison High School. Harlene, by all accounts was luscious, cute and just arriving at that age when young girls begin to have their greatest sexual allure for rampant teenage boys. She was also a good natured girl with a big heart and sweet temperament.

Before long he was dating Harlene on a regular basis, and she was to become his first steady girlfriend although Woody still harboured romantic ambitions for the leggy, dark and devastatingly attractive Bryna Goldstein, the aspiring artist.

Harlene's mother Judith was not keen on the relationship. Judith was an extremely attractive woman who had met her husband Julius when she was a singer in a band and he played the trumpet. They had married and prospered, running a children's shoe shop on the King's Highway. By Woody's standards they were rich, with a large corner house, and even a boat which they kept at the nearby docks.

Like Sadie, Bryna's mother, the last person Judith wanted Harlene to marry was a weedy little lad who had changed his name to the ridiculous sounding Woody.

The feeling was mutual. 'Woody always disliked her mother. Although she was a singer, she was a very cold woman and she made it clear she would have preferred someone from a higher social strata! Her husband was successful and she had ambitions for Harlene to marry someone very wealthy indeed,' says Jack.

Nevertheless, Woody and his pals ended up spending a lot of time around at the Rosen's spacious dwelling. United in their love of good music and with the encouragement of Harlene's trumpet-playing father, the gang formed a band and played to their hearts' content at her house. Harlene played the piano, her father the trumpet, Woody the clarinet or soprano sax, Mickey the drums, and Elliott the drums or sax. Elliott was a very good drummer, and Jack had the best voice of anyone so would occasionally burst into song. It was his habit to do this in situations which sometimes proved embarrassing – like in the middle of the street – when Jack would suddenly be overcome by a desire to hold forth. 'But we were chickens at heart,' he confesses. 'We would always be talking about performing at one of the clubs in Brooklyn – or even Greenwich Village! But it was day dreaming.'

Harlene and Woody's eventual engagement at the beginning of 1956 proved a disappointment for both sets of parents – or at least the mothers. The easy going Julius and laid back Martin didn't interfere, but Judith and Nettie were not happy. Nettie was not happy because she was never happy, and consequently a quiet engagement celebration over dinner at her home broke out into a row, with Woody snatching the ring off his mother and storming out of the house. They went over to Jack Victor's house where Woody presented Harlene with the ring.

Later, a more formal 'reception', on the lawn of the Rosen's house, was marred by the friction between Judith and Woody. She tried to persuade his manager Harvey Meltzer to do something about the match. 'There was great trepidation in her mind about her daughter marrying someone she regarded as a *schmuck*. Judith was very anxious for me to intervene but I told her it was none of my business. I was his manager not his mother.'[1]

It's hard to imagine it now, but Woody was considered a loser by many people then. The neighbourhood norm for a middle class boy was to go into one of the professions, and here he was writing jokes for some sort of tabloid ad agency. It was the height of McCarthy's 'reds under the bed' era where communists were imagined being in every nook and cranny. Not least in Woody's old school where his friends Alan Lapidus, Shelly Greenberg and Bryna were leading something of a revolt, that nearly led to the place being closed down when Lapidus organised the annual Sing Show, which satirised a new school rule calling for students to salute the flag every day.

'We were livid because we thought this was an enormous infringement of our civil rights, especially since the rule stipulated 'under God' and we said: "Well, there are some people who don't believe in God", a very precocious thing to say in those days. We were 40 years ahead of everyone else,' says Lapidus.

After he, Shelly and Bryna went to the *New York Post*, which turned the controversy into a big story, the State Board of Education backed down and with a few compromises on the students' part, the Sing Show was allowed to go ahead. It was a controversy that made Lapidus the writer look around for some form of outlet in the big world outside, where he could pursue a career of political satire. But there was nothing, even Mort Sahl had not yet made an appearance.

'I talked to Allan about it 'cause I knew he was going to be a comedy writer. So I said, "But where's the market?" and he said, "I'll write gags". I told him I couldn't do that because I was a serious writer. I was astounded that a brilliant guy like that had decided to do that, and for myself, I decided there was no practical way of becoming a writer, so I chose architecture.'

Mort Sahl was a political satirist yet to become popular in the States, and when he did, Woody Allen's eventual act would owe much to Sahl's casual appearance and staccato delivery on everything from psychiatry to women to politics. But when he was leaving school and working at Alber's, the state of American comedy was by no means sure. Charlie Chaplin and Buster Keaton and the likes of Laurel and Hardy had kept audiences laughing until the talkies took over, when vaudeville entertainers like W.C. Fields and Jimmy Durante would make it in the movies. And when TV became popular, it was essentially vaudeville comedians like Jackie Gleason, Sid Caesar and Milton Berle who became the big names. In these circumstances, and without Sahl around to show the way, it was difficult for any serious minded writer to understand how there was any potential in the showbiz world for his type of talent which is why Lapidus became an architect – and a very successful one. But he acknowledges now, that Woody could see way ahead of him.

'While we were writing our serious essays for the school newspaper, he was writing for Earl Wilson, he was writing throwaway gags, and I couldn't understand it because I knew he was brilliant and had a great mind. These were funny gags but I mean we all looked down on him because it wasn't great literature. But in reality, he could zing right to the heart of the matter with his humour.'

It was this ability which won Woody a place on NBC's prestigious new writers' development programme at the youthful age of 20, and thanks to his manager, Harvey Meltzer, within weeks he was off to Hollywood to write for the 'Colgate Comedy Hour' under a team headed by Danny Simon, elder brother of the playwright Neil Simon.

The 'Comedy Hour' writing crew – which was later called 'The Colgate Variety Hour' – stayed at the Hollywood Hawaiian Hotel in downtown Los Angeles, the sort of motel-style accommodation that proliferates in this peripatetic town. It was not exactly the heart of Hollywood, and Woody would quickly discover that writers in Los Angeles are the lowest of the low.

But it was an encouraging break for a high school drop-out who had suffered the disdain of his teachers and the contempt of his more studious colleagues. And Woody was suitably impressed by his new surroundings to boast to Jack Victor that he had a two room suite with pool. In fact he was sharing a one room suite with an older writer who was paid much more but wanted to split costs.

According to the account of one of his fellow writers in L.A. Woody was soon out 'looking for girls'.[2] (In vain, as it turned out. He returned to his hotel at 12.30 in the morning after having failed to find a woman willing to go with him.) Nevertheless Woody phoned Harlene and invited her out to get married to him.

His later animosity to Los Angeles was not immediately apparent from his initial effusive description of the West Coast paradise. Its constant sunshine must have seemed exotic and in contrast with the usual freezing winter of New York he had left behind. Just as Woody had been bewitched by Manhattan when he was a boy he was equally amazed by LA and its legends: Sunset Boulevard; the famous Chinese Theatre where stars flocked every year for the Oscar ceremonies (which Woody would ultimately not attend), and the stunning Pacific Coast Highway sweeping past Santa Monica and the Malibu homes of the rich and famous. His initial reaction to Hollywood was positive, although he admitted to being lonely and compared marriage to bachelorhood with the one added pleasure of being able to have sex whenever he wanted. Which actually, considering the years he and his friends had plotted and planned just that, was not such a minor consideration after all.

It was, says Jack Victor, Woody's flair for the dramatic. 'I always thought it was a spur of the moment thing, a romantic gesture from the bright new writer in Holly-wood, summoning his girlfriend out to marry him!'

Alan Lapidus says, 'We were always making grand gestures in those days – I asked my wife to marry me when we were 16 and I first unhooked her bra – so I'm sure Allan would have seen it as a particularly grand gesture to say to his sexy young sweetheart, "Look, I'm not the *schlemiel* everyone thought I was! I'm in Hollywood. Come and marry me and you'll be the first to escape Flatbush".'

Woody and Harlene were married in the hotel on March 15, 1956, and, as must be the case for many, they were at one another's throats immediately. By the end of the month, Woody was confessing to his best friend Jack that they had been fighting daily and – worse – he believed that he'd made a big mistake the day after their wedding. Woody was, he admitted, concerned that Harlene was not 'with it' and compared her negative attitude to that of his old next door neighbour. Soon, Woody was compiling a mental list of Harlene's best and worst points, with the latter out-weighing the former. Even her cooking did not please him. He complained that everything she made tasted like ham – even the coffee.

They were young. He was in the middle of his first experience of living away from home, alone and in a completely alien place. It was natural that they would want to be together, and in an age which frowned on 'living in sin' the only way a couple could live together was by getting married. It was an impetuous marriage, and to a certain extent, one of convenience. There are many such unions that last and prosper, but theirs seemed doomed from the start. Louise went as far as to say that Woody 'hated' Harlene, and she him, but this does not accord with the recollections of Bryna and Jack who knew the pair in the early stages of their romance and marriage and witnessed genuine love and affection. The mixed emotions of the relationship, and the perplexity of two young people being suddenly thrown into intimate, permanent and constant contact for the first time in their lives, were apparent to Jack, with whom they stayed in touch after they were married.

At the start, Jack Victor was probably their best friend, and during the trials and tribulations of their first weeks together, they would both confide to him their fears and worries.

Within three days of getting married, Woody set the tone for what was to come, by writing to Jack and referring to his new bride as 'her' and immediately inquiring after Nancy Kreissman, the girl who, in a roundabout way, was responsible for his theatrical name. There's no doubt what was going through his mind. Not an auspicious start to what on the surface should have been a dream: a young writing genius on the verge of glittering success in Los Angeles, with his teenage sweetheart flying from their home in Brooklyn to join him in an exotic new land at the beginning of a fabulous new adventure.

Hardly a fortnight had passed before he was talking about divorce and the humiliation and stigma attached to such a move. But Woody's woeful and plaintive complaints to Jack have to be taken in the context of the time and the circumstances, and he was the first to acknowledge this. He was not sure whether it was the distance from his home in New York that was causing his morbid thoughts, or simply the rapidity with which he and she had become inseparably attached to one another. He also admitted that his parents had been hurt by the sudden and unexpected union. He asked himself whether it was best to admit failure right away and pull out, or persevere to see if things got any better.

The complaints were by no means one sided, and Harlene had her fair share of reservations about her new husband. She loved him, but he was, she told Jack, a 'bastard', and out of the blue, at the height of their disenchantment with one another, Woody had even told her that it would be 'okay' if she wanted to sleep with Jack. They argued repeatedly, and although the arguments invariably ended on a conciliatory note with the two of them trying to make the marriage work, Jack was left with the impression that Harlene was trying to be more conciliatory than Woody. There he was in the heart of the entertainment business, a rising star in one of the country's most prestigious companies, an up and coming writer surrounded by some of Hollywood's most fertile young talent. At this time in his life, when everything seemed to be going just as he had dreamt it would when he was an unknown and ignored high school student, he had found himself permanently anchored to a vivid reminder of his past. It's not hard to understand how Woody felt, and how others caught in similar circumstances would feel.

At one stage it looked as if the worst was over, until Harlene's mother threw a spanner in the works by arriving at the Hollywood Hawaiian and checking into a room directly beneath the newly weds. What prompted Mrs Rosen to travel 3,000 miles to the other side of the country, can only be guessed at. But whatever raging arguments the newly weds must have been subjecting each other to, and whoever was the chief trouble maker, few bridegrooms would blame Woody for his reaction. He immediately suggested leaving Los Angeles.

Unfortunately, he was not at liberty to do so and had to endure several more weeks of arguments with his new wife exacerbated by the close proximity of a mother in law he had never been terribly fond of. His misery though, was soon to end, when it was announced that

the 'Colgate Hour' was to fold, and the services of Woody
Allen would no longer be required in Hollywood.

Things were made decidedly worse for Woody and
Harlene when 'The Colgate Variety Hour' folded in May
1956 and they had to return to New York. It was a toss-
up between moving in with the disapproving but loving
Judith who at least had a spacious and well-appointed
house, or the stricter confines – physically and mentally
– of his mother's place.
   They chose Harlene's home but delayed the day of
reckoning with a gambling trip to Las Vegas, and
spending the summer at a holiday resort in Pennsylvania
where Woody landed a job writing comedy routines for
evening cabaret acts. Tamiment summer resort was one
of the many predominantly Jewish retreats which
offered, for 90 dollars a week, a complete vacation
package similar to today's Club Med. Everything was
included in the price except drinks which were extra. It
was 'Borsch-belt' resorts like Tamiment that spawned the
likes of Mel Brooks, Carl Reiner, Sylvia Miles and Danny
Kaye.
   Woody was not quite in their league yet and his paltry
150 dollars a week pay hardly covered the cost of
accommodation. But the experience got the newly weds
out of Harlene's house, and it gave him valuable writing
experience. They would both return there for two more
summers as he built up a solid reputation for producing
good gags. But for some time during the off season,
Woody and Harlene had to live at the Rosens. He
desperately wanted a place on the Upper East Side but
they eventually compromised, leaving Brooklyn for a
small apartment on West 75th Street. The West Side did
not have the social cachet of its counterpart across
Central Park, but it was better than Brooklyn.
   Woody was still managed by Harvey who would often
buy his client a deli lunch and listen to his complaints

of inertia. 'He was always unhappy, because he never thought he had got as far as he had deserved to get,' says Harvey. He was regularly getting writing assignments, but times were financially tough, and Harlene had to work to keep them afloat, on one occasion taking a job at a paper factory.

Jack, Jerry and Elliott were all beginning to start their own diverse careers, but the friends still kept in regular touch, Jack often spending the night over at Woody's place. And Woody continued to be the leader of the gang, up to his usual tricks. For a while he was taken by the vibraphone, an electronic xylophone, which he practised on in secrecy with his characteristic tenacity. It was a phase that did not last, but Woody turned it to his advantage in a game of one-upmanship with Elliott who had no idea Woody had been practising on the new instrument. The two friends were browsing through a musical shop one day, and Woody steered Elliott to a prominently displayed vibraphone. Casually Woody said, 'That looks interesting! I wonder what it sounds like,' and began to play like a virtuoso to Elliott's amazement who emerged from the episode believing his companion truly *was* a genius.[3]

The fanatical interest in women continued, with Woody putting his new photographic skills to the test, photographing Harlene nude, a habit which was later to hit the headlines when Mia Farrow discovered nude pictures of Soon-Yi Previn in his apartment. Woody had signed on a photography course but never attended. He knew how to use a camera though, as one of his friends found out: 'He could do some crass things. He had some nude pictures of Harlene and was showing me them once. They weren't lewd in any way, just naked. It was very embarrassing because she walked in while I was looking. Woody turned several shades of red which was unusual for him because he normally had an answer for everything.'

Woody also continued to impress with his psychic abilities of 'Looking Up'. An acquaintance of Woody had long believed Woody *really was* a 'Messenger from Mercury' with supernatural transcendental powers. The friend was by now madly in love with a girl detested by Woody and several other friends, not least because she had the sort of intellectual accomplishments he mocked yet secretly aspired to. None of the gang particularly got on with the young lady but for a variety of reasons, this one friend was besotted by her, and announced his intentions to be wed. This struck horror into Woody who tried to talk him out of it. Woody could never understand why he was so obsessed with her. At one stage she announced that she was 'off to Alaska' on a research trip. 'Don't worry she'll freeze her ass off and be back in no time,' he told his friend. (A similar line would crop up in *Play It Again, Sam* when Linda would announce that she was going off to Alaska.)

When it emerged that their friend was intent on getting married, Woody gave up hope of dissuading him, did an about face and confirmed for him that, indeed, having utilised his psychic powers of 'Looking Up', the girl really *was* the girl destined to bring him everlasting happiness. They married, and although they were divorced in the mid 1980s, Woody's friend, a respected professional in his field, remains convinced that Woody really does have psychic powers, and took 'The Look' very seriously. 'He knows how to create an illusion. He studied mental magic, but the information he gave me about my future wife was so accurate he could not possibly have known from another source. He described certain things to me that it would not have been possible for him to have known otherwise.

'He tried to dissuade me initially simply because he didn't like her. He's a smart guy with a very high IQ but he flunked school so much he never really got a formal education and he was exceptionally jealous of my wife because she was a PhD in comparative literature from an extremely respected school [university] and graduated with high honours. He was always competitive with her and full of jealousy which I think is one of his biggest problems.'

They were married in 1958, and despite Woody's dislike of the woman, they all continued to socialise together. In fact Woody and the woman joined in extra sensory perception experiments together. The relationship tapered off around 1970 when Woody's Broadway production of *Play It Again, Sam* was a big hit and he was dating Diane Keaton. The plot revolved around a sexually insecure movie magazine writer, obsessed with Humphrey Bogart, who has a brief affair with his best friend's wife.

Woody's friend says: 'There was some friction, not so much between my wife and I as between she and he. It did have an effect on our relationship, mine and my wife's, and of course that was the subject matter of the Bogart movie. He interweaves his life with fiction but unfortunately he gets to the point where he doesn't know the difference between the two.'

The year 1958 was an auspicious one for Woody. Although he had been writing regularly, and had worked for the *Tonight Show* and Pat Boone's TV series, he was desperate for the exposure of working for Sid Caesar, the comic giant of America whose Saturday night TV show was the most widely watched in the country. He had been offered a job to do so once, but because it was below union rates he was forced to turn it down. Then in 1958 he was hired by Caesar and by the end of the year co-wrote a show that garnered prestigious awards. In the coming years, Woody would write TV and comic sketches for other big-time comics of the day – Herb Shriner, Buddy Hackett, Bob Hope and Garry Moore.

Jack Victor would regale his parents with stories of how young Allan Konigsberg was making it big in showbusiness. The little red-headed nobody that everyone thought was a write off was writing for Sid Caesar, America's King of Comedy! 'You believe every word that little schmuck tells you, don't you?' said Jack's dad, unimpressed by the credits at the end of the show listing 'Woody Allen' as a writer. 'Then how come the family are called the Victors?' demanded Jack, at which his father began to realise maybe his son had a point.

The Sid Caesar show did feature a family called the Victors, and there would have been more family references in all his work if Woody had had his way. He explained to Jack while he was working for Buddy Hackett: 'I've put everybody's name in everything but Buddy Hackett rubs them out and puts his own family names in.'

With the money coming in – by 1960 he was making 1,700 dollars a week working for Hackett – Woody arrived at his own personal mecca, and moved into an apartment on the Upper East Side, first to East 66th Street, and later to East 78th Street. With this new financial comfort, Harlene was able to enrol on a philosophy course at nearby Hunter College. Woody was to embark on his first serious education here too, learning philosophy with her and hiring a lecturer from Columbia University to teach them about literature. At home she would work on a sewing machine and he would practise his vibraphone, much to the delight of downstairs neighbours who were regularly entertained by the music during their evening meal.

But all was not domestic harmony and in 1958 he made a decision that would soon end it between him and Harlene. He did not renew his contract with Harvey Meltzer as his manager and, on the advice of his comedian friend Len Maxwell, took up with Jack Rollins and Charles Joffe who had shaped the career of Harry Belafonte (a former short order cook). Harvey had wanted to develop Woody's talent slowly but the latter refused to listen to his advice. ('He was making me sick what he was putting me through,' says Harvey today. '... What you put me through today. Unbelievable!' says Danny Rose before his main act dumps him.) 'People have always told me what to do. And I always listen politely and I'm always nice to them, but I always do what I want to do,' said Woody.[4]

He hoped that Rollins and Joffe could wave the same magic wand they waved for Harry Belafonte for him, but Rollins and Joffe knew that if he was ever going to fulfil his talent, he would have to perform his own material rather than write it for others. Under their guidance he decided to become a stand-up comic. The Brooklyn boy who had been so shy that he walked down back alleys to avoid other children, was going to stand up in front of a drinking crowd and tell them gags.

It was generally acknowledged that Woody was useless – by friends and audiences alike. Charles Joffe even had to persuade the manager of Greenwich Village's 'Duplex' to give Woody a regular slot there – much against the manager's best instincts. Night after night Woody would leap at any excuse not to perform before the often belligerent crowds of ill-wishers. It was yet another throwback to his childhood and the excruciating stomach aches that he got when faced with difficult situations. Only this time Joffe was no Nettie: the excuse that his temperature was at fever pitch did not persuade Joffe to let him off the hook.

It was as torturous as his dating days, only this time instead of the subject of his attentions pretending to be in 'washing her hair' on a Saturday night, it was out and very much in front of him. More often than not in his early days the gags would be greeted with blank stares and a stomach churning silence which was even worse than when they booed.

Soon he was without an income too, when he was fired

from *The Garry Moore Show* because he failed to turn up for work. He would stand outside their apartment in the freezing winter weather trying to get a cab downtown and wonder why he was putting himself through purgatory. At first he was working for nothing, but as time went by and his comic potential slowly emerged, pay was forthcoming. But never more than 100 dollars a week which was nothing compared to TV writing. And it would involve two, sometimes three shows a night, six nights a week.

The intense work was one thing, Woody's growing lack of privacy was another. 'It was difficult. When you're a writer, you're alone most of the time. Your eccentricities become charming, theatrical. Writers tend to be terribly theatrical – they claim not to be, but they are, with their beards, turtle-necks. It's a radical departure to go for eight or ten years as a writer and then become a performer. You're the opposite of alone. Your private life is laid so open to the public that the tendency is to behave slightly more normal or people will think you're an oddball. Everything you do, you do knowing you're doing it publicly and not anonymously.'[5]

The gruelling work schedule and pent-up anxiety of every day began to take their toll on his marriage. Harlene was furious that he had given up a lucrative living and the potential to realise his writing genius, to waste his talents on a low form of comedy. Harlene was a serious woman who aspired to serious ideals and she could not understand why Woody thought stand-up comic gigs could ever lead to anything intellectually satisfying. And she was supporting both of them and attending her Hunter College course. Evenings would end up in blazing rows.

Harlene was still in love with Woody, but for him the marriage was unravelling. The brief experience he had had of Los Angeles, and the life he was now leading in Manhattan had vision and hope of an even better future which did not include her in it. She was either at college or working to pay their way, while he was out meeting a fascinating new set of people, the likes of which he had never really met before. Now, instead of spending his time writing in the seclusion of his own home, or in a writing den, his afternoons and evenings were spent in the coffee houses and clubs of Greenwich Village which thronged with the Swinging Sixties generation. These were the days of Bob Dylan and the American comedian Lenny Bruce, who had shocked America by using 'dirty' words in his act. Dylan and Bruce were regulars down in Greenwich Village haunts like Cafe Wha, The Black Pussycat, Playhouse Cafe, The Village Gate, The Bon Soir and The Bitter End, where beauties like Faye Dunaway would hang out. These were the vanguard of counter culture rebellion. The men unkempt, unshaven, and long haired; the women, in Woody's new stamping ground, were beautiful, exotic and liberated.

It was during this new era in his life that Woody met Dick Cavett, today one of America's best known TV celebrities but then an up and coming comic writer who hero worshipped Woody (and would go on to imitate him in his own comic career). Cavett would watch Woody's shows with wide-eyed admiration, even while the rest of the audience – if there was one – would sit there silently. During the day before performances, Dick and Woody would hang out at billiards' halls.

Woody began to mix with the sort of girls he had seen from a distance in his Brooklyn school days, but were now everywhere in his new world. He confessed an admiration for 'tall, Teutonic-Prussian girls. Villagey looking blondes. I like a girl who's arrogant and spoiled, but brilliant and beautiful.'[6] He was also attracted to the 'Jules Feiffer' type of girl with long black hair and leather clothes. Invariably Woody could only watch these girls from a distance, as they hung themselves around their hairy rebel boyfriends smoking dope and downing beer, while he sat in the corner with his spectacles on, sipping soda.

If it hadn't been for girls, the great 'intellectual' Woody Allen would never have been either. He would take them out and they would ask him all sorts of questions about writers he had never heard of. When he told them that he read Mickey Spillane novels and comics they were incredulous. In order to keep up, Woody had to read an incredible amount of literature which he was totally unfamiliar with, and which was hard-going at first. Intellectuals and pseudo-intellectuals have always been victims of his jokes, so he didn't relish indulging in their favourite pursuits, but the thought that he would be winning the hearts of the women he loved pushed him ever onwards. After a while though, he discovered he actually enjoyed much of what he read, particularly Faulkner and Hemingway.

One such 'Jules Feiffer' girl was Vicky Tiel, now a famous dress designer, but then a waitress cum cash collector in the Greenwich Village coffee shops where Woody would sometimes perform. Studying fashion by day, she worked in the Village at night. She was known as 'Peaches La Tour' and owed her peculiar occupation to an obscure rule which prohibited folk singers from soliciting donations. Instead, Vicky would introduce the act, serve tables while it was on, and collect money afterwards. At the time she was dating a Jim Morrison-style rock singer who was the most popular guy in the Village, when she began to notice Woody, a quiet, funny, but by no means obvious presence among the boisterous talent of the time. Vicky noticed the development of the traits which are now familiar in Woody. 'He was formed in the Village. It wasn't just the girls he fell in love with – it was the whole milieu. At the time we all loved Ingmar Bergman's *The Seventh Seal* and it became the movie to watch and know about. Don't ask me why, it was just the trendy thing to be into. Well of course, when Woody finally got *carte blanche* to make whatever film he wanted, he was always trying to recreate Ingmar Bergman. It was the same with women. He fell in love with the women he saw around him – that kind of weird, dysfunctioning, hippie kind of girl. He always wanted to get the girls he couldn't get, the girls who were beyond him – the sort of ones who would go with Axl Rose today. Then he formed what became his act, the guy who couldn't make it with all these sex-pot girls.

'He was making fun of who he really was, but because it was who he was, it wasn't a joke. He never wanted something he could easily have, so he created a persona that was doomed to automatically have its heart broken. Those babes in the Village, the Britt Ekland types, they became Woody's ideal and they've remained his ideal. As he gets older, his vision of female beauty remains the same.

'When he got successful, he still wanted the women who were above his reach. He wanted Warren Beatty's girls. So because he was successful, he would get them because they were interested in being with a rich and successful person who could put them on the screen. But once that happened they were doomed to walk out on him. Whereas with Warren, they would fall in love with him because he would dominate them sexually, and Woody couldn't. His relationships with Diane Keaton and Mia Farrow were both beneficial to those women. Keaton's always been a good friend and I believe she's always loved him, but I don't know about Mia.'

It was in these Greenwich Village comedy clubs and coffee houses that Woody's 'intellectual' image began to bloom. Fuelled in part by his own pretensions, it was in spite of the fact that his comedy was in the classic style of quick-fire gagsters like Bob Hope and the Marx Brothers.

'I was always a big deal in Greenwich Village, but they were sceptical uptown. I was constantly being called cerebral. How many people came up to me, and said, "I like you, but other people won't know what you're talking about." If a joke is funny, it can go anywhere.'[7]

In a 1980 BBC interview, he said how exasperating the image was – and how it had led him to getting rid of an expensive car that he owned. 'It astonishes me what a lot of intellectualising goes on over my films. They're just films. Yet they treat me like a genius at times, at other times like a criminal. Because I've produced "bad art".'

'And I've never been that kind of person. Never. I never lived in the Village. I always ate at good restaurants. When I went to buy a car I said, "What's the best car?" Just automatically.

'But people always found that at odds with my image. They thought, "This is the guy who's a regular guy and who wears jeans to formal dinners and who must live in the Village some place."'[8] So he sold the Rolls Royce.

At this time in the Village Woody was also developing humour about taboos. One of his routines went:

'In the Faroe Islands where lovemaking is as casual as conversation, sleazy natives sidle up to strangers on street corners and try to sell them pictures of food. A piece of corned beef with just a little fat on it is considered very provocative. A girl is asked if she would like a little cream cheese with her bagels, and she says, "I don't do that sort of thing."'

Woody was on the outskirts of this 'underground' Village cultural movement, bursting with sexual promise and allure, that continued to elude him. He was on the outside looking in, beaming with curiosity and false hope just as his first screen character Victor would be in *What's New, Pussycat?* Victor was the striptease dresser at the Crazy Horse Salon surrounded by beautiful and half-clad women unwilling to join the bespectacled back-stage buffoon on cultural trips to Paris.

But one of the girls in Greenwich Village would soon be

falling into Woody's arms. She was Louise Lasser, beautiful and blonde, with whom Woody would eventually share many of the best years of his life. He had met her when a mutual friend introduced them at his own apartment which he was still sharing with Harlene. The marriage to Harlene was withering and when it was over, Louise and Woody became 'an item'. Although from a wealthy background, Louise would start serving tables at the 'Bitter End' much to Woody's chagrin, who complained that it was impossible to do his act seeing Louise working in the room.

'He tried to persuade me to stop but I liked the job,' says Louise. 'So he said, "Why don't you be my maid instead?" In the end I agreed, and for 50 dollars a week I became his maid but only on the understanding that I couldn't work for him when we were going out. One night when he was working in the Village, I arrived at his apartment to do my "maidly" duties and found stickers everywhere saying, "Don't do the washing-up", "Don't move the books", "Don't do this", "Don't do that".' The relationship with Louise was to be a far happier and lasting one. Woody's marriage was finishing and in the spring of 1961 he moved out of their apartment. A year later they divorced and met only briefly after that, around the time Harlene sued him over his *Tonight Show* jokes.

A standard routine of his became:

'It was a toss up between a vacation in Bermuda' – his references to hot, sunny island resorts are generally unfavourable – 'or divorce.' We decided to split up reasoning a vacation is over in two weeks, but a divorce is something we'll always have.'

There is, friends agree, a dark side to Woody, although that hardly makes him unique. There has been some suggestion that his financial treatment of Harlene was an example of this. She received hardly anything and there was no 'escalator' clause in the final agreement which would have guaranteed her a greater share of his later substantial earnings.

But realistically, Woody was making little money when he split up with Harlene, and Louise Lasser was to say, 'I didn't get much either'. There is no question that he's an exceptionally generous man when he wants to be, and is certainly not niggardly with respect to money. Vicky Tiel explained, 'He was Jewish, and all the girls wanted to go out with Jewish men because they're the most generous. Whatever a girl wants, she gets with a Jewish "papa".' This would seem to be true. Louise was always being invited to spend Woody's money; and one day he would write a million dollar cheque out to Mia Farrow. If there was any parsimony with regard to Harlene, perhaps it was unconscious, perhaps born out of his reduced financial circumstances then – or part of the bitter residue that seemed to afflict their union.

The relationship had been a loving one but had hit the rocks thanks to the inevitability of their situation. It was common in those days for young couples to marry, purely to get out of their parents' home, and once they did they found themselves woefully ill-equipped emotionally, sexually and financially to face a grown-up world. Woody was himself to say that nowadays he and Harlene would at least have had the chance to experiment with living together before making a decision to marry. Added to that was his advancing career – even though it may temporarily have appeared in a quagmire – which was taking him into a different orbit to Harlene's.

'She was his ticket out to have his own life, and he hers. As the saying goes, she married him so she could have her own set of Christmas ornaments not use her mother's. It was typical in those days for women to marry the first man they were attracted to in order to get the hell out of the house,' says Bryna Goldstein.

'But I'm sure knowing Woody that he wouldn't have

gone into it if there hadn't been any love there. He used to tell me about all the instruments she played and he really had a crush on her. He was very proud of her and she certainly stood by him through the worst.

'He was leading a very schizophrenic lifestyle when they were together. In one year he would be making lots of bucks working for Garry Moore or Bob Hope – but especially Moore – and the next year he'd be out of work and she'd be supporting him. She'd go to Hunter College every other year, get straight As, and in the middle she'd be working to keep him afloat. He would be the first to admit how hairy that marriage was because of both of their personal problems. Don't forget how many years of therapy he had and the fact that except for a short bout with Louise he never really married again.

'Maybe she loved him too much. She put up with a lot of very hairy creative insecurities and neurotic *schtick* and then didn't get around to any of the gravy. She was the one who got him where he is, and she was with him until months before his ship came in.'

Shortly after the split-up Woody said: 'We're still friendly but we don't see each other. It was really a great experience. It was enlightening to see what it was like to move out of my parents' house and be responsible and have to manage finances and live with another person. But our interests grew diverse. It would have been that much better had it worked out, but it wasn't destructive in any sense.'[9]

After the split-up Jack Victor got the impression Woody was trying to encourage him to date Harlene. The two had been great friends and did continue to see one another afterwards, but never became romantically involved. They corresponded every so often and shortly after the divorce Harlene left for Italy where she had a passionate involvement with a Florentine artist, which she wrote to Jack about. For a while she lived at an Indian guru camp in Canada.

'Harlene is a kind of depressive person anyway. She led the life one would have predicted had she not married, what was a kind of bohemian lifestyle. She continued pursuing those things which Woody would have liked, and she studied philosophy and art. I think she was genuinely interested in art and had talent.

'It was a loving relationship with Woody, very definitely, and even if they did have a few rows at first, that's not uncommon for a young married couple. Reading back over letters they wrote to me, you at first think they're pretty nasty about one another, but afterwards they're very warm together,' he says.

'There were problems. She was always trying to take courses in philosophy and this and that, to live up to him, to try and be smart. I remember she took a course with a well-known South African professor – she went out with him without realising that many considered him to be a racist.'

'We're divorced two weeks, she's dating a Nazi.'
Play it Again, Sam

'She tried hard to please and she dabbled at a variety of artistic and intellectual pursuits, in at least part to please him, but didn't quite have the intellect or talent to be successful at these, although she was very talented at art.

'That was the problem with their marriage, it wasn't quite working out and people could tell because they never seemed happy with one another. Guys would hit on her because they could tell she wasn't happy with Woody and she was a very attractive woman. They could tell there was some sort of strain.

'Woody's since tried to say the marriage was really over after four years but from whose point of view? They were together. I mean he may have felt that the marriage was too strained after four years but they were married, living together and she was trying to make it work. She even had some misgivings about leaving him. I think it was a lot more complicated.

'It didn't break up over his relationship with Louise because she did not know about it. He may have instigated things because of Louise, you know? When you're seeing someone else and you don't really want to make the move you make things so tense that the other person does make the move which could well have occurred.

'After they split up, Woody hinted that maybe the two of us would be a good match but I felt funny about it. I got the impression he would be relieved to off-load her on me. It would be a weight off his mind. I was terribly shy anyway, and although I thought Harlene was a lovely, adorable creature, I didn't like the idea of being with someone that was his. But Harlene and I remained close friends until I married and I believe in a way we loved one another.'

Lucky I Ran Into You

'Why did I turn off Allison Portchnik? She was beautiful.
She was willing. She was ... intelligent. Is it the old
Groucho Marx joke? I just don't want to belong to any club
that would have someone like me for a member?'

Alvy, Annie Hall

Louise Lasser was the woman Woody could not live with,
and the one he could not live without. They were together
for many years, married briefly, and remained friends
long afterwards. Woody still has a picture of Louise
prominently displayed in his home. Although they
divorced, there has never been any acrimony between
them, and she is, he has said, one of the few people who
can cheer him up.

Louise had everything he had never had: privileged
parents, a huge Manhattan apartment and a giant white
convertible to drive to college with – a gift from a
sophisticated dad who talked to her about sex and was
not constrained by the taboos of the time. But when it
comes to emotional health Louise and Woody could have
gone to the same psychiatrist. 'Sometimes I get depressed,
but then I'm not a model example of a person. I'm riddled
with anxieties that don't seem to bother a lot of people,'
she once told the writer, John Wilson.

Their marriage, she has said, was doomed from the
start. They were happy and unhappy before they were
married, and they were happy and unhappy afterwards
when he finally cast her in some of his movies. But they
remained lovers and good friends afterwards. 'I was the
ex-wife he always depicted in his pictures,' says Louise

Lasser, laughing at the dozens of cinematic put-downs he delivered about her after they were divorced. Louise may also have been the inspiration for Woody's trademark trenchcoat image. He started wearing one after noticing hers, which she wore wandering around museums and art galleries.

The ice maiden ex in *Annie Hall* who refuses to make love to Alvy while 'there are people from the *New Yorker* magazine next door' and Nancy in *Play It Again, Sam*, who walks out on Alan Felix because she wants to live life, be free and go skiing. These were Louise Lasser.

From *Annie Hall*:
Alvy: 'I'm so tired of spending evenings making fake insights with people who work for *Dysentery*.'
Robin: '*Commentary*'.
Alvy: 'Oh, really, I heard that *Commentary* and *Dissent* had merged and formed *Dysentery*.'

But Louise was always soft and vulnerable to Woody. She was never the shallow or mean ex-wife often portrayed. The words were hers, but the characters were out of context. Unlike Harlene though, Louise never took his screen jibes seriously. She says that: 'I did say some of those things like "I wanna be free! I wanna laugh all the time! I wanna go skiing!" but he was so *horrible* and took them all out of context.

'And then he would turn it into this idea that the reason we broke up was because we never went skiing places, which wasn't strictly true of course, but there were things like that which I wanted to do.

'The person I see in these movies is a sort of disembodied me. He portrays me as this hard, cold person that rejected him, yet he doesn't show any of the softness that held us together for so long – the stuff that made him fall in love with me.

'It wasn't just a bright mind, it had to be something else.

And I think that's why he never re-married after me. Without something sensual or stuff like that there's something missing and it makes things really hard. And if you *only* have something sensual, it's hard too.'

Nancy: 'I can't stand it, the marriage. I don't find you fun. I feel you suffocate me. I don't feel any rapport with you, and I don't dig you physically. Oh, for God's sake – don't take it personal!'

Play It Again, Sam

Louise Lasser came from the sort of background Allan Konigsberg had spent his childhood dreaming of. The glittering metropolis he worshipped was her home. The Upper East Side with its wide sidewalks and elegant apartment buildings he longed for, had been her natural territory since childhood.

While the young Woody fantasised about authors, celebrities, Hollywood stars and the glamorous New York society world he heard over the radio, Louise did just the opposite and imagined what it would be like to lead a simpler life. One of her favourite pastimes as a blossoming young woman was to take boyfriends along East 70th Street between Madison and Park Avenue where, standing imposingly at one end is the huge chateau-like home of legendary tycoon Andrew Mellon.

'I would walk my boyfriends along the street – which I think is the most beautiful block in Manhattan – and stop outside Andrew Mellon's house. I would tell them that that was where my mother worked – cleaning the floors. I insisted it was only the ground floor black and white tiles that mother cleaned because they needed exquisite care and attention. Sometimes, I'd tell them, the people in the house would be real nice to me and give me milk and biscuits. And my boyfriends wouldn't believe that my mother really worked in that house.'

So accustomed was Louise to her indulgent background,

as the only child of privileged parents, that she had little idea of how other people lived. 'When I was dating and someone took me to a restaurant, I would order the best steak and I always presumed the reason my date said he didn't want anything was because he wasn't hungry. Of course it was because they didn't have enough money.'

Louise grew up wanting for nothing. She was born in the heart of Manhattan's wealthiest district, and lived in a duplex apartment on the 11th and 12th floors of a modern building overlooking Fifth Avenue and Central Park. The sidewalk outside glittered with tiny fragments of crushed glass mixed into the concrete, which Louise grew up believing were diamonds, because that's what her father told her every time they walked out on to the Avenue. It was the richest strip of real estate in the land, and only few blocks away from the penthouse apartment Woody has today. 'This was my world,' says Louise of the compact oblong of city blocks taking in Madison, Park and Fifth Avenues, that forms the Upper East Side. 'All my school friends came from buildings around Central Park, and I can remember thinking the rest of New York may as well have been Siberia. Forget it! I didn't know anyone from there. Once you've lived on the Upper East Side there's no real reason to live anywhere else.'

She was the daughter of the highly successful and distinguished accountant S. Jay Lasser, renowned in the United States for writing one of the country's most popular income tax self-help manuals. The epitome of the American Dream and a conspicuous success. Although the Lassers were Jewish, the family was as solid as a rock in a WASP-like way that was to prove both an allure and a mystery to Woody.

Educated at the exclusive Fieldston private school, Louise grew up to be a beautiful, waif-like blonde, with an air of innocent seductiveness that men found extremely sexual. She later went on to Brandeis University in Massachusetts where she would turn up in the white convertible her father had given her.

Brandeis was a liberated college where most of the students lived off the campus. There she fell for a brilliant intellectual and musician whom her father suggested she share a house with, a suggestion she declined, although she was very fond of the man. 'He kept re-inforcing how I was all these great things, and I always thought I was just a dumb blonde.'

For the Fifties, this liberated upbringing was a far cry from the suffocating domestic constraints of Allan Konigsberg's early years. Louise's mother was a very beautiful, rather inaccessible and extraordinarily original woman, but she spent much of her life in and out of hospitals. From her early teens Louise learnt that doctors had diagnosed her mother as 'incurably insane'. It was a diagnosis that if made today would certainly never have been passed on to the family. But in the Fifties doctors simply did not know how to cope with Mrs Lasser's illness.

It was left up to Mr Lasser to be both father and mother, and he went out of his way to let Louise know that if the worst thing in the world ever happened to her, she would know enough to go to him and talk about it. Because of his heavy workload, he was home late many nights and in compensation arranged for extraordinary Sunday breakfasts which would sometimes go on for four hours. Father and daughter would talk for hours, and he had a subtle way of bringing up the thorny issues of pregnancy, abortion, and menstruation. It would be an unusual role for a father today; it was an extraordinary one then and one that Louise has never forgotten.

In many respects, the relationship Louise would eventually have with Woody was that of the child-father type: he the ever indulgent father liking nothing better than pampering his spoilt little girl.

Louise majored in political theory at Brandeis before dropping out through depression. She was first introduced to Woody by her own boyfriend who was a mutual acquaintance. Her boyfriend said, 'You two are so much alike one another, you really ought to meet each other.' They went around to Woody and Harlene's fifth floor apartment on East 78th Street. Louise and Woody were soon seeing one another. Jack Victor met Louise for the first time down at the Duplex. He says, 'She was a stunningly beautiful girl when I first met her ... and she was extraordinarily talented with a terrific sense of humour. She had a sort of Judy Garlandish appeal to her. She had a perfect figure and I remember being surprised that she never appeared as good when she was later on television.'

Woody and Harlene had already agreed to split up as soon as her college course was over, but he was still discreet about his new relationship with Louise and the two did not become 'lovers' until many months later. It was a raging love affair, the pair of them acting like two kids who had been set free for the summer vacation. Louise says, 'We were very smitten with each other. It was in the fall and I was living at home with my parents just a few blocks from where he and Harlene were. I invited them to a New Year's Eve party and Harlene was very hostile toward me so I guess she must have known something. But our relationship didn't start until some time later – I guess because of the situation. He asked me to go with him downtown once to go shopping for records, which we did, running through the streets and jumping over park benches like two kids.

'Then, after a few months, he asked me out on a date, date. I remember thinking that if he tried to kiss me I *mustn't* say, "But you're married!" So we went out together and he took me in a hansom buggy through Central Park where he turned around and tried to kiss me. And I *did* say "But you're married!" But he explained everything. He said it was over between he and Harlene and they would be splitting up after she had finished college. That was always the nice thing about Woody. He would always be in control and had a way of taking the anxiety out of a situation. He would say exactly what was going to happen, the reasoning behind it, and when. If he said he'd phone you at nine o'clock, he would phone you at exactly nine. He was very reliable and that was very comforting to me coming from the sort of background I did come from, where someone was always in control. We met in the fall, in the spring we went out, and in June after school they separated, which was his plan.

'But they were still living in the same apartment and once I needed some bed linen and called Woody to borrow some. Harlene answered the phone and I went around to pick the sheets up. She said to me after they split up, "I knew you had your eyes on my husband from the moment you came around to my house for those sheets."

'And there were other times. All three of us were at a restaurant one night when he offered Harlene a glass of wine and asked her, "What would you like?". Then he turned to me, and said in this Peter Sellers-style sensual way (with his eyebrows rising above those big glasses) "And what would *you* like?" I guess she must have known then.'

Harlene did not know. Louise herself says that although they fell for one another straightaway, her relationship with Woody began long after that first meeting. Jack Victor remembers that after Harlene and Woody finally divorced, she was surprised to hear he had been so heavily involved with Louise.

'I had a big *faux pas* with that. I was out with Harlene. She had left him really ... and she was saying maybe she shouldn't have divorced him, maybe it would have worked out. And I said, "But what about his relationship with Louise?" And I realised Harlene didn't really know that he'd been seeing Louise. They overlapped for some time. I felt very bad for Harlene ....'

Woody would have more 'overlapping' relationships in a romantic career as prolific as his artistic one. In the sort of showbiz world he began to move in, where the artificially intimate situations actors and actresses find themselves in, often become real, it's hardly unusual or surprising that relationships bloom. What *is* unusual in Woody is the way he will bend over backwards to do the 'right thing' and to be seen to be doing the right thing. If a long term relationship is over, fine. Do the right thing by the old partner and commit yourself to the new one only when it's appropriate. He would go to great lengths to emphasise the specific dates upon which a relationship had floundered, and the exact date a new relationship was born.

Woody and Harlene continued living together on East 78th Street while he would make a regular, if discreet, trek four blocks down to the Lassers' impressive high rise household. His fledgeling success though was not enough to impress the doormen. 'I was still living with my parents,' Louise says, 'and the thing was that the doorman would never want to let him up. He would arrive in his rumpled corduroys and polo shirt and a couple of times they made him use the delivery entrance.

'We would go for long walks in the park and talk about art and philosophy and life and all those things you find out months later that neither of you likes to do. But I had had a tremendous cultural upbringing and he learnt a lot of that from me.

'Harlene had a rough time with him and he with her. They do now and they did when they were married, at least that was the distinct impression I got. I don't know why – maybe they were just too young ... When they realised it wasn't going to work out, they decided to split which is where Woody's characteristic generosity came out.

'He stayed with her as long as he did, purely to see her through college. Woody wasn't hard on Harlene. He even took care of her after they divorced. He's never overtly negative or punitive to anyone. I think he's a very true person, he knows his obligations and sticks by them, and if he really cares for someone he looks after them. That's just the way he is.'

When Harlene was out of his life Woody and Louise were to share several different apartments during the course of their relationship. First it was a studio apartment at the back of a building a few paces away from Fifth Avenue on 77th Street where Louise would occasionally stay, although she still lived with her parents a stone's throw away. They dated more openly, hanging out at billiards' halls with his new best friend, Dick Cavett. He also started playing high stakes poker with friends like Ken Roberts, the father of Tony who later was to appear in many of Woody's plays and movies, and was to become a close friend.

Unable to overcome the inbred habit of constantly swapping homes, Woody kept changing addresses while living on and off with Louise. During their relationship, which eventually became a marriage, he lived in four East Side apartments. At first Louise stayed with him at the 77th Street studio which the two of them loved. But some time later when Louise moved there full time, he decided to move out into a bigger apartment on East 80th Street before deciding to live in one on Park Avenue, an address that provided him with the glamour he longed for, but turned out to be deeply depressing because of a chronic lack of light. When they finally married, they moved to East 79th Street, a rambling duplex on the top two floors of a town house. The homes were always in a limited area of Manhattan which they associated with their literary heroes, and for some obscure reason the couple were both bewitched by the 77th Street studio which inspired them to have a nostalgic feeling for Zelda Fitzgerald. 'We lived in this fantasy of being Scott and Zelda Fitzgerald,' she said.

'The studio on 77th was beautiful but I didn't live there full time until when my mother died and the family split up. After a while I was driving Woody crazy and he couldn't put up with me any more,' says Louise. 'So he moved out which was nice of him because really it was his place. As usual, he was generous and I was selfish. The day he moved out, I found an old photograph in the bottom of a closet, of Gertrude Stein and her lover Alice B. Toklas, and I was amazed. I called him up and said, "Woody! You'll never guess what I found! Didn't I tell you there was something about this apartment!" He said, "Really?" in that mock innocent way he has. Suddenly I realised that of course he'd left it there for me to find, like a father would leave a little gift for a child to come across unexpectedly. That's the way he was. He denies it to this day, but I know he put it there.'

Another of Woody's women has less romantic memories of that time. Sadly, for Harlene at least, it was just as she disappeared from his life that Woody's ambitions began to see fruition, and the success he craved slowly but surely came his way. His name began to be well-known outside New York. At the end of 1962 he began to get rave reviews, and Woody Allen, the obscure name that used to appear in newspaper gossip columns, was fast becoming Woody Allen, the New York comic phenomenon.

Jack Victor's memories of Woody's first wife are fond ones, and he thinks that the marriage was far more than a match of convenience for a young couple to get out of their parents' houses. 'Harlene was hurt that his success happened after her. Not just for financial reasons, but because she didn't get a chance to enjoy any of it with him, to go to the finest restaurants with him, and attend social functions, to mix with the other wives and so on.'

Woody Allen has made much of his dislike of television and the blatant commerciality of mass media. On the one hand his stance is admirable and honest, on the other it's blatantly disingenuous. After all, he made his name by writing gags for the biggest selling newspapers in New York, and in the early stages of his playwriting career he would tell one critic that whether the show was any good or not did not matter. All he cared about was the box office. One of his most famous works, *Annie Hall*, was totally re-engineered to sell to a mass market because the original was too esoteric. *Hannah and her Sisters* and *Crimes and Misdemeanors* were carefully designed to be 'art' films which appealed to big audiences. His early friend, Vicky Tiel, says he is a very commercially conscious performer and director. He has since acknowledged that he is one of the few directors to be lucky in having feet in both camps. But in the early Sixties, there was only one camp that mattered, as Allen embarked on self-exposure and publicity.

First, Rollins and Joffe – who had already signed up Louise and Dick Cavett – signed Woody for several advertising deals for products like Foster Grant sunglasses and Smirnoff Vodka. In the vodka ads he appeared with statuesque Monique Van Vooren, contrasting her glamorous sexual poise with what was rapidly becoming his trademark – a baggy and dishevelled appearance. Unlike the TV commercials he has done in recent years – one for an Italian supermarket chain paid him 3 million dollars – these early commercials made him next to no money but were intended to get his name better known on a national scale. And Smirnoff did give him many cases of their product which he off-loaded on grateful guests at the first New Year's Eve party he and Louise threw together at their newly decorated East 79th Street apartment.

And it's often forgotten that in the 1960s he played several memorable roles in *Candid Camera*, the hilarious TV spoof show that plays tricks on unsuspecting members of the public. Woody says he's still 'irresistibly drawn' to *Candid Camera* because of its spontaneity, but he also admits that it was 'degrading'.[1] The show, created and hosted by Allen Funt, ended with the victims bursting into laughter – or sometimes not – when their persecutor revealed that they had been caught out by Allen Funt of the dreaded *Candid Camera*! In one of the best episodes Woody plays a bookshop clerk who infuriates the customers by telling them all the plots of their books.

Other TV shows he either wrote for, appeared on, or presented in the Sixties, include *The Kraft Music Hall*, *The Tonight Show*, *The Laughmaker* and *Hippodrome*. He was also a regular on the big audience winners of Garry Moore, Joe Franklin, Ed Sullivan, Steve Allen, and Merv Griffin. So much for his distaste of TV. To be fair, it was practically impossible to earn a living otherwise, let alone get the widespread exposure critical to success. Then again, doesn't Woody perpetually harp about how he's not interested in widespread exposure?

By the mid Sixties he would be comfortably making more than 5,000 dollars a week appearing across the country in Washington DC, San Francisco, Los Angeles, St Louis and Chicago, flying across and around the country with a regularity which is alien to him now. He spent endless nights in hotels, but formed several friendships along the way, including a close one with the statuesque folk singer Judy Henske from Chippewa Falls, Wisconsin. This was a town that was to become the birthplace of his fictitious Annie Hall years later. When Woody was 'on the road' he also met a woman who was to become a very close friend. Jean Doumanian, a former model, met Woody when he was appearing in Chicago's Mister Kelly's and they have remained good friends to this day although never lovers.[2] At the time she was married to Jack Doumanian, who has appeared in small roles in several of Woody's movies.

In fact Jean is the most enigmatic woman in his life. Millions of words have been written about Keaton and

Farrow, and hundreds of magazine articles have probed his love life. Yet the woman he is closest to remains a mystery. There are no profiles of her, and press coverage was limited to an incident when she was hired by NBC a decade ago. For several years, she has been linked to Jacqui Safra who has had some small roles in Woody's films. But according to Louise, Jean once wanted to marry Woody – and maybe still does. 'I love Jean, and I know she loves Woody. I'm sure she wanted to marry him. But I could never be jealous of her. He had a very special relationship with her. When we were together, I'd sometimes wake up in the middle of the night and he wouldn't be there. The light would be on under the door and I knew he'd be on the phone to Jean talking about his problems.'

In 1963 came another big break. Warren Beatty, then an unknown and struggling actor, had been trying to get a script produced about a compulsive Don Juan, a character Warren described as 'pathetic' but 'funny' – the victim of his own successes with the opposite sex. He was working on it with Charlie Feldman, the high living and high spending movie mogul. They could not find a good writer until one night the two of them arrived at The Blue Angel and saw Woody who was 'brilliant', said Warren. 'We asked him if he wanted to do it. Charlie said, "I'll pay you 30,000 dollars." Woody said, "I want 40." Charlie said, "Forget it." And Woody said, "Okay. I'll do it for 30 if I can be in the movie." Charlie said okay.[3]

What's New, Pussycat? became the biggest grossing comedy of the time, making the then astounding sum of 8.3 million dollars. It also descended from being a fine script to becoming a sleazy and stupid adolescent fantasy later dismissed as a 'prolonged dirty joke'. Woody publicly washed his hands of it, although discerning critics noticed that he saw the project through to its end and took the money. It had the effect that Rollins and Joffe had hoped for – of jettisoning him out of the relative obscurity of the night club circuit and into international prominence.

Interestingly, it was Warren Beatty who displayed more artistic angst over the hatchet job on Woody's script. He had been due to star in the film but walked out before filming started. 'Woody finally wrote the funniest script I've ever read. I finally walked out in a huffing bluff or a bluffing huff, thinking they wouldn't let me go. Woody stayed. He was very unhappy with the movie ... I was even unhappier, because I would have gotten rich on it. The picture was a big hit. After that, Woody was always in control of what he did. And so was I.'[4]

At the time of their brief liaison, Woody and Warren's appreciation for each other was mutual, but their feelings were said to change after Diane Keaton fell for the legendary Hollywood Lothario. Woody cruelly satirised him as Tony Lacey in *Annie Hall*. He is the ludicrous record producer who lived in a spacious mansion, liked to be 'mellow' and ultimately pinches Alvy's girlfriend in a triumph of hedonism over intellect.

Feldman hit on the title for their project after he was around at Beatty's house one day, and the handsome actor took a call from one of his many female admirers, charmingly inquiring, 'What's new, pussycat?'.

Feldman agreed on Woody's fee and told him to 'write something where we can all go to Paris and chase some girls.' This is more or less what happened with cast and crew jetting off to the Continent for several months of work in 1964 interspersed with glamorous parties and beautiful women. For Woody, it also meant a welcome reunion with one particular beautiful woman, Vicky Tiel. She had moved to Paris to study fashion and was hired to be a costume assistant to Woody and the movie's director Clive Donner. 'Peaches La Tour! What are you doing here?' he demanded after bumping into Vicky on the set. She said, 'When I saw Woody I thought, "Oh my God!" because in the Village he had really been no big deal. Just a very funny comedian, but nowhere near as popular as people like Lenny Bruce.'

Away from home, it was an international extravaganza for everyone with a seemingly bottomless pit of expenses to fund an extravagant lifestyle in the best hotels of Europe. Except for Woody who was still the 'scared rabbit' Len Maxwell has observed. On location he took Vicky out for two months, never so much as attempting to kiss her. They would go to the same restaurant every night, Woody always eating the same course. 'He was nervous about everything. It's a Jewish thing,' explains Vicky. 'And I'm just the same. If you go to a place and you don't get ill, then it must be safe to go back there again! Night, after night, after night, he would eat the same thing because it hadn't made him sick the night before. And in all those two months Woody didn't make a move to get me.'

Until, that is, her birthday when she willingly became a sexual 'pawn' between Woody and Donner. She had not slept with Donner either and was still theoretically dating her 'Jim Morrison bad boy' back in Greenwich Village, but the crew decided that whoever gave her the best birthday present could take her to bed. Vicky says: 'We were both fresh faced novices on our first film set and both of us were like fish out of water. We were both overwhelmed by the presence of Peter Sellers and Peter O'Toole. Both of us couldn't believe all these important people with their fancy entourages. The crew told us, "Look, this is the movie business. Everyone sleeps with everyone else in this business, so you two had better start joining in." That's when they devised the competition between Clive and Woody, both of whom had dated me, but neither of who had gotten so far as first base.'

On Vicky's birthday that October 21, everyone gathered around at her new apartment for a big party. Donner gave her a gigantic box of Lady Godiva chocolates but was trumped by Woody who splashed out on a pinball machine which was so fantastic *everyone* voted Woody the winner. Feasting his eyes over his winnings, Woody instructed Vicky to be in his hotel suite the following evening as agreed, where she was to strip off in the bathroom, and join him in bed. Vicky was perfectly prepared and happy to go through with it, when on the appointed day of the liaison, alas, she fell in love with another man over lunch. It was Liz Taylor's make-up man and Vicky's future husband Ron Berkeley whom she decided to stay the night with instead.[5]

'I fell in love with Ron on the spot and went to bed with him straightaway!' says Vicky now. 'It was only in the morning that I realised I'd been supposed to spend the night with Woody. The next time I saw him was the following morning on the set and I just didn't know how to apologise to him. He was absolutely devastated. He'd spent the evening getting himself ready and planning what we were going to do. I tried to explain: "I've met the man of my dreams, I've fallen in love with him and I'm going to marry him!" He said, "You met the man of your dreams? Where?" I said, "Over lunch." He was incredulous. He said, "Over lunch!" He reproduced that moment in *Manhattan* when he warns the Mariel Hemingway character that she might meet someone at lunch.'

'You'll be with actors and directors. You know, you go to rehearsal and you hang out with those people. You have a lot of lunch. And ... attachments will form.'

Ike, *Manhattan*

Vicky and Ron split up 20 years later, but she has remained a close friend of Woody's, he often pointing to his extensive collection of porcelain at his Fifth Avenue apartment and saying, 'See how much porcelain you could have had?'

'I guess it must have affected him to put it in a movie, but everyone becomes part of his material. But what's interesting is that I went out with him for two months and he wouldn't even kiss me because he was too timid and afraid. The only way he could have sexual contact with me was by winning me in a bet!

'He's not capable of seducing anyone because he's such an unaggressive person. He may have a lot of professional aggressive male ego, but personally he's a very sweet guy and can't bring himself to initiate anything sexually. He's the antithesis of a seducer.'

At one stage at the height of his relationship with Vicky Tiel, he tried to get *her* a part in the cast. 'It was ridiculous. I was a dress designer not an actress. In any case Woody was a nobody on the set. He was totally eclipsed by Sellers and O'Toole. Nobody was listening to a word he said,' she says.

What's New, Pussycat? was to star some of the biggest box office pulls of the time: Peter Sellers, Peter O'Toole, Ursula Andress and Romy Schneider. Rollins and Joffe later agreed they had demanded ludicrously little for Woody, but he needed the publicity. The production switched between Paris and Rome with plenty of time off for weekends at star-studded parties on the Riviera or on touring trips around Florence.

As Woody checked into Paris's exclusive Hotel George V, along with Sellers and his wife Britt Ekland, he found himself checking into the sort of luxurious and cosmopolitan world that must have seemed beyond the reach of many of his friends back in Brooklyn. He later told Jack Victor about one of the sensual delights of being a movie star. On first arriving in Paris, Britt Ekland had commented how Woody looked just like her husband. This was not just wishful thinking on Woody's part – Sellers wears thick black glasses and a long black wig for the movie, and *does* look a little like him. It must have been a strong resemblance because shortly afterwards during shooting, Britt walked into a changing room where Woody was, and began to disrobe, talking to him as if he were Peter Sellers. She realised her mistake quickly enough not to cause herself too much embarrassment –

much to Woody's frustration.

But despite this new international jet setting environment and the company of stars, Woody's boyhood insecurities remained with him. He asked United Artists to send him regular packages of American steaks across the Atlantic because he had been warned that European meat was sub-standard. 'He ate fish all the time because he didn't trust the steaks,' says Louise who was soon to join him in Paris in tragic circumstances.

Louise was 21 when her mother attempted suicide. She spent five days in a coma and when she emerged from it asked the doctors who had been responsible for saving her life? When they told her that it had been Louise, Mrs Lasser replied, 'I'll never forgive her.' In the middle of *What's New, Pussycat?* she tried once more to kill herself and this time succeeded. It was a devastating blow to her daughter. 'It was a tough time,' says Louise, who flew to be with Woody in October 1964.

Woody's days were consumed with arguments over the script and settings, and he was to say later that although he liked Feldman, the movie would have been twice as funny if it had been done the way *he* wanted it. Much of what he later said about *What's New, Pussycat?* must be taken with a pinch of salt. He clearly revelled in the new found fame his role brought him, and as a minor player and lowly script writer, he was not in any position to argue much with his Hollywood bosses.

But it was true that Woody had already developed a well worn dislike of Hollywood excesses; and it is also true that his lines shine through in what is otherwise an embarrassing Sixties' slapstick farce.

Michael (O'Toole): 'Did you find a job?'
Victor (Woody): 'Yeah, at the striptease – I help the girls dress and undress.'
Michael: 'Nice job!'
Victor: 'It's 20 francs a week.'

Michael: 'Not much.'
Victor: 'It's all I can afford.'

Except for these few sparks, Woody Allen regarded *What's New, Pussycat?* as a big, expensive disaster which bore little or no resemblance to the screenplay he wrote. Nevertheless he enjoyed his first sojourn out of the country and it served its purpose, earning him a small fortune and bringing his name worldwide recognition. It would also bring him his first taste of celebrity gossip. As his name became better known, rumours about his sexuality flew around. Jack Victor remembers, 'There was talk of him being gay at one stage which was just as ridiculous as the later claims of child abuse. It drove me berserk at the time when you would hear it a lot. I was at the opening of *What's New, Pussycat?* and there was this guy seated in the next stall to me intimating that Woody was gay. It annoyed me no end and I contemplated going over to the balcony and belting him but thought better of it.'

Woody used to joke that he once took part in a neurotic exchange programme: when he was shooting a movie in Italy he would see an Italian analyst, while an Italian went to see his. Not true, but according to Eric Lax, there was one occasion when Fred Weintraub, Hilda Pollack and Woody decided to tell their individual psycho-analysts each other's dreams. After their sessions they each asked one another what the result had been. 'Woody, you're gay,' said Hilda.[6]

But homosexuality is something that has never sur-faced in Woody's emotional make-up and it is noticeably absent from his movies. Jack Kroll observed him one night at Michael's Pub where a stream of young women propositioned him, the man who had made anhedonia – the inability to experience pleasure – a virtue. 'This notorious proponent of anhedonia appeared somewhat more hedonistic when presented with a pretty girl.

Noting how a strawberry blonde "with eyes like candles" approached him and offered him a brass heart, she asked him: "Can we go out?" He replied: "I'm living with someone: she's not much but she's all I have".[7]

In 1965 Woody was soon back in the States, the toast of an increasingly appreciative town and of the new administration of President Lyndon Johnson, whom Woody had endorsed in Paris and London. In the long-standing tradition of America's inaugural bashes Woody was invited to perform at the winter spectacular with other celebrities.

Shortly afterwards he was invited back to Washington for a celebratory dinner. The invite did not include Louise – presumably because nobody realised she was his girlfriend – but Woody went anyway and mixed with the likes of American music legend Richard Rodgers and master comic Jimmy Durante. The White House waiters served *filet mignon* to the strains of 'Hail to the Chief'.

As the evening wore on Woody charmed the Johnson girls and their mother with his self-deprecating quips. They would be upset to know he later told Jack Victor, 'They were two of the ugliest sisters I've ever seen.' They were at an awkward age, Jack explains, but Louise Lasser reveals another side to Woody. 'He was always very hard on ugly people. I don't know why, but he was.' Later he asked if he could use one of the mansion's phones to impress Louise. 'He wanted to say he was calling from the White House but I was on the phone all the time. He called me for two hours and was so annoyed that he could never get through.'

His mother also continued to be annoying, being totally unimpressed by her son's burgeoning achievements, according to Mickey Rose. 'We all went to see *What's New, Pussycat?* but she didn't find it amusing. She just thought it was a bunch of nonsense.

'Being a freelance writer or a comic certainly didn't

have much of a cachet. it's not as important as being a doctor or having a steady job. A school teacher married with a job in Brooklyn – that was the ideal.'

Louise and Woody were finally married on February 2, 1966, a day dedicated in American folklore to the ground-hog – an oversized rat from Pennsylvania credited with predicting exactly how long the winter will continue for. As far they were concerned, the question was how long their marriage would last for. Both of them had taken blood tests long beforehand in case they were over-powered by the sudden urge to swap vows. Character-istically, Woody had collapsed in a faint at the sight of his own blood during the test. They decided to get married the day before her father left for a worldwide tour, while Woody was performing at the Royal Box auditorium at the Americana Hotel.

'I never used to think in terms of getting married, and can never remember my parents saying anything like "when you get married" or things like that,' says Louise. 'We had taken blood tests but at the time we were reluctant to do it. He was reluctant because so many times before I'd backed away from the commitment. It wasn't that I was being mean – although he might say so – but I was troubled by a whole lot of stuff and I kept asking myself, "Should I or shouldn't I?".

'In the end I think we both decided to do it because the relationship wasn't moving forward and we thought if we give marriage a try maybe that will make things different. We were irresistibly drawn to one another, but we were both hesitant to commit.

'The second I got married I started asking myself, "Should I stay married or shouldn't I?".'

The ceremony was a quiet one at Louise's father's apartment to which Woody's own mother and father were not invited although he told them it was going to happen. Louise's new stepmother was there, and the only

119

other guests were Mickey Rose and his wife Judy, and Woody's great friend Jean Doumanian, who was to be by his side at most great junctures in his life.

Mickey Rose recalls, 'I remember the judge was a personal friend of Louise's parents but wasn't familiar with who, exactly, Woody Allen was, and when he wed them in holy matrimony, he called him "Woody Herman".' Louise says, 'When the judge asked me if I would marry Woody Herman, I said "no" and always thought that would be my get out clause later on. I'd never agreed to marry him technically'.

The 'honeymoon' was to be at the Plaza Hotel where Woody was temporarily billeted while waiting for the 79th Street apartment to be decorated. But one of the biggest blizzards in memory put an end to that and the couple spent their wedding night in his suite at the Americana. Beforehand, in between performances at the Royal Box, Woody held a makeshift reception at the Americana for the likes of Rollins and Joffe, and later, his old – and surprised – friend, Jack Victor.

'I called Woody up one day and said I'd like him meet my fiancée. He immediately asked my fiancée and I around to the Americana where he was performing and told me dinner was on him. I had my doubts and towards the end of the meal was getting worried about the impact of the cheque on my graduate income, until the waiter said it was all on Mr Allen who wanted us both to go upstairs. We did, and found a wedding party. I think he possibly married Louise Lasser to get one up on me! He then wanted to know if I thought he should call Jerry.'

Other friends and acquaintances were equally badly informed. At the time, the comedian Len Maxwell was working with Woody and Mickey on *What's Up, Tiger Lily?* but didn't hear about the marriage until he opened his newspapers on February 3.

Woody was certainly a 'catch'. He has never been much interested in money, but in 1966, he was due to make up to half a million dollars – a huge amount by the standards of the time.

The marriage was off to an unclear start, with Woody wondering whether a second trip down the aisle was likely to be any more successful than the first. And with Louise characteristically being unable to make her mind up from one moment to the next. Since he was still appearing at the Americana, sometimes in two shows a night, there was no time for a honeymoon.

She says: 'I simply had never thought in terms of weddings, wedlock or anything like that. And neither of us had high hopes, but it turned out to be not such a bad thing after all. We even called my father after a week to tell him it wasn't such a bad thing.'

And it *did* prove not to be such a bad thing, certainly not as bad as they had imagined. Married life took on a happy pattern that to a certain extent would be repeated for Woody time and time again in his later relationships, with heavy demands from work interrupted with leisure hours devoted to museums and the movies, and Upper East Side restaurants. But in other ways it was markedly different. With Louise for instance he could barely spend a moment apart from her; whereas with Mia Farrow he was later to claim that he rarely spent an evening at her New York apartment, and Diane Keaton's period of living with him under the same roof was very brief.

Louise says: 'I found that he didn't like to be on his own at all – he always wanted to be together and to spend time together. He wasn't the sort who would say, "I'm just going out for a walk," you know? Everything he did, he wanted to do it with me.

'People would call late at night suggesting doing something, and he would say, "Come with me" but I'd always say, "No – but you go." The theatre, the movies, everything, he always wanted to do it with me.

'We spent a lot of time in Paris and later London together and we were alone for long periods of time. Of all the people I've known he's the last one to want to spend time alone, and when we were in bed, he was very close and cuddly. He was the first person who accepted and loved me unconditionally, and he was the first person I wasn't embarrassed with physically. I would wander around the apartment naked and he would accuse me of flaunting myself but really, I was just enjoying that liberated feeling.

'He liked us to be together every second. I don't know about the other people. Mia Farrow's demands may have been different, and with Keaton it was a different kind of relationship.'

Woody was by now, in Louise's words, 'New York *rich* – rich, rich'. His gamble to give up writing jokes to try to forge a career as a stand-up comic had begun to pay off handsomely. He had pocketed the 35,000 dollar writing fee for *What's New, Pussycat?* plus more for his acting part, and he and Mickey Rose were working on a script which would eventually become *Take the Money and Run*, the first unadulterated 'Woody' movie with himself as writer, director and playing the lead. He was being paid 66,000 dollars to do the wacky Japanese James Bond-style spy caper, *What's Up, Tiger Lily?*, and on top of that he was making 5,000 dollars a week for stage appearances. TV specials and movie roles were constantly being offered. Despite Woody's bad experience on *What's New, Pussycat?* he flew to London a few months after marrying Louise to do another movie for Feldman, this time a British based James Bond spoof, *Casino Royale*. The six week shoot ended up being six *months* during which time Woody wrote *Don't Drink the Water*. By the time he got back to New York, David Merrick had agreed to produce the play for Broadway.

The money was pouring in. 'These were the days when 200,000 dollars would set you up for life,' says Louise who lived with him for a month in a London flat during the marathon *Casino Royale* shoot. 'He was gambling and winning a lot, and bought me a beautiful Emile Nolde watercolour with his poker winnings once. He kept it after we divorced though.

'We met the Queen at some sort of benefit full of entertainment people like Raquel Welch. It was the most nerve-racking experience of my life. It was so uncomfortable getting dressed up for the whole thing because I didn't feel I belonged there at all. There was a picture of me standing behind Woody with my eyes closed and looking as if I had tons of make-up on.

'We had to go to a screening with them all, and we couldn't breathe, so when we finally got in the elevator away from everyone afterwards, we both let out a sigh of relief and said, "Thank God we're outta there!". It was just so tense and we weren't very good at social situations so it was a relief to be let go and suddenly we were very high just to be free. We never did see the movie. We just went straight home and put some comfortable clothes on.'

While Woody was in London he dined with the Dean of Westminster Abbey who was a fan. According to Eric Lax, when he met the Queen, he asked, 'How do you do, are you enjoying your power?'.[8] Although Louise Lasser says Woody's witty recollection may be wishful thinking. 'When I was with him and we met the Queen, he was too nervous to say anything clever.'

On returning to the United States, renovation work on their East 79th Street brownstone apartment was complete and Louise and Woody moved out of their temporary residence at the Plaza. On the walls was the Emile Nolde watercolour, a drawing by Oskar Kokoschka which he had also bought with his gambling winnings, and three oils by Gloria Vanderbilt. But despite his conspicuous financial success, then as now, money did not play a big part in his motivation beyond the purely practical one of allowing him to do more or less what he wanted to do. Louise was often surprised at his frugality.

'Woody never cared about money, all he was concerned about was his work and his relationship with me. I've never known a writer who could be so caring personally. He insisted we had a sort of formal dining area at the end of the house, and we bought a beautiful antique table for special occasions. But he didn't buy the chairs to go with it.

'I couldn't believe it and I said, "What do you mean? Everyone in New York knows who you are, and I thought you made a lot of money anyhow?" He said, "Well, I suppose I do, but I guess it all goes in taxes or something." Of course he could afford the chairs but he didn't have a clue how much money he had or what he could do with it. He didn't care, and I don't think he does today either.

'We had a beautiful bedroom which was decorated with antique French furniture, but in a cosy sort of way. But none of the rooms were really finished or anything.'

Dick Cavett liked the place so much that he was going to move into it when they moved out. Then he remembered that it had a half-furnished quality about it, with a giant billiard table in the 'library' – so big that it was impossible to use the correct sized cue. Another room looked like the Athenaeum Club with very little furniture but a complete ensemble of apparatuses for performing magic. There was also the film projector which Louise's parents gave them as a wedding present. A jukebox stood there also which Woody bought her for a Christmas present, and she presented him with an organ and a milkshake mixer which went down a treat with the sweet toothed Woody.

Jack Victor has vivid memories of their domestic arrangements. 'They had this Filipino valet who was found to have a drink problem so Woody fired him. The valet said, "I just want to tell you one thing: Miss Louise – she is the sloppiest lady I ever saw".'

Writing in 1967, Nora Ephron reported how a quiet New Year's Eve get together with close friends turned into a 500 person bash, mainly because a newspaper item publicised their private do and no one else was holding a party.[9] Woody filmed them all as they came in and had to order more liquor to supplement the supplies of free vodka, before he and Louise left for a sandwich at a nearby drugstore. The catering at home had been slow because the chef who had been hired insisted on waving at the home movie camera instead of cooking the food. Woody told Ephron: 'But there was surprisingly little damage. And the next day one of our neighbours found our Matisse drawing on the stairs and returned it.'

He did not tell Ephron that he had been nauseous the night after the party – not because of drink or food, but because of the realisation that he was now famous. Having been closer to him than anyone else, Louise understood exactly what he was going through. 'The party had been meant for just a few friends, a very small dinner party. But all these people turned up and we didn't know one of them. They were only there because it was Woody Allen's do. When we looked at the film later on to see which of our friends had turned up, there wasn't one face we recognised. We had a couple of sodas that night and the next morning Woody was truly nauseous at the thought of fame.'

'There's no satisfaction to fame. When you're a kid you think there would be,'[10] he told William Geist years later. And he confided to Frank Rich, 'I was telling my analyst just a while ago that I had a certain admiration for Howard Hughes – I mean, I'm certain he was a *terrible* man – but what I was referring to was that he was living out a certain reclusive quality that I liked. My idea of a good time is to take a walk from my house to the office and not for the entire walk have to worry about hearing my name being called from a passing car or being spoken to at all. That would be perfect.'[11]

For most of their married life together though, life for Louise and Woody *was* a private affair rather than a public riot. Almost all of his time was sacrificed to work, and little time was ever spent outside the island of Manhattan. What breaks there were, were dedicated to exploring the city's museums and art galleries, dining in a few select restaurants, and taking long walks in Central Park.

He has since acknowledged the debt he owes to Louise. Before the years they spent together he was an outsider trying to make his way in a notoriously unrewarding profession, in a strange city. With Louise he was transformed from being an awkward suburban Brooklyn boy to being a fully fledged member of New York's elite social set. It was her who taught him the sort of social sophistication that he had thought about in Brooklyn. He gave her a love for modern jazz, she taught him about classical music and art. His taste in home furnishings was 'contemporary Danish' but Louise gave him a love for the traditional furnishings of France and England that he has today. His relationship with Louise transformed him from a suburbanite to a fully-fledged Manhattanite.

Their married life was spent in some seclusion, recalls Louise. 'We liked playing poker a lot, but we didn't mix with friends. On Friday nights we would never have any cash – these were the days when you couldn't just go along to a automatic teller and get money whenever you felt like it. But we had a cook in the house who would have made us brownies, pies and tuna fish, so we'd stay in the house all weekend and work our way through that.

'He would shut himself away and get on with his work and I would try not to bother him. But if I knocked on his door, he'd be very welcoming. He would say to me, "Hiya Louise, come on in" just like a father talks to a little girl. With me, he never minded his work being interrupted and would share his thoughts with me. Even during the week – in other words most of the time – we'd be alone together.

'He needed to work all the time. It wasn't just that he

was disciplined, he was addicted to work. Even if we went on holiday, he'd get up first thing in the morning while I was still in bed, and write.

'We rarely went on holidays together although we spent a lot of time in Paris and London for *What's New, Pussycat?* and *Casino Royale* – but even then he'd get up first thing in the morning and work. He's a very serious person, probably more serious than any other person I've ever met.

'We borrowed his father's car once and drove out to Montauk to stay at Gurney's Inn. We were there three days and it rained non-stop, but Woody got sunstroke. He's the only person I know who can get ill from the sun when it's pouring down with rain. When the sun finally did shine through, I had the best of times jumping around on the beach in the sand like a little kid, but he was sitting inside with his typewriter looking very glum and covered in sticking plasters.'

It was a stable life for both of them, with Louise's rich Manhattanite parents adopting a long and lasting affection for Woody's family, in stark contrast to the coolness between them and Harlene's mother and father. Louise and Woody would often go down to Brooklyn for dinner with Nettie and Martin. She loved being with Letty because 'she was just so funny' and Martin was 'a really sweet guy'. Louise never shared Woody's annoyance at Nettie, but recognised the traits in both of them which were mutually antagonistic. 'She was always interfering with him in a worrying kind of way. Everything was always, worry about this, worry about that.'

With Martin it was different, father and son enjoying a close and affectionate relationship. 'Nettie always called Woody "Allan", but Martin always called him "son", and Letty was always "sugar". When we were living together, he called *every* day always with some hysterical warning. If there was a blizzard outside Martin would call to warn Woody to make sure there were enough canned foods in the kitchen in case we were snowed in. He used to worry when we borrowed the car and always warned us to keep the windows open in case there was a fire. That way we could get out safely. And Woody would never let me take the wheel even though he couldn't drive. He could hardly see through the windshield. Always something would go wrong and Woody felt so embarrassed because his father was so undemanding.

'He ... would walk with Woody from uptown to downtown when he was working in the Village. They never said much to each other but they were close in an unspoken sort of way. Martin worked at Sammy's Bowery Follies, and always had access to plenty of cash which was really useful because Woody was always running out at crucial moments – like half way through dinner at expensive restaurants. So Woody would call Martin on the phone and Martin would always send a bum with some money. We were at this really smart restaurant, The Chambourd, when Woody realised he didn't have a cent. Half an hour later, a street bum turned up and put a few five dollar bills on the table, "Your dad sent this, Mr Allen." Everyone in the restaurant turned and stared, because in those days it was rare to see a homeless man in such a nice part of town, whereas it's common today. In those days, bums as they were called, only came from the Bowery in lower Manhattan where Martin worked. Martin was a nice guy, and like the fictitious father in *Radio Days* who did not blame the black maid for stealing, he sympathised with the downtrodden.

'When he [Martin] was out of work in the Seventies sometime, he took a job with Woody's managers, Rollins and Joffe, as a messenger. Everyone was aghast thinking "how humiliating! What could Woody be thinking to subject his father to such a demeaning role?" But to Martin it was just another way of earning a living and getting to do one of his favourite pastimes – walking around the city and meeting people. He even dropped a

128

package off with me once, after we were divorced. "Here you are, honey," he says. "You wanna come in for a coffee?" I said. "No, got to go, Louise darling.".

'His parents were very close to mine. My father was this great guy who'd made such a success of his life, and his [Woody's] parents lived in this little house in Brooklyn, but he made a point of calling them all the time to ask after them and see how they were. He loved them.'

Woody once proclaimed Louise was 'brighter than I am, funnier than I am ... the only person who can cheer me up.'[12]

But despite the wealth and privilege of her family background, Louise was a woman deeply disturbed by the tragedy of her mother's death. She blames their final break-up on her violent mood swings and changes in temperament. Even today, Louise is a difficult woman, often suffering from a croaky voice for one reason or another.

As Lewis Grossberger said in a 1980 *New York* magazine profile of Louise, 'Funny things happen to Louise Lasser.' He went on to detail the problems of arranging an interview with her because of her fragile health. 'Her throat had cleared up,' he reported. 'She'd now caught the flu.'[13]

After the marriage with Woody was over, in the Seventies she was the star of *Mary Hartman, Mary Hartman*, a hugely popular America soap series which fearlessly dealt with subjects like venereal disease and exhibitionism, a big topic in those days. And in terms of visibility at least, *Mary Hartman* proved to be the height of her success. But that too gradually floundered amid family trauma, television station politics, and overwork. In the middle of it all she was arrested for cocaine possession which she claimed was given to her by a fan. 'Star of Hartman Suds is in Real Hot Water' screamed the *New York Daily News*. Even the outcome of the court case was a joke: she was sentenced to visit a psychiatrist, but since she was already doing so, she just carried on seeing the same doctor.

Louise's father was a brilliant, loving man, who cherished his daughter and had given her an enviable lifestyle. But neither she nor her mother could live up to his strict self-control. They bottled things up. Arguably, the scars of Louise's mother's suicide, the circumstances surrounding and leading up to it, are at the bottom of Louise Lasser's neurosis which destroyed her marriage to Woody.

Woody wanted to have children – girls, and lots of them. But Louise did not feel ready for it. He was always cheerful, but she was invariably in a mood about something. He was always positive. She mostly saw the dark side of things. He always wanted to do something in the city. She wanted to lie in bed. He was always adventurous and highly-sexed in bed, she was unsophisticated and in her own words provincial – ironic considering her father's liberated attitude.

After they were divorced Louise became famous in a series of TV advertisements promoting a popular cold remedy as 'Mildred', the compassionate housewife who nurses her feverish husband back to health. 'You're a good wife,' he would groan at the end. Louise said at the time, 'There are always these women coming up to me and saying, "My husband wants to know why I can't be as good a wife as you are" which is funny, because in reality, I was a terrible wife. I just wasn't mature enough at the time to handle the responsibility for myself and my marriage.'

Today she is more frank. 'I had problems that pursued me, they weren't problems that got cleared up like I thought they would ... Sometimes we'd get up on a Saturday and he'd want to go to a gallery but I'd just want to sleep, and I would literally have to go back to bed and I would sleep for hours and hours ... He would call the doctor over and ask if these pills he'd given me were really meant to make me sleep for hours and hours. He was really concerned that I was having a lot of problems ... He was the one who would make the food, and I was the baby. It was great but it also probably contributed to my depression although I don't know how.'

(Years later, a book exposing the backstage history of *Saturday Night Live* portrayed Louise as the most difficult guest host, childlike, pouty and very uncooperative. Her response was, 'Whatever trouble they had with me, I had *more* with me.')

'I was also with an analyst at the time and he said I shouldn't be with Woody because he felt I wasn't getting a chance at a career or to fulfil myself, and that's how I felt ... At times Woody *did* say I ought to do comedy, but I thought the whole idea of standing up in front of people trying to make them laugh was humiliating. Basically, he wanted me to be with him all the time ... He wanted me to be happy being his wife. "You love going shopping, you love spending money, you love first class restaurants! Just be my wife," he would say ... He was really happy to see me spend money. He said I should do poetry or paint, but I said, "Woody I've never written a poem in my life!" "Well," he'd say, "Write a story or something like that".

'It was a suffocating thought to me as it would be to many people I guess. Basically I'm a suffocated person. But he didn't stop me from doing it ... And when we were together, he wanted me to have little girls but I wasn't ready. He adored little girls, and that was his big dream ... But I was never able to be there for him. I was very depressed a lot, and I had a lot of problems, and he was always the one who had to cheer me up. I was always the disturbed one.'

The problems got worse and worse as the marriage progressed. It was not as if Louise was by any means a human liability. She was talented, resourceful and funny, with money of her own and making more out of a string of TV commercials. She was to go on and appear in one of

America's top TV shows. Her stage career had been impressive, and she had been Barbra Streisand's stand-in in *I Can Get It For You Wholesole*. But she could never shake off her depression which came in ebbs and flows at a time when Woody's career was going in one direction, and one direction alone. A constant pill popper and victim of colds, flu and laryngitis, she would often say, 'If I ever feel optimistic, that means I think I can get through the end of the day'.

After a year or so they decided to try a trial separation and Louise moved out although they continued to see one another. 'We remained close because we knew one another so well and certain affectionate feelings remained. But Woody still couldn't tell the truth. My bookcases were so big they had to be hoisted out of the window. Woody didn't want his parents to know what was happening because he didn't want them to be unduly upset, so he hadn't told them, but Martin arrived at the front door when they were hoisting the books on to the street. "What's happening son?" Martin said. "Nothing's happening dad, are you crazy? What do you mean?" Woody can fail to see the reality of the situation despite the fact that something is obviously wrong. There's an awful lot of denial in his life.'

She moved into a temporary place before buying the 20th floor apartment she now has on the Upper East Side, and at about the same time, Woody bought the Fifth Avenue penthouse he still lives in, only a few blocks away. Covering two floors of a post-war block, the apartment has a top storey with a wrap around terrace and panoramic views through giant plate glass windows across Central Park and to the north and south of the city. The underneath floor is a rambling warren of rooms. Woody moved into a hotel while the new property was gutted and completely redecorated in a French provincial style. To the terrace were added dozens of trees and plants which are no longer there today. Significantly, the top floor with the light pouring into it was completely altered to become one room – Woody's bedroom.

'He spent thousands of dollars on a place and the whole top of it is the only bedroom in the house,' says Louise. It was a Seventies version of the typical playboy's penthouse. The sort of thing Warren Beatty would have.

But the typical playboy films of *What's New, Pussycat?*, *What's Up, Tiger Lily?* and *Casino Royale*, were things of the past. By now Woody was flexing his creative and financial muscle. First came the movie *Don't Drink the Water*, based on his stageplay of the same name. A bland and unimaginative tale of an American family trapped behind the Iron Curtain, *Don't Drink the Water* had originally been written by Woody while holed-up in London for *Casino Royale*. It was based on his own first hand impressions of what it was like to be in a foreign country deprived of the everyday necessities of New York life. (He said subsequently that the plot was roughly what would happen if his own family were let loose abroad, a theory which has never been tried on Nettie and Martin but did transpire much later on with Woody, Mia and a gaggle of her kids. They flew to Scandinavia to pay homage to the homes of his heroes, from cinematographer Sven Nykvist to the classic artists and musicians Bergman, Greig, Ibsen and Strindberg. Taking a side trip to Russia, the entourage found themselves on a holiday in hell, stranded at the Hotel Pribaltiskaya. There is no point in going into details, but anyone can imagine what happens when a group of rich American kids, and one particularly big kid, used to ordering take outs from Dominos Pizza and every other conceivable fast food outlet, have to stay in a communist hotel. Hours after arriving Woody was on the phone demanding the time of the next plane out.)

More importantly in 1968 came *Take the Money and Run*, often referred to as the first unadulterated Woody Allen movie. He co-wrote it with his friend Mickey Rose, and directed and starred as the lead in the story of failed crook Virgil Starkwell. It was important also, because Woody set a precedent which would guarantee him creative freedom from that day on. In a day and age where directors regularly bust budgets, Woody brought *Take the Money and Run* in at a significant 400,000 dollars less than its already modest budget of 2 million.

Some critics panned the film which was shot in the same sort of pseudo documentary style as *Zelig* although not as professionally. But for Woody Allen addicts it is a great movie and has many of his best lines. (When one of his psychiatrists asks Virgil if he thinks sex is dirty, he replies: 'It is if you do it right'.)

Alas for him, his private life was not going quite so well. In the spring of 1970, Louise and Woody flew to Mexico to get a quick divorce the next day, telling friends that they had got in this mess together, so they had better get out of it together.

Louise says: 'We stayed together that night in the same hotel room. We had a lot of what now appear a lot of contradictions like that. Because at the time we were still drawn together.

'We had a good time,' she says laughing, 'we stayed overnight and then in the morning we went to get it over and done with. We just sat there clutching each other's hands because we were both very nervous.

'The guy came out and said, "Which one of you is getting the divorce?" and we both said, "I am". "Are you sure you want to do this?" he said.' And neither of them could really answer that question just like they couldn't three years before when they got married on Groundhog Day. 'It took no time really, and it didn't really feel much different at first, but afterwards it became very real.'

Strangely enough, Louise might be wrong. Quickie Mexican divorces were popular then because they saved a lot of hassle. But they are challengeable, and Louise and Woody later talked with lawyers about the possibility that that may very well happen one day. The issue is clouded by Woody's first *Who's Who* entry which says 'dissolved' rather than 'divorced'.

'I like the idea of it dissolving,' says Louise. 'Divorce is so final, but dissolving sort of means gradually falling apart.'

After their marriage, just as Harlene had hung on to the second name 'Allen', Louise continued to call herself Louise Jane Allen, at least on her driving licence.

'Before I met Woody, I always felt like Marilyn Monroe, like girls were supposed to be stupid or something ... like it was somehow unfeminine or something to be too smart ... The smart boys always liked me because they could see through my whole dumb act. I mean, can a woman who married Woody Allen really be dumb? That's not dumb, that's smart, right?'[14]

The Girl From Chippewa Falls

'Grammy? Grammy Hall? What did you do, grow up in a Norman Rockwell painting?...Your grammy!...Jesus, my grammy never gave gifts. She was too busy getting raped by Cossacks.'

Alvy to Annie, *Annie Hall*

Diane Keaton *did* grow up in a Norman Rockwell painting. It was the clichéd American lifestyle of picket fences, clapboard houses and oversized station wagons which has been immortalised in movies and television shows. Steeped in New World optimism, a puritanical innocence and simple religious faith, it may as well have been a different planet to the one self-obsessed Woody Allen occupied among Manhattan's media elite with their intellectual pretensions and perpetual social dilemmas.

The contrast served as a basis for one of Woody's most enduring comedies, *Annie Hall*. It is the whimsical Oscar-winning love story of Alvy Singer, the world weary and cynical New York comic who falls for Annie Hall, the goofy mid-western girl who loves and leaves him. He never intended the movie to be a romantic story at all, and Diane Keaton's part was originally minimal. But perhaps through some osmosis of the subconscious, it ended up being a touching fictional treatment of Diane and Woody's real life relationship, which began when the two of them were working together on the stage version of *Play it Again, Sam*. He, the tortured soul labouring to find some meaning in a seemingly senseless universe; she, the wide-eyed innocent from out west, struggling to make it on stage in the Big Apple.

'When I first met her, her mind was completely blank,' Woody said of Diane Keaton.[1]

He maintained the usual fiction that his work bore no relation to his real life. 'I was playing myself, but not in autobiographical situations for the most part. I was not born under a roller coaster on Coney Island, nor was my first wife politically active, nor was my second wife a member of the literary set, nor did Diane leave me for a rock star, or to live in California.'[2]

Of course not. But like Alvy and Annie, the pair enjoyed an unlikely love match for several years, and continue to be best friends today. Woody *did* take Diane Keaton under his wing and show her a different way of life. She *did* move into his Upper East Side apartment for a while before the two of them found it impossible sharing the same space. Diane *did* leave Woody a sophisticated and worldly woman, and she *did* fall for the charms of a narcissistic Hollywood schmoozer, albeit Warren Beatty rather than the record producing Tony Lacey. And her real name is Hall: there's even a Grammy Hall, who once met Woody when he paid a Thanksgiving visit to the Hall family home – just like Alvy. The real Grammy Hall would say of Diane's boyfriend, 'That Woody Allen, he's something! I can't make head or tail out of half of what he says!'

'I can't believe this family. Annie's mother. She's really beautiful ... and the old lady at the end of the table is a classic Jew hater. And they really look American, you know, very healthy and like they never get sick or anything. Nothing like my family. The two are like oil and water.'

Alvy, *Annie Hall*

'Woody's had a very positive influence on her, very much like *Annie Hall*,' said Diane's mother, Dorothy Hall. 'It's 85 per cent true,' said her father Jack, 'even to

Dorothy and my mother!'[3] Keaton, incidentally, also began seeing an analyst several days a week on Allen's advice.

Keaton is a classic Californian girl brought up in the sun kissed suburbs of Los Angeles. She was born in 1946 in central Los Angeles where she lived until the age of five, before the family moved out to Santa Ana, a booming new community to the south which was rapidly becoming part of the city's vast concrete sprawl.

Jack Hall was a municipal engineer for Orange County, and the family, though comfortable, was not rich at first. It was a typical middle class Southern Californian childhood with trips to the beach for swimming and scuba diving, water skiing and surfing, and camping expeditions into the desert or down to Tijuana in Mexico. Jack was eventually to set up a business of his own, and along with some shrewd real estate investments, became independently wealthy and eventually capable of backing his eldest daughter's acting ambitions.

Her mother once won the 'Mrs Los Angeles' title but her beauty was not immediately inherited by the young Diane who was an awkward girl shy of her gangly body on the beach. 'When I was a surfer, it was not a pleasant time with other surfers in the water. I've always had a little bit of trouble about swimming gear. I totally loathe and despise it. I have definite opinions about my body … My mother is beautiful, my father is very good looking, my brother and two sisters are very attractive and real American.'[4]

This sand and surf lifestyle bore little resemblance to Woody Allen's Brooklyn up-bringing but Diane Keaton is similar to him in other ways, not least in her appalling school record and the way she chose to escape school in flights of fancy. While Allan Konigsberg read comics and watched the movies, Diane Hall, her younger sisters Dorrie and Robin, and their brother Randy, put on plays for Dorothy and Jack. Diane channelled her school efforts

138

into choir singing and amateur dramatics. And during the holidays, the kids made home movies using a primitive video camera. Ironically, the family favourite was *Bonnie and Clyde* in which she played the Faye Dunaway role and which Warren Beatty would love to watch re-runs of later in life.

'School? I went to school as a social occasion – it was nothing more than that. I was more interested than anything to be in the choir and the talent show. I was always motivated in performing. I was shy and didn't have a lot of friends. I really didn't have an education – I was a bad student. I compensated with personality! ... I don't think that helped much, either.'[5] The highest score she ever got in school was for interpreting the meaning of photographs in a test that went by the name of 'Abstract Reasoning'. 'I went home and asked my mother what abstract reasoning was so that I'd know what I was good at,' she said later.[6]

Diane was also like Woody in another significant way: frustrated by her persistent failure to entice into her arms the bronzed basketballers at school, she resorted to unconventional fashion in a bid to attract attention. She eventually won the title 'Miss Personality' in her last year thanks to her bizarre clothing.

'Diane had an absolute panic to be different,' her mother said. 'She wore black stockings and eye make-up as black as her stockings.'[7] One old school friend remembers, 'We were the high school weirdos. We thought of ourselves as two beatniks, but even then Diane had a great sense of style – her mother made lots of her dresses.'[8]

While other students went on to higher education, got jobs or found a husband, Diane set off to try her hand at acting on the other side of the country where she had won a scholarship under Sanford Meisner at Manhattan's Neighbourhood Playhouse. To complete the picture of the wide-eyed innocent abroad, Diane did not go alone.

Dorothy, Jack and her brother and sisters accompanied her in a Ford van for the 3,000 mile trek across America to make sure she would be safe in the country's capital of corruption.

Not only was she safe, she was soon at home in the Big Apple, living in the usual squalid walk-up populated by would-be actors, managing time to join a rock band and study dance under Martha Graham, while taking her courses at the Playhouse. Among the thriving New York theatre community she also met a good looking young actor with a soft, gravelly voice and mournful demeanour whom Diane immediately became very close friends with. Al Pacino was not a name that would make women go weak at the knees then, but he impressed the impressionable Diane with his knowledge of Chekhov and Emily Dickinson and his passion for poetry. Pacino, even then in his late teens, was an admirer of the method style of acting, and would look upon Lee Strasberg of the Actor's Studio as his guru. It was an obsessive form of acting that would become associated with a group of young up and coming stars of the time – the likes of Dustin Hoffman and Robert DeNiro. Although its insistence on immersing the actor in a part for 24 hours a day is sometimes seen as pretentious and absurd, Pacino's dedication to his art touched Diane. In the meantime she graduated to discover the first obstacle to her name ever appearing in the bright lights of Broadway – Actor's Equity already listed a 'Diane Hall'.

So the first time her name did appear on a bill, it was as Dorrie Keaton – her mother's maiden name and her sister's first name – in a production of *Oh! What a Lovely War!* at a small theatre in Woodstock, the upstate New York community beloved by bohemians and artists. The production was a great success and Diane was thrilled until it closed. Unemployed for the first time she returned, dejected, to Los Angeles. It was Grammy Hall who told her to go back and try again. Which she did, in early 1968, when the newly named Diane Keaton won a part in *Hair*, the revolutionary rock musical which began as an off-beat and off-Broadway show and was to become a theatre phenomenon.

Diane made her name in *Hair* for two reasons. First, she declined the 50 dollars a day inducement to appear totally nude, remaining covered up throughout, unlike the rest of the cast who were revelling in the new found sexual freedom of the Sixties. She did confess though, to taking a peep at the others during shows. And as a result she was immediately the subject of interest grabbing headlines in the trade papers. Second, she took over the star role after being ordered by the producer to lose weight and appear more attractive. She did, and for the first time the name Diane Keaton appeared over Broadway. Soon after, still modest about her new found fame, and uncertain about her abilities, but wanting to make a bigger individual impression, she auditioned for the role of Linda Christie in *Play it Again, Sam*, the play destined for Broadway.

Woody Allen's career had received a big boost after *What's New, Pussycat?* and he had been able to make *Take the Money and Run*, co-written with Mickey Rose. And the two of them were beginning to enjoy the possibilities of laughs at their old friends' expense.

'I think the conflict in his personality disorder started from his formative years ...'

The words are those of Dr Julius Epstein, the prison psychiatrist in *Take the Money and Run*, a mock documentary tracing the decline, fall and further decline of Virgil Starkwell. Starkwell is the poor New Jersey kid whose life of crime started at age six when he would break into chewing gum machines to pay for cello lessons. An early heist of one such dispenser was thwarted when Virgil became stuck to it and was caught by the cops, a humiliating failure foreshadowing a series of bungled bank raids which did not even get him on the Top 10 Most Wanted List. 'It's very unfair voting – it's who you know,' explained his long-suffering lover Louise.

Virgil is clearly Woody and Dr Julius Epstein is based on his friend Jerry Epstein, according to Epstein himself. The fictitious psychiatrist continues...

'I think that gave evidence in his choice of cello – studying the cello at the age of six which is just coming out of the formative years but the conflict is there within the choice... Because it's generally assumed that the cello is a phallic symbol with the grasp ... lower structure certainly feminine – if anything *motherly* – in fact the utilisation of the bow I would imagine is the sublimation of stroking a torso ... So we see between the grasping of the phallus and the stroking of the torso creates what I would imagine was great conflict – even at the age of six.'

Jerry Epstein good naturedly acknowledges the sly dig today. Woody has been in therapy since he was 17, and has had at least five specialists according to some accounts. The idea has raised eyebrows, but Woody has always displayed every sign of not taking psychiatry in the least bit seriously.

In the meantime, thanks to Warren Beatty spotting him in The Blue Angel and giving his career a boost, he was now to be introduced to Diane Keaton. But as they met for the first time, neither of them could have any idea that their artistic collaboration would bring *her* to the attention of Warren Beatty. Years after the audition, they discovered that they had each been terrified of the other. He thought she was a legitimate actress who had starred in a hit show while he was an unknown quantity: Diane thought she had just been lucky and he was a comic genius.

'She was a Broadway star, and who was I? A cabaret comedian who had never even been on the stage before,' he said.[9] She almost did not get the part because, at 5ft 7ins, she was almost an inch taller than Woody and he did not want the joke to be simply their difference in height. But after slipping off their shoes, the two decided the height difference was small enough and all else being equal, Diane got the part.

Play it Again, Sam, is a romantic comedy about Allan Felix, the ineffectual film reviewer with a Humphrey Bogart fixation whose wife walks out on him because she 'wants to go skiing'. Adrift in the lonely singles dating scene, Felix fails miserably with the beautiful dates that his best friends Linda and Dick Christie line up for him – but finally ends up in bed with Linda.

Off stage though, Woody's inhibitions got the better of him and at first he was too scared of Diane Keaton to even talk to her. In any case, Woody was still in the final stages of his relationship with Louise Lasser, and although he had been seeing other women – including an actress he had offered a small part to in *Play it Again, Sam* – he wasn't in the mood for plunging headlong into another romance. Meanwhile though, his co-star Tony Roberts, who was to become a great Woody Allen companion, had a riot with the many other glamorous girls who were in the cast.

In any case Diane Keaton was enjoying her new found success in New York like any young actress would do, and spent much of her time with contemporary drama student friends like Al Pacino. The fact that she departed every evening with a mystery man also torpedoed any romantic ambitions Woody may have had, but gradually she, Roberts and he began to socialise more and one thing led to another. 'We'd hang around together, nothing big, have dinner,' said Woody.[10] 'Tony and I couldn't stop laughing at Diane. It was nothing you could quote later; she couldn't tell a joke if her life depended on it. Tony tried to figure it out one time – what it is she does. He says she has this uncanny ability to project you back into an infantile atmosphere, and you are suddenly a little kid again. There is something utterly guileless about her. She's a natural.'[11]

Although Tony Roberts was having a great time with the many other good looking women in the show, Woody, according to one report, did not join in the skirt chasing because he 'didn't like to mix business and pleasure'.[12] But evidently he did, because while the production was in Washington DC, Woody began an affair with Diane who was 11 years his junior. 'Maybe it was the Freudian lifting of ambitions or something, you know, being in a different city from the one where my mother lived,' Woody later said.[13] Or maybe he just did not want Louise to catch him. Louise did go to Washington several times but was oblivious to the extra-marital meanderings going on under her nose.

Soon after their return to New York when *Play it Again, Sam* opened on Broadway in February 1969, the two started living together. But Louise was still around when Diane arrived, and although they were estranged – with her moving out of their East 79th Street apartment for a 'trial separation' – they were still man and wife, extremely fond of one another, and regularly in touch. They would continue to be very close friends on and off long after Diane and Woody had become 'an item'. Whatever other reasons caused the break-up with Louise, she still had something many of the other women in Woody's world never had. And to this day he still has a photograph of her in his apartment.

But for the most part at this stage, Woody's relationship with Louise had deteriorated almost to that of doctor-patient, he being the benign and fatherly doctor taking care of a disturbed patient.

'There's disturbed disturbed, and there's cheerfully disturbed. I was always disturbed disturbed whereas

144

Keaton was cheerfully disturbed for him,' laughs Louise. 'He was really taken by her. We had a separation of 18 months before we divorced but I only found out that he had been seeing her after we were divorced, although he would talk about her.

'For a long time I wasn't threatened by anyone and then along comes the girl that even I thought was special. That was a very painful experience. Woody kept saying that we would be such good friends if we got together.

'She was more like a great, great friend to him in the beginning. I don't think he loved her or that he was deeply attracted to her because if he were, he would have got married in a second. I think he had a wonderful relationship with her. It was romantic but it was different to mine.

'I like her very much but at the time I had a real hard time because I'd had seven years of knowing I could do whatever I wanted, go wherever I wanted. Then he flaunted her in front of me. Nothing like that had happened to me before. He would talk about all the things she was like and that I would never be like. He was for her career but against my career.

'I had a rough time about Keaton because I could see all those things about her too and this was the first competition I'd had – even though I'd made my own bed to lie in. But he used to push it in my face and he'd actually flaunt her. I thought she was charming and everything, but I didn't think she was a wonderful actress, she was okay and all that, but the way he would pillar her against me, you know?

'And it wasn't as if I was useless: I contributed a lot to his nightclub act, his movies, his *New Yorker* pieces, his writing. You know, I contributed an awful lot.'

It was during his years with Lasser that he contributed his first stories and essays to the *New Yorker*. Three collections of his writings – *Getting Even, Without Feathers* and *Side Effects* – have subsequently been published and many of the comic ideas in them have appeared in his films.

'I used to say to him but why do you like her so much? We have a great time together. He helped her with her career but he didn't want me to have a career ... It was a difficult thing: it was a case of when you can't live with somebody and you can't live without them and I think the two of us were like that for a long time.'

After Louise and Woody divorced, they remained in touch not least because he gave her a cameo role in his movie, *Take the Money and Run*, and later bigger parts in *Bananas*, and two years later in *Everything You Always Wanted to Know about Sex, But Were Afraid to Ask* (in the segment 'Why Do Some Women Have Trouble Reaching Orgasm?'). Louise's cinematic partnership with Woody was to continue to as late as 1980 when she had a small, uncredited role as a secretary in *Stardust Memories*.

Despite Louise's sometimes wild mood changes, (Woody once said that she was the only person capable of cheering him up) she could make him laugh. Her unscripted part for *Take the Money and Run*, called for a scene where the crook's former neighbours spoke about the 'quiet man next door' who became a hood. Louise was one of the neighbours and Woody told her to say into the camera whatever came into her mind first.

'Everyone thought he was such a *schlemiel* and it turned out he's a criminal! You have never met anything like this in all your life, such a nothing.'

Woody burst into laughter at the invocation of the dreaded schoolyard put-down which Louise knew would irritate him. But Louise was irritated with *him*, because while she believed she was capable of developing an acting career for herself, he was using her for one-liners in roles that did not even qualify as 'bit parts'. She was infuriated that her husband would not fight for her career.

Nevertheless, that simple little display of ad-libbing did win her a credited role in his next project, *Bananas* after everyone else at United Artists realised she was good. 'She was extremely talented, and had a terrific sense of humour,' says Jack Victor. 'Louise had a Judy Garland-ish air to her.' Louise was very serious about her acting, and is a respected acting coach today, but Woody was more interested then in boasting about the new love of his life.

Louise says: 'Diane was a great friend of Woody's but he was not greatly attracted to her in a sexual sense. He'd feel for her, and it wasn't as if he didn't do stuff with her, but it wasn't like with me. He has a great sexual appetite, and she had one too, but for some reason he didn't have it for her.'

Louise's role in *Bananas* was entirely New York based and she had no reason to visit the set in Puerto Rico where Woody was staying with Diane in a hotel. But one weekend she flew down to the Caribbean island to visit her ex-husband.

'I was devastated about the situation with Diane and I was determined to do anything he wanted. I went down fully prepared for *anything*, but it wasn't what I wanted. That little inner person in me wanted to be taken care of like a child.

'But he was awful to me, and flaunted Keaton. As soon as I walked into his room he pointed to a chest and said reverentially, "That's Diane's drawer". He spent the rest of the weekend telling me what an unbelievable actress Diane was. He told me, "Diane is America's greatest actress", and I would say, "Come off it, Woody?" He knew how much I really cared about acting. I took it seriously but he was determined to undermine me. Then he rubbed it in further when he would say time and time again, "Diane is the greatest companion I've ever had".

'I was awful to Woody at times so I can't blame him. It was a matter of bad timing but at that particular juncture

I was devastated and I phoned my dad in a hysterical mood. He said, "Come on home." So I did.'

Louise flew back to New York where she now had a new apartment, but continued on her work in *Bananas* throughout July and August of 1970. She suffered many emotional difficulties because of the break-up with Woody, and it wasn't helped by Diane's unseen but acutely felt presence. 'She never visited the set but I got to know what they were up to thanks to Woody. He told me once they were off to the Hamptons for the weekend and I couldn't help laughing. "You're off to the Hamptons?" I said. Apart from that one time we went to Gurney's Inn at Montauk, Woody avoided the countryside like the plague, and the idea of him driving out to *the Hamptons*, this WASP stronghold with his new girlfriend was hysterical to me at least. I embarrassed him I like to think.

'The one thing that I was lucky about was that he carried on insisting that he was really attracted to me and that I was the one he wanted to have sex with, which was true, I know. Obviously they had sex, but he led her to believe he wasn't interested. He was keeping me dangling, but I'm happy he did because otherwise I would have flipped.'

By now Woody was living in the cherished Fifth Avenue apartment he still owns today. Diane had moved in with him, but the arrangement was not working out and she was looking for her own place nearby on the Upper East Side. *Bananas* wrapped later that year and Louise was still recovering from her break-up with Woody, when Diane announced she was returning to California for a month that December to see her family during the Christmas holidays. Woody invited Louise to come around and stay, which she did for a month. But it was the end of their romantic relationship. Louise says, 'I related more to him as a father than a lover.'

Bananas is a big hit with Woody Allen purists who pine for his early movies with their giant doses of rapid fire,

idiotic humour, big breast jokes and none of the pseudo
intellectual pretensions of his later efforts. But critics gave
it a cool reception, noting that Woody still had not
distinguished between his ability to make stand-up comic
jokes, and his ability to direct and act in a film. It's the tale
of a nurdish products tester Fielding Mellish (Woody)
who falls for a political activist Nancy (Louise Lasser)
who rejects him because she wants a more politically
active man. Consequently Fielding becomes a rebel leader
in San Marcos in an ultimately successful bid to win back
and marry Nancy.

Louise acquitted herself commendably, and her humour showed through in at least one scene which appeared ad-libbed:

> *Fielding*: 'Have you seen the X-rays of me?'
> *Nancy*: (Laughing) 'I've seen the X-rays of you.'
> *Fielding*: 'I fail to see the humour in this.'
> *Nancy*: 'You didn't see the X-rays.'

Although there are no *messages* in *Bananas*, the movie
contains cautionary warnings about the dire state of
married life, an institution Woody had just struggled out
of, and was intent on avoiding in the future.

Wearing his false revolutionary's beard, Fielding finally beds Nancy who is ecstatic after making love to her
impression of the ideal man. 'That was practically a
religious experience,' she says before Fielding whips off
his beard to reveal who he really is. 'I knew there was
something missing,' she adds disappointedly. The two do
marry but sex is never quite the same again. 'It was the
worst I've had,' she says to the camera afterwards.

The same theme crops up in his next film, the big screen
version of *Play it Again, Sam*, directed by Herb Ross.
Nancy wants to go off skiing and motorcycling complaining that everything went wrong with their marriage.
'During courtship, things are different,' he explains. (In

Sleeper Luna warns, 'Meaningful relationships between men and women don't last. There's a chemical in our bodies that make it so we get on each other's nerves sooner or later.')

The theme was the same but it was not Louise Lasser playing the part. Ross chose Diane Keaton for a reprise of her stage role, and although by now her relationship with Woody had cooled, the two were still 'intermittent lovers' as they headed out to shoot the film in San Francisco (because of a union strike in New York). In the same year Diane had been united for the first time on the big screen with her great friend Al Pacino in the first *Godfather* movie. Diane had signed up for a tiny fee hoping the multi-million dollar budget of the movie would turn it into something special and guarantee her some recognition. *The Godfather did* become a great hit hailed as 'the greatest gangster picture ever made'. But unfortunately, her own role in *The Godfather* was lost amid Francis Ford Coppola's sprawling cast in which Pacino too, was a relative unknown. Coppola had wanted a more aggressive actor like Robert DeNiro but Pacino would eventually become synonymous with the part of Michael Corleone, and Keaton would grow in acting stature in the two more *Godfather* epics that they would both appear in as their love for one another bloomed.

Meanwhile Keaton was in a damp San Francisco with the *Play it Again, Sam* cast. Woody had washed his hands of any part in the direction of the movie partly because he felt that *Sam* had been created for the stage and he would not be able to recreate it successfully on celluloid. Also, the offer of a handsome sum of money for the screen rights was too tempting to ignore. (For his 10 per cent cut he eventually made more than 1 million dollars.)

Thanks to Ross's direction, the final product was stylistically different from the sort of film Woody would become best known for. Yet ironically it is a quintessential Woody Allen movie, witty and intelligent with touching twinges of lost romance and nostalgia for the days of the silver screen. It united for the camera, the team of Keaton, Allen and Roberts, and had it been set in New York would probably fall more neatly into place with his own paeans to the beloved city, *Annie Hall* and *Manhattan*.

Play it Again, Sam has everything of these later fully fledged films, the autobiographical references to his youth … 'that little co-ed from Brooklyn College who passed out' when she saw Felix and the pangs of anxiety when Felix has to call a date – 'the old tension is beginning to set in – my stomach is jumping …' There are the references to image and reality, Felix the film reviewer who is 'one of the world's great watchers' and his hero-mentor Humphrey Bogart who overcomes romantic disappointment with a shot of bourbon and soda.

Dick like Bogart, is the Hollywood ideal of what a man should be, while Felix is hesitant and inept who gets migraine headaches and sores like Linda to whom he's gradually drawn and has a brief affair with. In imagining how he can explain the affair to his best friend, the idea of 'sophistication' crops up. Recalling *Separate Tables*, Felix imagines two English gentlemen discussing the affair over tea at their club.

Play it Again, Sam, ends on a happy but unresolved note at San Francisco airport as Linda and Dick fly off together. It echoes Bogart's farewell in *Casablanca*, and leaving a sense of lost but somehow sanguine love, similar to the ending of *Annie Hall*, as Annie walks away from Alvy.

In his article, 'How Bogart Made Me the Superb Lover I am Today', Woody talked about how the original idea for *Play it Again, Sam* had come about …

'The first Humphrey Bogart movie I saw was *The Maltese Falcon*. I was 10 years old and I identified immediately with Peter Lorre. The impulse to be a snivelling, effeminate, greasy little weasel appealed to me enormously and, setting my sights on a life of mealymouthed degradation and crime, I rapidly achieved a reputation that caused neighbouring parents to appear at my doorstep carrying torches, a large rope and bags of quicklime ... I wrote *Play it Again, Sam* to honour Bogart for at least giving me a few months of smooth sailing, and also to get even with a certain girl (or a particular sex that gives me trouble, to tell the truth).[14'

Perhaps *Play it Again, Sam* marks the stage that Woody is beginning to feel more confident in himself. He had come a long way from the days when parents in Brooklyn would look down on him. When the Broadway version of *Play it Again, Sam* came out, he dined one evening with Bryna Goldstein. She laughs now at her mother's reaction: 'She wanted me to go to Connecticut and marry him!'

In the film the gags continue with assurance:

Dick: 'The other night she [Linda] spoke about having an affair in her sleep.'
Alan: (Worried) 'Did she mention any names?'
Dick: 'Only yours. I woke her and questioned her and she said it was just a nightmare.'

Woody's relationship with Diane Keaton has often been painted as a 'Svengalian' one, a comparison that crops up time and time again with his women. Many critics saw their biggest hit together, *Annie Hall*, as the ultimate proof of this one sided relationship. From the perspective of these critics, he is the talented maestro who turns her into an overnight star and she is the ungrateful beneficiary who rejects her mentor. Unfortunately for these critics though, this comparison hardly fits the facts. Allen may have turned many women into stars, but they invariably returned his kindness albeit not necessarily in a romantic way.

Allan Konigsberg (left) and Jack Victor in the Midwood High School year book.

Allan and teenage sweetheart Bryna Goldstein.

Right: Louise Lasser outside the Russian Tea Room in New York.
(AP/Wide World Photos)

Below: Woody Allen stands with Betty Ford, wife of the American President, choreographer Martha Graham, and Diane Keaton at a benefit performance in New York of the Graham Dance Company in June 1975.
(AP/Wide World Photos)

Diane Keaton and Woody Allen outside an Upper East Side restaurant in New York in September 1992. *(Alex Oliveira/DMI)*

Above: Diane Keaton and Warren Beatty arrive at the Winter Garden Theatre in New York to see the Broadway musical *42nd Street.* Accompanying them are Diane Keaton's mother and father. *(AP/Wide World Photos)*

Below: Frank Sinatra and Mia Farrow at the first game of the Orioles-Dodgers World Series. Sinatra's daughter Tina is to the right. *(AP/Wide World Photos)*

André Previn and Mia Farrow at home in Surrey. André holds his son, Fletcher(three), while Mia sits at the piano with Summer Song(two) in the foreground, and Lark(four). *(AP/Wide World Photos)*

June 4, 1982. Woody Allen and Mia Farrow outside the Astoria Film Studios in Queens, New York. *(Ann Clifford/DMI)*

Above: Woody Allen and Mia Farrow with children outside the Russian Tea Room in March 1986. The children are, left to right, Fletcher, one year old Dylan, Misha and Soon-Yi. *(David McGough/DMI)*

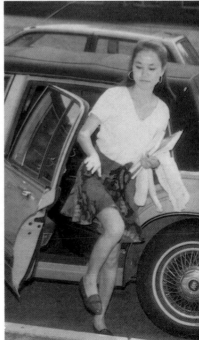

Right: End of a school day. Soon-Yi Farrow Previn arrives back after her literature class at Rider College. *(AP/Wide World Photos)*

January 1988. Woody Allen and Mia Farrow with their new born son, Satchel, and Mia's daughter, Dylan, photographed in Mia's New York apartment.
(David McGough/DMI)

Diane Keaton was far less educated than him in many ways, and totally in awe of his knowledge of philosophers, writers and artists that he had grown to admire through his own self-education. He became her mentor, teaching her about the intellectual world he likes to see himself as part of. He also introduced her to analysis which was an alien concept to this wide-eyed girl from sunny California, but it is something that she continues with today.

Annie Hall was undoubtedly a portrait of Diane, and it was autobiographical in that it would draw on many strands of his relationships with Diane, Louise and many others. It is true that he has always shown a penchant for wives or lovers who seem to be more dependent on him than he is on them. But Diane was never a weak willed or easily manipulated woman. He would help her become a star, but she was the teenage girl who set out to succeed at a business in which she had no family background. She was the one who pushed herself to stick at it after initial disappointments.

Just as Louise Lasser had given him a taste for traditional music, art and literature, Diane Keaton gave him a sense of visual style that he was entirely lacking. 'She has an utterly spectacular visual sense. I see many things today through her eyes, textures and forms I would never have seen without her. She showed me the beauties of the faces of the old people. I'd never been sensitive to that before. And there's a certain warmth and poignance associated with young women I would never have seen without her. She's increased my affection for women in general,' he said.[15] And Diane introduced other forms of art. After they had split up, in 1973, she persuaded him to dress up in leotards and take dance lessons with Martha Graham, an experience that he said was 'embarrassing'.

'It was interesting, but it wasn't fun. It was quite embarrassing for a 38-year-old person to put on a dance belt and leotards and sit in there. I didn't mind being there but once you had to get up and prance across the floor with the others and do the open steps, I couldn't make it! My sense of shame just overtook me!'[16]

She also had a huge appetite for life. 'She had the largest appetite of anyone I've ever known. After a ball game or a fight I'd take her to Frankie and Johnnie's and she'd have a steak and potatoes and marble cheesecake. Then we'd come home and she'd go into the kitchen and turn on a TV movie. She's always cold, so she'd turn on the stove, take her paintings out and put them on the kitchen table. And Bette Davis would be on and the stove would be wide open and she just had a steak dinner and she'd go to the freezer and take out frozen waffles and she'd start making them and have three or four of those. And I'd go into the kitchen later and find her frying up tacos. I couldn't believe it – I was awestruck by her appetite.'[17]

Some accounts of their relationships maintain that Woody and Diane were together for years, even up to *Annie Hall* which was made in 1976. But he has always insisted they were together until March 1970 when she moved into her own apartment on East 68th Street. 'She lived here and at one point we talked about the idea that we had been living so closely for years and it might be nice, we thought, to try it with her *not* living here. That was a mutual decision. And if we didn't like that, we'd move back in together ... I mean, we were still lovers intermittently after that for a while. Gradually we sort of cooled down and drifted apart more. But it was *nothing* like in the movie.'[18]

Diane is quoted as saying: 'I'm comfortable with him. We're very good friends. I talk to him a lot, and we see each other every week. We laugh and share things. He's very good to his friends, he's always been tremendously encouraging to them, always giving them a big push. We're beyond getting involved again with each other. He's my closest and dearest friend.' But when asked why they split up, she says she's not sure. 'It's very hard to say.'[19]

'Friend' is a far better description of Diane's relationship with Woody. She was an independent soul who certainly loved him once and continues to have a great love for him. But while he enjoys living in Manhattan with only a few trips out of the city, usually to the cultural capitals of Europe, she likes driving to places like Graceland in Memphis and the Grand Canyon with old friends who treat the trips like college kid vacation jaunts. One of her best friends once said, 'She's a middle class girl with the soul of an artist.'[20]

After their joint success with the movie version of *Play it Again, Sam*, Diane did not rest on her laurels and wait for her mentor to dish up another hit. *The Godfather* came out a month before *Sam*, and was to be one of the biggest box office hits ever. Although her part had been buried in a huge cast, her performing abilities were not questioned, and Coppola signed her up for the sequel which was also to star Al Pacino. Their relationship was developing in much the same way that her and Woody's was crumbling. They would not be lovers for many years, but they enjoyed a marvellous camaraderie which is unusual for men and women. Diane enjoyed working with Pacino just as she loves acting with Woody even today. But Pacino found the idea of working with a lover suffocating. 'I'd prefer not to, frankly,' he said.[21]

Diane saw Pacino go through one of his most self-destructive stages in the months after *The Godfather* came out. The sudden success went to his head as the struggling actor who had had to do odd jobs, then become an overnight star, and would soon be a wealthy man. He turned to drink during the making of the movie, the high pressures of Hollywood unfamiliar to a man who saw himself as a stage actor. When the film was a hit, he hit the bottle further and became immersed in a sea of booze, tranquillisers, women and unsavoury characters. Over the next few years while his friend Diane watched despondently, Pacino would often fall into endless periods of melancholy, sickness and often exhaustion through drinking. It was a remarkable contrast to Woody, who rarely touched drugs of any sort, drank wine only sparingly and could go from one major project to the next without collapsing into the self-destructive crazes which were familiar in Hollywood.

Woody was re-united briefly on the screen with Louise Lasser for *Everything You Always Wanted to Know about Sex, But Were Afraid to Ask*, his hilarious parody of Dr David Reuben's sex manual which was hugely popular at the time.

The series of vignettes such as 'What are Sex Perverts?' and 'What is Sodomy?' contain some of the most memorable Woody Allen sketches in which he appears variously as an inept royal jester and a bespectacled sperm in 'What Happens During Ejaculation?' Woody is the reluctant sperm, worried at what he may meet when shot out of the erect penis – the pill, a condom, or, worst of all, 'supposing it's a homosexual encounter!' he wonders aloud. And, 'What if he's masturbating? I'm liable to wind up on the ceiling!' He finally goes off to his fate commenting, 'Well, at least he's Jewish.'

Louise appears in a couple of the segments, including one on homosexuality which for some reason was left out of the American version. 'To prove how I can really hold a grudge,' Allen wrote in a later *Playboy* article about the movie, 'the girl playing the part of my wife is my ex-wife, Louise Lasser, who was not frigid when we were married and could come at the drop of a hat – the big problem was that I rebelled against wearing a hat to bed, although I didn't mind earmuffs.'[22]

In the same magazine, he explained that he had been given the chance to film *Everything You Always Wanted to Know about Sex* or the Old Testament and he chose the former because it made more sense: 'The picture expresses my feelings about sex: that it is good in moderation and should be confined to one's lifetime. I have tried to remain faithful to the book, which is more than I did with my wife, and have attempted to delineate for all time the various perversions, along with tips on what to wear.'

In fact the movie had a serious point to make about the 1960s counter culture of increased sexual awareness. Developments like the Kinsey Report had revealed the truth about rampant behind the doors sexuality in the U.S. But the spate of 'sex manuals' that followed, desensitised sex by reducing human emotion and the human body to a series of technical and scientific terms.

'It's a society with so many shortcomings – desensitised by television, drugs, fast food chains, loud music and feelingless mechanical sex. Until we find a resolution to our terrors, we're going to have an expedient culture that's all – directing all its energies toward coping with the nightmares and fears of existence, seeking nothing but peace, respite and surcease from anxiety ... Until we reach some understanding of who we are, what the purpose of creation was, what happens after death, we're caught in a maze of certain hysterical desperation ... Even sex won't improve until we've deciphered these ultimate meanings.'[23]

Later on in *Hannah and Her Sisters*, Elliot (Michael Caine) has presented Lee (Barbara Hershey) with a book of poetry by e.e. cummings. When he anxiously asked her if she had read a love poem she said she had, and it had made her cry '... it was so beautiful ... so romantic ...' At which point Elliot makes a ham fisted attempt to kiss her. Once more, perfect love and purity of thought ruined by base human desire and lust.

In April 1973, Woody flew to Los Angeles to start the filming of *Sleeper* with Diane Keaton who had not yet started on the second *Godfather*. *Sleeper* was due to be made in the Mojave Desert and on the old Culver City *Gone With the Wind* lot where United Artists supplied him with the pleasant three bedroomed house which had been used years earlier by Clark Gable as a dressing room.

Filming started on *Sleeper* on April 30, 1973 budgeted at 2 million dollars and with 50 days to shoot it. Unfortunately (Woody was a perfectionist) it took more than twice that time. In so doing it consumed his own 350,000 dollar fee which he was due as actor, director and co-author, and cost him the end of a blossoming relationship with the producer, who walked out in exasperation.

It was to become one of his best films, but at the time looked like a disaster with Woody and Ralph Rosenblum working around the clock on last minute editing in the Clark Gable cottage. At one stage Diane Keaton, who was by now working on *The Godfather*, had to be called back for re-shooting just two weeks before the picture was released. 'It was only through a whirlwind of overlapping labour that we made the Christmas release,' said Rosenblum.[24]

The reclusive, obsessive and occasionally morose Woody struck a chord with Ralph Rosenblum the moment they met, and he has worked with the director on more films than any other film editor. The two shared so much in common besides their Jewish backgrounds and Brooklyn youth. Ralph would describe the two of them as 'both perennially joyless, pessimistic about our chances of happiness, and easily sucked into low spirits.' 'Woody,' he said, was 'consumed by his alienation.'

Ralph had once suffered from a stammer, an embarrassing affliction which helped him to understand Woody's own social timidity. He noticed how Woody, like him, avoided eye contact with fans or even colleagues, and dealt with difficult situations by using *silence* – something Ralph described as 'his primary tool for both protection and control'.

Yet he observed the courage too, and admitted to being captivated by the power it must have taken Woody to overcome his natural inhibitions, and break into the cut-throat showbiz world by confronting his worst fears, and standing before rowdy nightclub audiences. It was something Ralph could never envisage doing. But while Woody's fears and frustrations became the bedrock of his work to the exclusion of a stable emotional life, Ralph had married and sought the security of a family.

Despite their long collaboration together, Ralph does not regard Woody as a close friend, to this day. In his book, *When the Shooting Stops*, which includes an account of their working relationship, he paints a vivid portrait of this private man and his working habits.

'Woody is very private, very reserved, excruciatingly – at times maddeningly – controlled. He never snacks when he works; he never betrays what he's feeling. His paltry lunches, sometimes no more than a glass of club soda, are symbolic of stoicism.' Ralph is an admirer of Woody's work, and grateful that he was able to contribute to many of its most glorious moments. But he has never claimed any false intimacy.

'The public reports stress his unhappiness, but despite all the words that have been written about his two decades of psychoanalysis, only a few intimates know the particulars of his pain.'

Ralph Rosenblum's experience with Woody is not unlike many of those who work with him closely, and would expect, with any other director, to assume a greater level of intimacy as a result. Rosenblum though, may be reading too much into Woody's extreme solitude and silence on set, which is sober compared to some of the childish trickery and pranks that some film directors encourage. Woody likes to get filming over and done wtih as quickly as possible, and he probably realises that the less time spent messing around on location, means more time in his beloved editing suite where he loves to while away the days, or back at the Fifth Avenue apartment. Interestingly though, he loosened up on the set of *Manhattan Murder Mystery* despite his personal travails with

Mia Farrow which were raging in the headlines at the time. Cast and crew on the movie reported that Woody, for once, did kid around.

It was on *Sleeper* that Woody began to develop the monastic work habits that were to become his personal imprint on movie sets from then onwards, and Rosenblum draws a vivid picture of the director at work: 'When he arrives at 8.58 am in a room full of sound engineers, sound editors, and assistants at the mix, he doesn't join in the morning ritual of coffee and conversation, does not pause to receive their greetings, but rather moves double time in the direction of his chair, keenly hoping to avoid small talk … All told, the impact of Woody's entrance will be to dampen whatever spirits existed in the room.'

The trials and tribulations of a movie set were never more so than on his next project, *Love and Death*. Woody embarked on this project with more enthusiasm than anything he had done so far, believing he was going to have a greater level of control than before. It is a story about a Russian pacifist, Boris Dmitrivich Grushenko, who ends up being executed for shooting Napoleon's double. It was to be a reasonably successful movie with some of Woody's best lines:

'How I got into this predicament, I'll never know. Absolutely incredible. To be executed for a crime I never committed. Of course, isn't all mankind in the same boat? Isn't all mankind ultimately executed for a crime it never committed? The difference is that all men go eventually, but I go six o'clock tomorrow morning. I was supposed to go at five o'clock but I have got a smart lawyer. Got leniency.'

Boris, *Love and Death*

In 1974 Diane and Woody set off for Europe as he enthused about the prospects of making a comedy that also said something significant. He was well aware of the fact that many audiences might find it depressing, with the title and the number of death scenes. And he knew the biggest failure is to make a movie which has a message but is not funny. The old Hollywood adage was in his mind: 'If you want to send a message, go to Western Union.' But he was determined to make amusing comedies while exploring serious issues.

He would go on exploring things with as much depth in the future, but never away from home after learning for himself the problems of location shooting. *Love and Death* was to be shot mostly in Hungary but also in France. It involved thousands of extras, none of whom could speak a word of English, and for many weeks Diane Keaton, Woody and the crew lived in cramped caravans in rain sodden fields.

Diane recalled: 'Only three people spoke English, Woody his secretary and myself. The rest spoke French. Woody speaks French too. We didn't have much to say, so we'd sit in a trailer and talk in between shots which took forever.

'And every day we would have the exact same meal in the hotel. Woody would have fish, and I would have chicken. No wine. The waiter thought we were the two most eccentric people in town.'[25]

I Miss Annie

'I've got nothing but feelings for you, but, you know, you don't wanna get hung up with one person at your age. It's charming and erotic. There's no question about that. As long as the cops don't bust in, we're gonna break a few records. But it's not a good thing.'

Ike to Tracy, *Manhattan*

After *Love and Death* Woody was in romantic limbo, dating one or two women and remaining very close friends with Diane Keaton. He would say of this period, that he dated many women both in and out of show business, but that none of them were very long-lasting relationships. He certainly had enough offers. By now he had a clique following suffering from Woody Allen mania, and his mailbag began to fill with fan letters and correspondence from adoring women. Like most stars who can become engulfed with this sort of adoration, he either ignored the letters or got someone to send a polite reply. Not always though. In 1976 housewife Judith Viorst was amazed when, two weeks after writing to say she loved him, a handwritten reply came through her letter box inviting her around to dinner.

The venue was his spectacular penthouse apartment, and the meeting reveals the growing distance that arises between a celebrity's private persona and the one which is invariably foisted on them by their fans. Judith, thrilled with the response, took the elevator up to his apartment and rang the bell of his door which opened directly off the hallway. Woody himself answered the door and showed her in, offering cocktails while a cook in the background prepared a sumptuous meal.

'It was truly the stuff dreams – and movie scripts – are made of: Woody Allen padding around, putting classical music on the stereo, making me a Martini on the rocks and leading me into the dining room, to a table set for two with wine and candles.'[1] It was a magical evening, but not the sort she expected. Far from being the piercing intellect she had imagined, and far from being as hilariously funny as he was in her children's favourite movies *Bananas* and *Sleeper*, the Woody Allen she talked to that night was subdued, intense, and much to her great disappointment, claimed to be more influenced by Bob Hope than any of the great thinkers she admired.

'People,' he told her, 'have always thought of me as an intellectual comedian, and I'm not. I'm a one-liner comic like Bob Hope and Henry Youngman. I do the wife jokes. I make faces. I'm a comedian in the classic style.' Shaken by this revelation, Judith was also disappointed to learn that Woody did not take his years of psychoanalysis in the least bit seriously. His reasons for doing it were, firstly that he could afford it, and secondly that 'it's nice to whine for 50 minutes'.[2]

Judith got into a cab on Fifth Avenue shortly after midnight after having disconcertingly observed that Woody had not smiled once since 8 p.m. when she had arrived at his apartment. His one joke had been about his new analyst – the third in his life – who was a woman. 'I thought that a change of sex might help – theirs not mine.' She had enjoyed the evening but left feeling a little sorry for Woody. 'There's no one I know – not anyone – who does well in love,' he told her.

When his love life with Diane Keaton finally fizzled out is a mystery, not helped by their frequent appearances together long after they both insisted they had parted. There is no reason to doubt Woody's insistence that she only lived with him on Fifth Avenue for the duration of the stage version of *Play it Again, Sam*, shortly after which she found her own apartment nearby. But his claim that they were no longer romantically involved by the time the film version of *Play it Again, Sam* was shot is open to question.

Woody's old friend from his Greenwich Village days and *What's New, Pussycat?*, Vicky Tiel, was still in touch with him. Vicky says she was never allowed in his apartment, she presumes because he was with Diane Keaton. Then – in 1976, the same year that Judith Viorst met him – Woody invited her around, saying, 'It's okay now, Keaton's clothes are all gone!'

Vicky would be linked romantically to Woody around 1976. Much to the annoyance of Vicky's husband Ron Berkeley, tabloid magazines in Europe and America announced his wife's happy news: she was pregnant. And the father, they suggested was Woody Allen. Vicky Tiel said that: 'The stories were completely wrong. They happened after a paparazzi photographer got a picture of us together and I told Woody that I didn't want to be photographed pregnant – so he tried to shield my tummy from the lens. It looked as if we both had a secret to keep. Ron was particularly upset about my relationship with Woody and he would warn me that he never wanted to read about us together. I think it's because Ron couldn't believe that a woman could be such good friends with a man without sex being involved. After that picture appeared Ron was furious. It caused a lot of havoc for everyone although Woody was pleased about it, it made him feel good.'

This paradox over Woody's claimed loathing of personal publicity crops up time and time again. And it was in evidence in 1975 when he and Diane Keaton were very publicly together with President Ford's wife Betty at a Martha Graham benefit in Manhattan. The shy and reclusive actor guaranteed himself national headlines by wearing black and white sneakers with his formal evening suit. He claimed the anxiety of the event caused him to lose five pounds, but as Guy Flatley was to comment in the *New York Times*, it seemed odd for such a timid chap to turn up in a pair of sneakers for a date with the President's wife. His own explanations for this attention grabbing stunt have varied over the years and include claims that he thought the sneakers would be more comfortable,[3] to the fact that he *knew* they would win publicity for Martha Graham. Could Woody Allen be an attention grabbing celebrity like all the rest?

Still, nobody doubts his explanation to waiting pressmen about his relationship with the President's wife: 'We're just good friends.' The event was full of characteristic anxiety attacks for Woody especially after he learned that he would have to escort Mrs Ford. 'Can I do this like unobtrusively?' he begged when told the presidential limousine would take him to the benefit. 'I just wanted to see some dancing, that's all.'[4] He told *Seventeen*: 'The anguish was unremitting, because I hate going any place. Then when I, who slinks to my seat in a theatre, walked in with Mrs Ford, everybody stood up and applauded!'[5] As soon as they could do afterwards, Diane Keaton and Woody fled to a Third Avenue restaurant for iced coffee and a break from the formality.

Regardless of her romantic disposition towards him, Diane had made a clear break from him as a mentor, branching out into stage and screen roles of her own making. Many would prove to be big mistakes, but she had made the conscious decision to be independent. In 1976, besides Woody's next movie which started shooting in May, she returned briefly to the stage, and signed up to do director Richard Brooks's film version of the bestselling novel *Looking For Mr Goodbar*. This is the story of a teacher of deaf children who leads a sordid private life, trawling nightclubs looking for sex. *Looking For Mr Goodbar*, for which she was paid a comparatively modest 50,000 dollars, involved some nude scenes and she consulted her father and Woody before making it. She did go ahead with it, but it was a role axiomatically opposed to the one Woody had in mind for her on his next movie.

This was the year for Woody that marked a break from his professional past where he had very much been a small cog in a big wheel. With the trauma of *Love and Death* out of the way, he was approaching the stage in his career where he would be able to have increasingly more control over his work – and the people around him. He was to act in Martin Ritt's *The Front*, a movie about McCarthy era blacklisting of Hollywood writers, but his thoughts were focused sharply on his own projects from now on. Projects he now had the clout to do in the way he wanted to do them. The image of a hapless loser for ever at odds with the world would continue on the screen, but in real life Woody Allen was taking charge of his own destiny.

He was now in a position to do something about the pet hates that had irked him since childhood, and would no longer commit himself to big budget extravaganzas like *Love and Death*, that required hundreds of technicians and extras, inhospitable locations on the other side of the earth, and expensive period costumes. He was in Manhattan, and he was there to stay. (Since then he has only travelled once out of the New York area to make a movie, and that was the forgettable *Scenes From a Mall*, which he didn't direct.)

Like any artist effectively given *carte blanche*, he embarked on his favourite project. He wanted to call this 'Anhedonia', a term meaning the inability to experience pleasure. He had been nursing the various strands of 'Anhedonia' in his mind for months if not years, and around 1975 it began to take shape with his friend Marshall Brickman as co-author. It was the story of Alvy Singer, a small Brooklyn boy born under the Coney Island big dipper which, along with his constantly battling parents, was responsible for a nervous state of mind which made relationships with the opposite sex difficult if not impossible. Alvy becomes reasonably successful as a stand-up comic and even has relationships with women, but he's constantly distracted by morbid thoughts of Nazis and concentration camps, and despair at the banality of the culture he lives in. True love or meaningful relationships seem to elude him. When he finds love in the form of a dizzy mid-west girl called Annie Hall who is unencumbered with *any* thoughts, let alone morbid ones, Alvy discovers it too late. He gets her to see an analyst; he educates her about literature, he takes her to see *The Sorrow and the Pity*, and he turns her into a sophisticated New Yorker. Which is when Annie walks out on him.

They started filming at a beach house on a stretch of Long Island's breezy South Fork on May 10, 1976.

'Anhedonia' never saw the light of day but *Annie Hall* did, and was to become Woody's first commercial and critical hit, a movie many people who had never heard his name before will always associate with him. 'Anhedonia' was the title he wanted for it right up to the very last minute when an elaborate but not very credible advertising campaign was planned across America to promote it. But at the eleventh hour he listened to wiser counsel and changed it to *Annie Hall*, the movie that would catapult his ex-lover Diane Keaton to stardom and garner four top Oscars *and* four British Academy Awards as well as a host of other accolades. In fact Woody had listened to wiser counsel throughout the making of *Annie Hall*, and the final product was dramatically different from the original film he made.

The original was an hilariously entertaining visual stream of consciousness centred around Alvy and his nerve-racking neurosis, a sort of two hour twenty minutes comic routine which featured Diane Keaton very briefly. It was his editing collaborator, Ralph Rosenblum, who immediately recognised that no matter how good the jokes were, the film would be virtually unwatchable as a movie except to a very dedicated following.

He set about slicing the celluloid into many different pieces, something that initially his co-writer, Marshall Brickman, was not happy with. But Rosenblum had waved his magic wand once more and when the film was spliced together again he had transformed a series of witty observations, interspersed with rambling monologues, into a cohesive story about two people who fall in love. What had been initially a surrealistic portrait of Alvy Singer's (for which read, Woody Allen's) tortured soul attempting to come to grips with the idiocies of the world, was transformed into a sort of Pygmalion love story with Woody as a Jewish Professor Higgins to Diane Keaton's mid-western Eliza Doolittle. Rosenblum described the first draft as a 'chaotic collection of bits and pieces that seemed to defy continuity, bewilder its creators, and, of all Allen's films, hold the least promise for popular success.'[6] It was a measure of Rosenblum's editorial vision and skill as much as Woody Allen's creative genius that *Annie Hall* became the film we know today.

Rosenblum had edited all but one of Woody's first seven pictures, and the job he faced with *Annie Hall* was similar to what confronted him when he was brought in to sort out *Take the Money and Run*. When he eventually congratulated Woody on the Academy Awards, the director told Rosenblum: 'You know what we had to go through to get it.'

Diane Keaton, who was no longer romantically involved with Woody, *became* Annie Hall in the minds of millions of fans. A short-lived fashion phase was started for women wearing baggy trousers and men's ties with waistcoats and droopy hats. But the girl Woody was dating at the time was nowhere to be seen in the final cut.

Stacey Nelkin, an attractive teenage brunette actress featured in a short scene in which the grown up Alvy

fantasised about a schoolhood girl he had always wanted
to date but had never had the courage to ask out. Stacey
was a well kept secret from the public at the time, and has
only ever spoken about the affair very briefly. But Woody
was to immortalise her on the big screen in the form of
Tracy, the teenage girl played by Mariel Hemingway,
who has an affair with Isaac Davis in *Manhattan*.

At the height of the Mia Farrow scandal, Stacey, by
now 33 and living in Los Angeles, spoke to support her
ex-love after hints that she had been underage when she
fell for Woody. 'I wasn't underage when I dated Woody.
It was a real relationship and a mature one that was
perfectly normal. We met on *Annie Hall* and became good
friends. I was 17 and he was 41, but the age difference
didn't come up. It was a non-issue.

'Because of my upbringing, I was extremely sophisticated. I grew up in New York and had lived in Europe. I
never dated boys my own age. It was a two year
relationship and it wasn't just about the bedroom. It was
a very moral relationship. There were a lot of wonderful
things about it. I learned a lot from Woody about music
and film. I was crazy about him.'[7]

Once more 'sophisticated' crops up, Woody's own
euphemism for unusual behaviour. In *Play It Again, Sam*,
Felix's dilemma of having to admit to his best friend Dick
that he had been sleeping with his wife, prompts him to
think of how two English gentlemen would discuss an
affair over tea at their club ... 'Because of our social
encounters a little romance has developed – it's a very
natural thing among sophisticated people.' Time and time
again, in his movies and private life, Woody equates
sexual experimentation with sophistication. Years later,
when it was discovered he had been seeing his lover's
daughter, Soon-Yi, Woody would characterise her and the
relationship as 'sophisticated'.

Woody is an autodidact, as one of his closest friends
observed, and like many autodidacts, once he latches on

to something or some idea, it's impossible to budge him because he has not the scholarly facility to deal with the material and possibly change his point of view based on the facts that come his way like a scholar can. His opinions, often about matters he has no experience of, become entrenched. A close friend was irritated once when, after he and his wife returned from a vacation in Mexico, Woody pronounced that Hawaii was a nicer place. 'How could he know since he'd never been there in his life? "I know," he said. He would firmly hold that opinion without ever having gone to that place just as he has an opinion about Israel and the Arabs but he's never been there in his life. I've been there 21 times. But Woody will talk endlessly about Israel and it's frightening because people listen to him. He's been told so many times he's a genius that he believes it and everyone else believes it.'

Woody's friends are used to the fact that his opinions about everything – ironically for a self-proclaimed 'liberal' – become watertight and irreversible. He was convinced that the Upper East Side of New York is the only place to live in a city with hundreds of pleasant neighbourhoods. He eventually acquired a Rolls Royce, because he was told it was the 'best' car available. He has his clothes tailored by Ralph Lauren, because he's the 'best' American tailor. He would boast that he had the 'best' cigarette lighter. (He doesn't smoke but after his hero Groucho Marx showed Woody his Dunhill, Woody got one of his own.) Fitzgerald, Hemingway and George S Kaufman were the 'best' writers. No argument.

One idea indelibly imprinted on his mind is that being brought up in New York City automatically endows that lucky person with 'sophistication' which, in turn, more often than not, means an in built tolerance for sexual situations which others would consider perverse or bizarre. He's acutely conscious of the fact that his own parents were never 'sophisticated' unlike, say, Louise

Lasser's parents. A scene clipped from the original *Annie Hall* contrasts Alvy Singer's perpetually battling parents with Annie's polite mother and father. (Father: 'Make me a Martini.' Mother: 'Of course, sweetheart. How would you like it dear?' Father: 'On white bread with mayonnaise.')

Stacey Nelkin therefore, having been born and bred in New York City, and having *lived in Europe*, (which for Woody is a much more sophisticated place than the United States) was a sophisticated woman regardless of her tender age. She could handle an affair with a sophisticated man like any other world weary woman. This is certainly what Stacey herself said when ambushed by reporters in 1993. But other versions painted a less rosy picture of her liaison with Allen, portraying Stacey as a 'sex toy'. She was sneaked into his apartment, never allowed to stay over, and was 'devastated' when the affair broke up and she began to believe that it had been used as material for his next movie.

'It was clear to me that she was desperately in love with Woody. I know she would have married him if she could. But the relationship was strictly one way traffic,' a source said. She was star struck by him and he swept her off her feet when he gave her a small part in *Annie Hall*.

The contrast between Woody Allen's screen image and real life was noted by *New York Times* writer Tony Schwartz in 1980. The Mia-Woody relationship was in its fledgeling stages and after the launch of *Stardust Memories* in which he is Sandy Bates, the successful, bright and witty film maker who is full of self-pity and cynicism. Schwartz noted: 'Mr Allen paints [an] ascetic portrait of himself so ingenuously that it seems almost impolite to disbelieve him. The catch is that what Mr Allen says is often at variance with the way he really lives and with what some of his close friends say about him.'[8]

In the article, Woody says that like Sandy Bates he does

find himself propositioned many times. 'The business I'm in is full of beautiful women, but what good is it if they have nothing to say? I've never been a big believer in going to bed with a woman that I don't have some feeling for.' Schwartz observes that that assertion evokes a big smile from Allen's friend Tony Roberts, who told him: 'Put it this way. Harpo Marx probably chased the most girls, I chase the second most and Woody is a close third.'[9]

The Marx brother was a good comparison, but increasingly Woody's life was beginning to resemble another of his great comic heroes, Charlie Chaplin. Whether through design or subconscious imitation, Woody was beginning to follow a public *and* private course similar to America's greatest film icon. Chaplin was badly educated and came from a cripplingly poor background in London, yet achieved rapid success when he burst on the scene in the earliest movies. Similarly, Woody has eschewed the conventional education available to him, and although his parents were not poor, his was an unlikely background for cinema success, and he was an unlikely movie hero.

Yet he had become a comic success with amazing speed in inexpensive 'slip on the banana' style movies; in a similar way, Chaplin had been very successful with his own brand of slapstick comedy produced for next to nothing by movie king Mack Sennett. And as Chaplin slowly transformed into a romantic hero, so did Woody. Before long, like Chaplin, Woody's directorial and acting efforts would become introspective and morbid, attempting, with little success, to recreate on celluloid those private neuroses which had driven him to the heights he had achieved, just as Chaplin tried to reach back into his sad and unhappy past. Critics would say of Allen – just as they had of Chaplin, 'he isn't as funny as he used to be.' And just as Chaplin tried to ignore his critics and the Hollywood establishment, so did Allen.

Chaplin was well-known for his film collaboration with wives and lovers who cropped up in dozens of his movies, just as Woody's wives and lovers would do in his. And Chaplin had a tremendous fondness for young women, ending his life in 1977, in blissful serenity with Oona O'Neill, the girl he had married in 1953 when she was 35 years his junior. Richard Attenborough's movie, *Chaplin* hints that Oona was Chaplin's recreation of the girl he knew as a teenager and loved for evermore – even though he had never even kissed her. Others have suggested that Woody consciously tried to imitate Chaplin in a bid to achieve his greatness, something that seems too far fetched and simplistic to be true.

But Woody, who always insisted his relationships were 'age appropriate' was beginning to show a hankering for younger women, perhaps in his own way, trying to recreate the love he had longed for but never had when he was a struggling comic in his late twenties surrounded by girls in their first bloom of sexuality.

Vicky Tiel saw this in him, and recalling the days when he appeared in the Greenwich Village coffee shops where she served, she said it was this stage that 'formed' Woody. 'Me and other babes in the Village – where Woody had come from he hadn't really ever seen women like that and that's his ideal. Britt Ekland types. As he got older his ideal remained the same.'

Annie Hall was released in April 1977 to immediate critical and popular acclaim, although there were one or two dissenting voices among the Jewish community apparently unhappy with the undertones of assimilation, and that Woody had turned a WASP-like *shiksa* goddess into a superstar. The grumblings would later turn into headlines like 'Is Woody Strictly Kosher?' after Mia Farrow became his leading lady. Alan Lapidus, who had been the Features Editor of Midwood High School's newspaper, was not one of them. He enjoyed an unusual perspective on Woody's life having grown up in the same community, attended the same school. 'It was frightening watching *Annie Hall* because I was involved in a similar situation with a girl called Pam – except she wasn't brunette, she was a blonde, blue eyed creature who lived in Oak Forest, Illinois ... We actually went back there just after Thanksgiving, and it was the identical family, the idiot son who'd just been kicked out Florida Air Academy of all places, and the mother who I swear to God looked like Coleen Dewhurst, and the grandmother who was known as Grammy Pam because everyone in that family was known as Pamela. The father with the crew cut, the sort of ex-airforce pilot.

'Pam and I were watching the film and just looking at one another. In fact when we broke up which was not in O'Neals where the film was shot, but across the street in the saloon. I looked at her when she was saying this isn't working and I immediately thought of the line in *Annie Hall*, when Alvy Singer says relationships have to be like sharks – they have to constantly move on. I said to Pam, "Please don't say the relationship's like a shark – I've seen that scene played before." She said, "Well relationships aren't any good unless they ceaselessly move on".

'It's not just me, a lot of my friends have led similar lives to Woody. The background was so similar with all of us, the vast majority of Jewish males married these adorable budding Jewish flowers and we all got divorced fairly rapidly after that and then we all went out with the Gentile goddess. When my friends all got married and divorced at the same times, they were all going out with the same blonde, blue eyed girls at the same time – all from the Midwest. I even ended up marrying one who is exceptional, wonderful and magnificent – a blonde, blue eyed girl from the Midwest.

'We went through the same horrendous experience of the first marriage, associated that with Jewish women, went through horrendous divorces and then said, "Never again! I'm going to fulfil my fantasy and go out with the wonderful Gentile blonde."

'It was always a fantasy when we were kids because it was forbidden fruit. In a Jewish family at the time when I was I guess 14, my uncle married a Gentile woman and the family went into ritual mourning. I thought someone had died! I said "My God, what happened?" And they said he married a *shiksa*. The *shiksa* was the forbidden fruit therefore it represented everything that was exotic, mainstream, American, undoubtedly far more savoury than the Jewish nymphs we were going to school with.'

Alan Lapidus's views are *not* shared by all Jewish males, and Jack Victor thinks Woody is definitely not one of them. 'As Jews become more and more assimilated into the American mainstream we meet more and more people who are not Jewish. This is especially significant because we are so few. Hence there is greater intermarriage. This is not to say there are no fantasies or motives towards greater assimilation or seeking out what is more "respectable" in society especially in areas where there are considerable social barriers. Also, there is an element of rebellion to not want to be pigeon holed in our limited world or do what our parents want. But I just don't think Woody is a good example of a Jew striving to find acceptance in a WASP world. His two marriages were to Jewish women; he is in a milieu where a high percentage of associates are or have been Jewish. And even when he developed relationships with non-Jewish people, they were Catholics rather than WASPs.'

When *Annie Hall* opened, the critics were indifferent to the obsession with assimilation which afflicts some of Manhattan's elite. It was recognised immediately as a resounding success, and Woody Allen was placed overnight on the pedestal preserved for America's greatest comic directors.

Variety pronounced: 'In a decade largely devoted to male buddy-buddy films, brutal rape fantasies, and impersonal special effects extravaganzas, Woody Allen has almost single handedly kept alive the idea of heterosexual

romance in American films.'[10] His four romantic comedies with Diane Keaton were compared to Tracy–
Hepburn films. And while *Star Wars* was the biggest box
office hit of the year, *Annie Hall* was proving to be no
mean performer. Diane Keaton was an overnight star,
inundated with requests for interviews with all the major
publications (which she responded to sparingly, describing a cover story with *Time* as 'the most painful experience' of her life) and lucrative offers of work flooded in.

Just as Diane Keaton was getting used to this new
found adulation, her second movie of the year, *Looking
For Mr Goodbar*, came out to be universally slammed
despite high hopes when the project was initially announced. But her performance was praised almost universally, so much so that one critic said that if she did not
win an Oscar for it there was no God.

But when the Academy Award nominations were
announced in February 1978, it was her role as Annie Hall
that was in the running for an award as best actress along
with *four* other nominations for the film: best picture, best
actor (Allen), best director (Allen) and best screenplay
written directly for the screen (Allen and Brickman).
Looking For Mr Goodbar was roundly panned and later
dismissed as 'an exploitative and very boring sex melodrama which doesn't even make one believe in its central
character' by the film bible, Halliwells. When the winners
were announced *Annie Hall* swept the board getting all
the trophies it was nominated for except 'best actor' for
Woody who still got an Oscar for best director.

Woody was not at the ceremony in Los Angeles but
3,000 miles away in Michael's Pub playing his clarinet.
Rollins and Joffe accepted the award on his behalf.
Legend has it he put himself to sleep that night reading
Conversations with Carl Jung, a suitably pretentious piece
of symbolism to contrast with Tinseltown's crass commercialism. His joylessness was not unexpected by those
who knew him, but still prompted the odd query. 'I was

very surprised. I felt good for Diane because she wanted to win. My friend Marshall and my producers Jack Rollins and Charles Joffe had a very nice time. But I'm anhedonic,' he said.[11]

Charles Joffe said: 'Woody is not basically a happy person. I felt badly that after the Academy Awards he could only say he was surprised. "No joy?" I asked. "I don't have time for that," he said. I thought, what a shame he won't allow himself that joy.'[12]

'Life is difficult for Woody,' says Louise Lasser. 'He's one of the unfortunate tormented people. His mind is working all the time. So is a sweet side and a silly side and a sexual side. One night I couldn't sleep and I thought "I am lying next to one of America's foremost humorists".'[13]

Diane Keaton insists that he isn't as morbid as people think. 'Woody has great capacity for joy. He's moved by things and he has a great sense of beauty. He's very sensitive and he has these feelings of guilt and anger and shame. Who's to say where they come from, or why?'[14]

But even enjoyable things for Woody seem to torment him with thoughts of mortality. 'I was watching [the basketball player] Walt Frazier one night with the Knicks. He was so beautiful and young, so dazzling, but I saw the death's head looming. I thought of the inevitable deterioration, the waning away of the adulation. I felt that anger and rage, not anything correctable, but at the human condition you're part of too.

'I was with Keaton, and leaving the Garden I had the underground man feeling, the decay at the core of existence. So I'm no fun to be with at parties because I'm very aware of this all the time.

'Sometimes I think I've got a good thing going. I'm in a culture where being funny is important. If I was an Apache and funny, where would I be? The Indians don't need comedians, you know.'[15]

It would appear success was not being kind to Woody Allen. Although he once said he had been visited by the

'blue bird of anxiety' at an early age, his morbidity really
stems from the time that he became internationally
recognised. His movie *Annie Hall* had a great joke about
pseudo intellectuals in it which most fans cherish. Alvy is
queuing for a movie with Annie and is getting increasingly agitated at the pretentious pontifications of a man
standing behind them, lecturing his girlfriend on Fellini
and Marshall McLuhan. Fed up, Alvy fetches the real
Marshall McLuhan from behind a screen, and McLuhan
declares contemptuously: 'I heard what you were saying.
You know nothing of my work. You mean my whole
fallacy is wrong. How you ever got to teach a course in
anything is totally amazing.'

'Boy, if life were only like this!' says Alvy to the
camera.

Annie Hall marked the stage where Woody would start
becoming a little pretentious, and critics started wishing
someone would whip Marshall McLuhan out on him.

His early films are full of madcap humour which he has
compared to 'Tom and Jerry' cartoons. 'A guy runs out
and you smash him on the head with something and he
doesn't die and he doesn't bleed and you clear the decks
for the next joke right away.' In *Bananas* there is a
memorable scene where the cowardly character, Fielding
Mellish, victoriously pushes two muggers out of the
stationary subway train when their backs are turned –
only to find the furious bullies jump back to beat him up
when the door unexpectedly slides open again.

In the same movie Fielding pathetically attempts to
acquire a pornographic magazine by surreptitiously hiding it among other purchases, only to be thwarted when
the newsagent shouts out loud, 'Hey Ralph! How much is
a copy of *Orgasm*?'. This is worthy of Benny Hill or
Ronnie Barker.

Take the Money and Run, Love and Death, Bananas and
Sleeper are full of obvious comic devices. There's nothing
'intellectual' or even serious about them. These have been

the tools of the trade for everyone from Buster Keaton, Charlie Chaplin, the Keystone Cops and Laurel and Hardy, to Frankie Howerd, Morecambe and Wise, the Goons and Monty Python.

Mickey Rose, talking about how critics over-intellectualise, referred to the reviews given to *Take the Money and Run*, and the sometimes deep meaning that critics attributed to scenes. The scene in which Virgil Starkwell volunteers to be a guinea pig and is transformed into a Rabbi is a case in point. Woody's references to the Jewish faith are often seen as some deep, dark hatred for his parents' religion.

According to Mickey Rose: 'The reason we have the Rabbi jokes is just that I guess Woody's not too religious, and certainly finds orthodox Rabbis funny, that's all. Originally he was going to be turned into a sports announcer, but we decided the Rabbi was funnier.

'These things are accidental … just come up, but reviewers read a lot of things into them. In *Bananas*, when we were visiting the palace and we had musicians up on the balcony they didn't have any instruments. Well, some critic said this was a brilliant piece of surrealism, but the truth of the matter is that the instruments never arrived, and these were people from an old age home in the village so we decided let's let them pretend they're playing … Critics see things in films and think it's a specific thing, but they just happen – there's no deep reasoning.'

Woody's later works like *Play It Again, Sam, Annie Hall, Manhattan, Hannah and Her Sisters, Crimes and Misdemeanors* and *Alice* are more *serious* movies and could be classed as 'intellectual' in the sense that they are 'thoughtful'. But they still rely on a sort of adolescent, schoolboy humour which was evident in his earlier efforts, the constant obsession with getting gorgeous girls, sexual gratification, 'scoring' and 'making the right moves'.

It appeared Woody was not getting any joy out of his increasing success or his private life. Stacey Nelkin was

still, according to the account of their relationship published years later, seeing her older suitor and enjoying his
company, visiting museums and swapping ideas. It had
been characterised incorrectly as a 'Svengali' relationship.
The Victorian fantasy melodrama of Svengali set in turn
of the century Paris, was about how a hypnotist turns a
girl into a great opera singer but she fails to return his
love. Strictly speaking, that comparison could not be
applied to Stacey Nelkin or any of the women in Woody's
life who *did* return Woody's affection but were ultimately
rejected by him. And 'Svengali' has sinister overtones. In
fact ever since Letty had been born, Woody had displayed
an unusual and touching interest in young girls, in
nurturing their interests and provoking them to use their
intellect. It was a relationship very similar to that of Cliff
with his niece in *Crimes and Misdemeanors*, in which he
would be endlessly taking her to old movies and buying
her books of bygone New York.

In 1978, after *Annie Hall* was finished, Woody took under
his wing a 13-year-old girl who wrote to him out of the
blue. As a precocious little girl at school in Coral Gables,
Florida, Nancy Jo Sales's life was an up to date mirror
image of Allan Konigsberg's in 1940s Brooklyn. She
skipped lessons and tried to avoid teachers and other
students by hiding behind stacks of books in the library.
Nancy ignored the school curriculum much to her parents' irritation, and immersed herself in 1940s movies and
19th century literature. She soon became the 'geek' of the
school wearing old-fashioned thrift store clothes which
her class mates would whip off while hurling insults. She
was a sensitive child with nobody to turn to ... until *Annie
Hall* came out and the concept of 'the sensitive man'
became popular. She found Woody's address on Fifth
Avenue, and wrote to him.

Nancy arrived home from school a few days later to
find a brown envelope awaiting her, and when she

opened it, to her astonishment, she saw the name 'Woody Allen' emblazoned across the top. It was an astonishingly open letter, the first of many, and even at that early age, Nancy was amazed to think that her idol could spare the time to write to her. He was starting *Interiors* and had *Manhattan* at the back of his mind.

The letters Nancy received are touching tributes to Woody's faith in human nature. Short and concise, they are nevertheless written in his own hand and are not the dismissive 'thank you for your interest' letters that many stars get their public relations people to write. In the first letter he tells her how it's hard to believe she can only be 13 when he could not even dress himself at that age and here she is writing about existential boredom. He ended it with a long list of questions about herself, the clothes she wears, what time in the morning she gets up at, and whether she's from a poor family. He's also curious to know whether Nancy broods a lot and whether the relentless sun and humidity of Florida has an effect on her.

They are amazing letters, with Manhattan's movie king telling a teenage girl how far he's got with his latest project – even admitting he's not particularly happy with it – and recommending that she study S J Perelman, Sartre and Kierkegaard. The correspondence became animated, more like two old friends who miss one another, exchanging argumentative but friendly letters to keep in touch. She asked him who he would like to have around for dinner – he said Zelda Fitzgerald and 'maybe' Charlotte Rampling, along with Dostoevsky and Tolstoy, Proust and Yeats. They got into an argument over Scarlett O'Hara whom she admired but Woody said that although he had too initially, he'd realised what a 'bitch' she was and that he had '... grown up regarding my taste in women.'

It got to the stage that Nancy was running home every day after school to find out if there was another brown envelope in her mail box, to be full of elation if there was, and infuriation if there was not. She finally met him on a trip to Manhattan with relatives when she left him a note to say she was in town and was delighted to get a call from him at her hotel, 10 minutes later. Nancy went around to his apartment shaking with a combination of excitement and trepidation, her two older relatives accompanying her. The meeting was short lived. The relatives proved to be an embarrassment, talking about Florida real estate values and the fact that they dined out at Elaine's too!

Nancy made an interesting observation of Woody during her short and embarrassing visit to his home. He was, she noticed, like a little boy, sitting upright in his armchair, politely listening to talk about Florida property prices while secretly trying to catch her eye. He had thoughtfully placed a huge bowl of sweets, chocolates and fruits on the coffee table, but they never got eaten in the atmosphere of nervousness during the meeting.

It was to be the end of their brief literary relationship, much to Nancy's disappointment. She had expected something like *Manhattan* where her hero would take her to art galleries and museums, and talk about books. But in the end, the moment of contact, like so many longed for meetings, ended up an awkward mess. She says, 'I have noticed that in Woody's films he often repeats a line about having your worst fears realised. It had been my worst fear, at 13, that I would lose this improbable friend. And here it was happening, as if I were watching our letters being shredded by wolves.'[16]

Nancy was initially saddened by the meeting with Woody, hoping for something more than what had transpired. But she followed the advice he had given her in his letters, read the books he recommended and studied his favourite philosophers. As he suggested, she went to prep school and then on to college, and strangely, as she progressed, the school boys and girls who had tormented her for the 'geeky' looks gradually began to disappear, and she met more and more people who would share her interests.

She remembers fondly something he had written: 'Your kind of mind and feelings is a prize to have even though you will have to pay a high price for it.'[17] She never heard from him again, although she did have strange sensations sometimes watching his movies. In *Husbands and Wives*, the 19-year-old English student Rain, whom Woody almost has an affair with, was born in a hurricane. Nancy too was born in a hurricane.

Annie Hall was a piece of good fortune for Diane Keaton. The Oscar win brought professional and private rewards. Woody had turned her into a major film actress. It also brought her to the attention of Warren Beatty, the legendary Hollywood Lothario with, as it has been caustically noticed, a penchant for Oscar winning actresses. Beatty counts among his many past loves Academy Award winners Julie Christie and Leslie Caron. Diane Keaton's *Looking For Mr Goodbar* director, Richard Brooks, had already drawn his friend Beatty's attention to her fine performance in the otherwise dismal movie.

Oscar night confirmed Brooks's prediction that Keaton would be a great star. Within months Beatty and Keaton would be dating, confirming two of Woody's long-standing convictions. Firstly, that *Annie Hall* could not possibly have been autobiographical since the girl ran off with the West Coast Lothario *after* the movie was made. And secondly, that women would love him and leave him.

A year later Beatty cast Keaton in what would be the fruition of a personal obsession, *Reds*. This is an epic story of American radicalism during the Russian Revolution and was to break its already massive budget and win 12 Oscar nominations. Beatty would get Best Director. It was a movie Woody would never have got made because he

did not have the clout to spend as much money as Beatty
even though his success as an auteur was undeniably
greater. But it was also the sort of large-budget multiple
location shoot that Woody would never have committed
himself to after *Love and Death*. While Woody was
obsessed with small intimate clashes of personality and
mind, Beatty was into the grand picture, the huge sweeping cinemascopic statement. He had been dreaming of the
story of John Reed, a journalist and radical who was the
only American to be buried within the walls of the
Kremlin, since the late Sixties.

He visited Russia in 1969 and the authorities put him in
touch with a woman named Eleanora who had been John
Reed's 16-year-old sweetheart. Finding Eleanora in a high
rise apartment on the drab outskirts of Moscow, the film
star demanded: 'So you were in love with John Reed?' She
replied: 'In love? I fucked him.'[18] After the conversation
Beatty was determined to make his film despite generous
offers from studio chiefs who advised him it would be
easier to make a 25 million dollar film in Mexico for 1
million – Beatty could keep the rest. But he was determined to make the epic and he wanted Diane Keaton as
Reed's wife Louise Bryant.

Much has been made of the stark contrast between
Woody Allen, the diminutive director, and Warren
Beatty, Hollywood's answer to Don Juan. But there are
one or two similarities. Both are intensely shy but at the
same time acutely conscious that self-promotion is
necessary for their chosen industry. Hence the apparent
contradiction between their screen and real life personae
both have been given by the media. Both have great
pretensions to intellect and both are choosy about their
work – Beatty once buying himself out of a movie studio
contract which he thought was not good for his career
when he hardly had a dime. It was Beatty too who
walked out on his starring role in *What's New, Pussycat?*
because he objected to the changes foisted on Woody's

script. The two of them are also intensely private people, Beatty living virtually reclusively in his hilltop house in much the same way as Woody does in his penthouse.

There the similarities stop. Beatty is one of the biggest heart-throbs in the business, and despite making many disastrous career decisions, has arrived at the pinnacle of Hollywood. He turned down roles in *Butch Cassidy and the Sundance Kid*, *The Way We Were*, *The Sting*, *The Godfather*, and *The Great Gatsby*. Yet his rise to fame and glory has been unstoppable. He could be mistaken for one of Woody Allen's many TV producer alter egos who went from strength to strength churning out pulp while the Woody character strove in obscurity for high art.

But Beatty's success was not just mindless. He's a thoughtful businessman and made a lucrative financial investment in *Bonnie and Clyde* which turned him into a wealthy man overnight. But he also has the sort of looks that could never fail in any society at any given time. He was the sort of guy Bryna Goldstein was dating while Woody was waiting forlornly at the beach house for his love to turn up. As Vicky Tiel has said: 'The girls that would go with Woody are the same that would go with Warren because they were interested in being with men that are successful. But with Warren they would fall in love with him because he would dominate them sexually and Woody couldn't.'

Woody had always been in the paradoxical dilemma of seeking yet despising fame, after *Annie Hall*. As the characters of Woody Allen and the real thing became widely known and inseparable in many fans' minds, his every move came under intense and sometimes comical scrutiny. Not just from reporters and photographers but from people in the street who would accost him in much the same way as Alvy Singer was waiting for Annie one day outside the cinema when two lowbrow thugs spotted him.

Ralph Rosenblum described one hilarious encounter at a restaurant which had his collaborator quietly seething. 'Two middle aged women passed our table and stopped about 10 feet down the aisle. After exchanging a few words with her companion, one began retracing her steps until she was alongside the movie star. "Are you Woody Allen?" she demanded. Quietly, without looking up from his food, he said, "Yes." At that she walked away, rejoining her friend, who was standing with her arms folded a few tables away. As Woody and I resumed our conversation, I noticed that the first woman, having conferred with her friend, was on the way back. "Are you sure you're Woody Allen?" she said, looking down at the top of his head. "Yes," he mumbled. Again she left, and I assumed his agony was over. But to my amazement, the second woman now loomed over us, staring boldly at the trapped man. "Can you identify yourself?" she said, whereupon I rose and made shooing motions, and the two of them left.'[19]

A dichotomy was emerging about his public and private persona. It had been there since the early days when he only had a small following. Judith Viorst, the fan whom he invited to dinner at his apartment, had observed how quietly serious he was. Lyn Tornabene discovered in private that he made few jokes. These people, like the two women in Ralph Rosenblum's story, had confused the lovable neurotic with the private and inwardly serious man he really was. Or at least, *the serious man he liked to think he was.* Accounts from personal friends from his childhood up to his marriage to Louise Lasser confirm that Woody was *never* the dull and morose character he portrayed. Jack Victor, Mickey Rose and Bryna Goldstein all say that he was always a bundle of fun as a kid, and one of Louise Lasser's fondest memories is of how much fun Woody was to be with. He may have been 'visited by the bluebird of anxiety' at an early age, but whatever inner neurosis he suffered emerged in humour.

It was only as critical praise began to be heaped on Woody Allen the film icon, that this dark, all-pervading misery began to emerge. Could it be, as one critic said, the result of the *New York Times* calling you a genius every day of your life? As *Annie Hall* wrapped up he let it be known that his next project would be a gloomy Bergman-esque drama like *The Seventh Seal*, the Swedish director's portentous medieval allegory. Woody confessed he had always felt 'indictable' as a film maker on the basis of triviality, that silly Chaplin-style slapstick yarns were 'okay' for entertainment, but now was the time for *serious* stuff.

'It's a terrible thing to say – almost masochistic in a way – but in *The Seventh Seal*, that constant, unrelieved gloom, the intensity of feeling, the religious solemnity, are very pleasurable to me – it's hypnotic. That slow pacing – well, a movie like that just can't be paced slow enough for me.'[20]

So, Woody's next movie was *Interiors*, a sombre, dark and brooding piece with no jokes, no musical soundtrack, and – it would transpire – no audience to speak of. The performances of all involved, including Diane Keaton, Geraldine Page, Maureen Stapleton and Mary Beth Hurt were fine, but although Woody will defend *Interiors* to this day, the general consensus is that it is a monotonous and pretentious movie.

It is the story of a disintegrating family and the frustrated attempts of three daughters to cope with a suicidal mother. It was later dubbed *Hannah and Her Sisters: The Dark Side* by Stephen J Spignesi. Geraldine Page played Eve, the mother who throws herself into the ocean after discovering that her estranged husband Arthur (E G Marshall) has married the flamboyant Pearl (Maureen Stapleton).

Interiors also demonstrated Woody's dark side. Not his brooding inner consciousness, but a disregard for other people's feelings and a lack of sensitivity. It was clearly a portrait of Louise Lasser's tragic family background. But the first Louise heard of it was when she went to see it at the cinema.

Someone very close to Louise recalls a telephone conversation that she is said to have had with her ex-husband after seeing *Interiors*. 'He said, "Hiya Louise!" in that annoyingly innocent way of his as if she didn't realise anything was wrong. "What's up baby?" he said. "I'm very, very upset Woody," said Louise. "That movie is about my family right down to the singlemost specific detail. That's my mother, and that's my father. I don't want to have any control over your life, but you could at least have warned me you were going to splash it across the screen." Woody said, "Hey! Louise, you will never guess how many people have phoned me up to say that *Interiors* is the story of their family!" "Oh yeh?" laughed Louise, "they must have all been relatives of mine".'

After a long conversation Woody pacified Louise, assuring her that the movie was definitely not based on her family situation. It ended with Louise saying, 'In any case, I don't think you got my mother right.' 'Really,' said Woody, 'I thought I was pretty spot on about her.'

Characteristically of Louise, she laughs the incident off and does not bear Woody a grudge. Jack Victor and his wife went to see the movie in Manhattan. 'It absolutely *was* about Louise. My wife and I discussed it afterwards.'

Woody had predicted that his first stab at a serious movie could be humiliating, and he proved to be right. 'The absence of wit does not necessarily betoken seriousness; it merely betokens the absence of wit ... Doubtless, a necessary movie for Allen, but it is both unnecessary and a minor embarrassment for his well-wishers,' wrote Richard Schickel, one of Woody's ardent admirers.[21] Other critics accused him of outright plagiarism of Bergman's work, a charge that was to dog Woody Allen from time to time. It was ironic that he had defied convention two decades previously by becoming a gag writer rather than trying for a 'serious' literary career, yet now that his comic talents had proved to be so successful, he was attempting something that he had scoffed at. Perhaps he should have stuck to what he told Alan Lapidus at the end of the Midwood School years: that serious writing would never have as much impact as comedy.

Woody had penned the role of Renata in *Interiors* specifically for Diane Keaton, saying that he saw much of himself in the part. By now his romantic involvement with her was completely over as she became increasingly involved with Warren Beatty, dividing her time between his house in Beverly Hills' Mulholland Drive and her own modest apartment in New York. Beatty's *Heaven Can Wait* came out a month before *Interiors*, and he already had her in mind to star opposite him in *Reds*. Woody's next movie, *Manhattan*, which started shooting in late 1978 also starred Diane Keaton.

Manhattan, which Woody co-wrote with Marshall Brickman, centred around Isaac Davis, a TV writer who quits his job to write a serious novel. He's involved with Tracy, a 17-year-old and at 42, he is self-conscious about the age difference. Also, he is unable to resist getting involved with Mary, the mistress of his best friend Yale, when he hears that they have split up. When the movie came out, many concluded it was the story of Marshall Brickman and the Manhattan journalist Susan Braudy who was romantically linked (incorrectly) with Brickman. The speculation may have been prompted by earlier disclaimers by Woody that *Annie Hall* was autobiographical – that it was in fact, based on many of Brickman's experiences, rather than his own. However, Susan Braudy and Brickman were not involved, and *Manhattan* was not a portrait of them.

It was disconcerting publicity for Susan, but Woody claimed that his own family was unconcerned at the constant claims that his work was autobiographical. 'The stuff that people insist is autobiographical is almost invariably not, and it's so exaggerated that it's virtually meaningless to the people upon whom these little nuances are based. People got it into their heads that *Annie Hall* was autobiographical, and I couldn't convince them that it wasn't. And they thought *Manhattan* was autobiography.'[22] In another interview, he pointed out that unlike Isaac Davis in *Manhattan* he had never wanted to marry a 17-year-old girl.

Which was strictly true: but he had certainly dated one. Stacey Nelkin surely *was* the woman Woody based the character 'Tracy' on in *Manhattan*? Tracy was played by Mariel Hemingway. Stacey said, 'But the thing that was always strange to me is that Mariel played it much younger. She acted in such an innocent way. That just wasn't me.'[23] And it was not her that walked out of the two year relationship. She had such a crush on Woody that she left to live on the West Coast to get over it and put her life in order. He was the one who tried to stop her from becoming involved with him.

> 'You don't want to get hung up with one person at your age. It's charming, you know, and erotic. There's no question about that ... Think of me as a sort of detour on the highway of life.'
>
> Isaac in *Manhattan*

According to one published account after Stacey had left New York for California, Woody asked her to return.[24] 'Stacey called her friends, all excited because he was flying her to New York,' a close friend said. 'She kept saying, "I'm going to see Woody".'

But Stacey was to be heartbroken. There was no future in it. And she was devastated watching her real life heartache being played out by Mariel Hemingway. Since then she's rarely discussed her romance with Woody.

Warren Beatty's *Reds* was now well into fruition, and in

March 1979 he and Diane Keaton flew to Russia to scout for locations and negotiate with the communist authorities over access and film rights. Thanks to a clash of egos – the USSR's and Beatty's – the negotiations reached an impasse and Hollywood decided to take its money to Finland instead. Production began later in the year on what would become one of the most expensive films in contemporary cinema by which the excesses of *Heaven Can Wait* would pale by comparison. The initial budget of 20 million dollars was big by the standards of the day and Beatty was to spend possibly more than twice as much flying crew and cast between the USA, Scandinavia, Spain and England. Beatty seemed to relish the sort of excesses that Allen despised. Shooting took place in several British locations – off the Lincolnshire coast, in Kent, around Manchester and at Twickenham Studios.

As the seams of the studio's pockets began to burst open, the tempers of all involved began to fray. Senior executives refused to talk to one another, and the formidable cast of stars like Maureen Stapleton, Gene Hackman and Jack Nicholson began to rebel openly at Warren Beatty's manic and extravagant demands. By the time filming ended in summer 1980, Keaton and Beatty were no longer sharing the same living quarters. It was a miracle that despite all its flaws, by the time *Reds* opened at the end of 1981, it did so to rave reviews for all the performances.

According to Stacey Nelkin, her relationship with Woody lasted some two years after which friends say she was in a state of some emotional hurt. She was not the only spurned lover recovering from the scars of a failed romance as *Manhattan* prepared to be screened for the first time in April 1979. On the cold and windswept island of Martha's Vineyard off Cape Cod, Mia Farrow was arriving at the end of a winter without her estranged husband, the composer André Previn. The marriage had effectively been over for two years, and Mia had returned from their home in Surrey to her mother's apartment in New York. With the end of the marriage in sight and a burgeoning brood of children to support, she had signed up for a succession of poor but lucrative movies before accepting the lead in Broadway's *Romantic Comedy*, with Tony Perkins, the actor most famous for Alfred Hitchcock's *Psycho*.

That winter she spent on the Vineyard at a rustic old house she had bought years ago after breaking up with her first husband Frank Sinatra. Her stay was briefly interrupted by a quick flight down to the Dominican Republic where she finalised the divorce from Previn. Bustling with tourists in the summer, this millionaire's retreat was quiet and almost deserted the rest of the time, and Mia spent her days driving through its deserted rutted lanes in a Jeep, and the evenings listening to classical music by a crackling log fire. The marriage to Sinatra had been a short and tempestuous one; the marriage to Previn had been longer but no more successful. There had been a series of romances and near romances in between with the likes of Peter Sellers, Roman Polanski and the director Mike Nichols. Mia's career had got off to a spectacular start with the leading role in one of the most popular American TV dramas, *Peyton Place*, and the controversial part of Rosemary in Polanski's *Rosemary's Baby*. But despite her involvement with so many film people, and despite critical successes in the theatre in London, her movie career had been fallow since parting from the protective embrace of Sinatra.

Then, in April 1979, Mia picked up a copy of the *New York Times* magazine which featured a glowing tribute to America's latest movie sensation whose latest film was about to open. There, in a large photograph, peering shyly from behind a pair of thick black glasses, was Woody Allen, the comic Mia had met briefly years ago in California when she was with Roman Polanski and he was with Diane Keaton. The two couples had exchanged pleasantries then, but little else. Now, after going to see *Manhattan*, Mia decided to write Woody Allen a letter saying how much she admired his new film.

Mother Mia

'You know, of all of us in the family, you were the one
blessed with the true gift.'
                              Norma to Hannah *Hannah and Her Sisters*

The scene is the Supreme Court in Manhattan on a chilly
day in December 1992. Woody Allen, suspected of child
abuse, has just emerged from another pre-trial hearing in
his custody battle with Mia Farrow. Flanked by lawyers,
and wearing his trademark tweed jacket and corduroys,
the director confronts a phalanx of waiting photographers and reporters.

An unlikely rapport has developed between this reclusive man and the celebrity chasing press he has spent
so much of his life avoiding. Thrown together in the
maelstrom of media sensation, these two spectacularly
different breeds had widely divergent motivations, yet
had developed a sense of mutual respect – and were
almost on first name terms with one another.

'Woody!' shouts one of the good natured crowd, 'would
you have begun the romance with Mia's daughter Soon-
Yi if you knew this was going to happen?'

'If I had known this,' Allen replied, 'I would never have
taken Mia to that first lunch years ago.' The cavernous
mock Roman court chamber echoed to cheers and laughter, and the perpetually depressed director for once
allowed himself a grin.

That lunch was at the fashionable midtown Manhattan
French bistro Lutece on April 17, 1980, a date which
marked the beginning of a 12 year relationship in which
the pair would be crowned the unofficial King and Queen

of the city. Characteristically, Woody could not bring *himself* to arrange the auspicious event, relying instead on his secretary Norma Lee Clark to somewhat imperiously telephone Mia and invite her to the restaurant. Nevertheless, it was a date to leave such an impression on Mia's mind that she made a needlepoint picture of it to present to Woody, like a child would present her father with a crayon painting in thanks for a memorable day out at the zoo.

But then, to all intents and purposes, Mia *had* behaved like a little child who had impishly asked her father for a special treat and had been rewarded accordingly. Although Mia was 35 years old, she still had that innocent child-like demeanour which had beguiled former husbands Frank Sinatra and André Previn, and dozens of other famous men. Men at the height of their fame and fortune. She has the frail, far away look of a waif-like convent girl whose only earthly concern is to remember to say her rosary at night. But Mia Farrow has never been quite as *lost* as she often appears. Earl Wilson, the New York columnist who had given Woody Allen his start in life was always 'dubious about Mia's radiant innocence'.[1] And at a Hollywood party once, Mia impressed her friend Kirk Douglas with amazingly accurate character appraisals of their fellow guests. Mia had always 'looked so naive, wide-eyed, angelic. But she was a rapier. Concise and to the point.'[2] He went as far as to say that he thought she could have the highest IQ of any actress he knew.[3]

Like a well-aimed rapier Mia spotted something particularly vulnerable in the face of Woody Allen peering at her though his black-rimmed glasses from the front page of the *New York Times* magazine. He had posed for the picture with an umbrella over his shoulder on the terrace of his Fifth Avenue apartment. There was something about the photograph, she later said, that made him look 'interesting'.[4]

Mia Farrow had not been remotely interested in

Woody Allen on the only occasion they had met at a party in California. At the time she had been dating Roman Polanski, Hollywood's *enfant terrible* of the moment and the toast of the fickle Tinseltown. Woody, who was with Diane Keaton, was not quite as well-known, and after a polite exchange of courtesies Mia had little or no contact with him until 1979 when the commercial hits of *Annie Hall* and *Manhattan* had turned his name into the one that was on everyone's lips. By her own account Mia was at the time 'low on funds'[5] although the possession of a 300 acre farm on Martha's Vineyard hardly qualifies her as 'hard up'.

Mia had taken a part in Broadway's *Romantic Comedy*. She carefully cut out the *New York Times* magazine picture and pasted it into a book. And then she wrote to the director.

The following autumn, when she was in *Romantic Comedy* on Broadway, she went with Michael Caine and his wife to Woody's favourite restaurant, Elaine's, where the director was sitting at his usual table. Bobby Zarem, a popular New York socialite and public relations man, introduced the two of them.

That Christmas Woody invited Mia to his New Year's Eve bash at Harkness House where she turned up with her *Romantic Comedy* co-star, *Psycho* actor Tony Perkins and his wife. For years Mia had been out in the cold; now, as the freezing December air chilled Manhattan, she was welcomed back into the warming embrace of the rich and famous. It was a night to revel in the company of Robert DeNiro, Andy Warhol and Mick and Bianca Jagger. In his diaries, Warhol noted: 'Woody's was the best party, wall to wall with famous people, we should have gone earlier. Mia Farrow is so charming and such a beauty.'[6]

After the evening was over Mia wrote Woody a note of thanks including a copy of Lewis Thomas's book of essays, *The Medusa and the Snail*. It was then that Woody's secretary Norma Lee Clark called to return the compliment, and ask if Mia would like to dine with him.

'We all feather our own nests, but Mia's got a gift for it more than most of us,' says Louise Lasser, who remembers talking to Woody after three or four years of his relationship with Mia. 'You know,' he told her, 'Mia and I have a great relationship. We *never* argue – never! It's a perfect relationship – it's better than I could ever dream of!' Louise looked at her old lover disbelievingly, as she had done so many times before when confronted with his high flying expectations of human behaviour. 'Woody,' she said, 'if you've never had a single argument in three years, it's the worst sort of relationship you could possibly think of.'

Mia Farrow grew up in a world of high expectations and fragile relationships. Like Diane Keaton she is a California girl, but Mia's home was in the heart of Beverly Hills, and her family grew up amid the theatrical legends of Hollywood's most golden days. Her father was John Villiers Farrow, a colourful combination that only Hollywood could produce, of Roman Catholic intellectual, screenwriter par excellence, movie mogul and notorious womaniser. He was the prolific director of films like *Sorority House, Full Confession, Married and in Love,* and *Easy Come, Easy Go.* His greatest success was as author of the bestselling inspirational book, *Damien the Leper,* and he was knighted by the Pope for his history of the papacy, *Pageant of Popes.* (Mia would say, 'My father wanted to be the Pope, a poet and Casanova.'[7]) Her mother was Maureen O'Sullivan, the Dublin born actress best known as Johnny Weissmuller's Jane in the *Tarzan* series, and Ronald Reagan's leading lady in *Bonzo Goes to College.* Maureen was later to play an unflattering version of a boozy old concert hall figure in Woody's *Hannah and Her Sisters.*

Mia was christened Maria de Lourdes Villiers Farrow, with gossip columnist Louella Parsons and another legendary director George Cukor as godparents. She was the third child of seven and they lived the usual lavish lifestyle of Beverly Hills with a constant procession of movie stars visiting their home: Ava Gardner, Lana Turner, John Wayne. They also had a house in Malibu, and would later acquire an apartment in Manhattan. Mia's best friend was Liza Minnelli, the daughter of Judy Garland and Vincente Minnelli. Hal Roach and Rosalind Russell were neighbours. It was the lifestyle of movieland legend, insulated from the realities of the outside world by chauffeurs, maids and nannies, the children living in a separate wing of the mansion set in sprawling grounds.

It was a luxurious but not necessarily happy existence for Maria who could not pronounce her name properly so became Mia. Despite her surroundings, she was a lonely child. Her sense of isolation increased when, aged nine, she contracted polio and had to be confined in Los Angeles's Cedars of Lebanon Hospital where her brothers and sisters would visit her every day but were not allowed to get too close. In those days polio was a crippling and potentially fatal disease, and Mia's clothes and toys had to be destroyed. The girl in an iron lung next to her hospital bed, died. She recovered, but the illness left an emotional scar.

On location, legend has it that John Farrow would make trips to LA every Saturday night to pick up a plane load of women for some weekend fun, but at home he would insist that the family should all attend mass on Sunday mornings. The first time Mia saw a nun she is said to have become hysterical. She later developed a love for the Roman Catholic religion, initially because she believed it would let her levitate and 'things like that'.[8] She had do gooder dreams of becoming a Schweitzer-like doctor in the Third World and each Christmas she staged a pageant with her brothers and sisters and the neighbourhood kids, charging a dollar entry, the proceeds of which were sent to a polio fund. Before she was 12 years old, noting these strange proclivities for isolation and occasional hysterical despair, her parents put her into analysis, or as Mia later called it 'a jiffy course' intended to 'stick me together'.[9]

The little girl may have been an emotional wreck, but she had already mastered the skilled art of gentle manipulation. One story says that at school she would always carry with her an old tooth which had fallen out, and if the class proved too tiresome, Mia would whip out the prop and ask the teacher for the afternoon off.[10] And despite her fragility, friends noted how Mia was emerging as the dominant child, a 'mother' to her brothers and sisters both younger and older.

The whole family moved to Spain for her father's movie, *John Paul Jones*, which starred Bette Davis and included little parts for all John Farrow's children. Davis was to make a perceptive observation of the little girl: Mia, she noted, 'was born with an old soul. She lived all alone in her own world.'[11] But her father was not keen on the idea of Mia going into the theatrical world in which he lived life to the full. When she said she wanted to be an actress, thinking perhaps of the casting couch he had subjected so many aspiring young things to, John Farrow ordered her to convent school in England. The whole family moved to England for a while, living in an imposing London townhouse which always reminded Mia of the one from *Peter Pan*.

Bette Davis had also made another perceptive observation about Mia, namely that she was intelligent and would always get her way. At school in England, later in Los Angeles, and back in London again, Mia pursued amateur dramatics with a passion. Her big break came when she was a teenager, partly through the good fortune of her mother, and partly through tragedy.

Maureen had unexpectedly become a big hit in a Broadway play at the grand old age of 51. Ever watchful for her children's careers, she capitalised on her new found fame to tip off agents and columnists to look out for her talented young daughter. The teenage Mia was soon mixing with the in crowd, briefly meeting Kirk Douglas (who later in life she became closer to) and striking up a bizarre friendship with the controversial painter Salvador Dali, then married and in his late fifties. Dali would become a mentor to this blossoming young woman. One story says that the two of them visited Greenwich Village where they (fully clothed) witnessed an orgy where Mia was to claim she really had no idea what was going on.[12]

It was exactly the sort of world John Farrow had tried to steer his daughter away from, but in 1963 he died suddenly and ceased to have any more influence over her. After burying her husband, and faced with no other means of support, Maureen chose to continue acting in New York where Mia was noticed by her mother's classmate Vivien Leigh in a production of *The Importance of Being Earnest*. Within weeks, with a little help from old friends, Mia had been signed up by 20th Century Fox for their ambitious new TV series, *Peyton Place*.

'Her life had been Hollywood crazy from the beginning. Her parents had shipped her off to convent school, then in her teens she became a total libertine, hitting the scene in New York at 16 as a wild child. Her rise was much too fast, more traumatic than it ought to have been on a young soul.'[13]

Peyton Place turned her and her co-star Ryan O'Neal into instant soap opera stars, but it was a meeting with a celebrity that really transformed Mia's life. And like Mia's meeting with Woody Allen years later, this meeting was no accident. On the 20th Century Fox lot towards the end of 1964, shooting scenes for *Von Ryan's Express*, was Frank Sinatra, approaching the pinnacle of his fame. Mia's version of events is that she met the singing star by accident one day when she had some time off, and spotting him she said, 'Hello, Mr Sinatra!' in a girlish voice.[14]

In her biography of Sinatra, Kitty Kelley gives another version. She says: 'A bewitching 19-year-old girl with long golden hair appeared every day at the door of the sound stage in a gauzy nightgown that fell to her ankles.'[15] 'She had borrowed the transparent gown from 20th Century Fox's wardrobe department said one writer noting she was 'not so naive'.[16]

Brad Dexter, an old friend of Sinatra's, tells a different version which has Mia inviting herself to the *Von Ryan* set every day for a week, where she would conspicuously observe and admire the crooner. 'At the end of the first week ... we were leaving for Palm Springs on Frank's little French jet. Mia was standing there looking up at him as we were walking out, so he said, "See ya later. We're going to grab the jet and hit the desert for the weekend." She nearly knocked him over when she said she wanted to go with us. "How come you never invite me to come along?" she asked. Frank did a double take. "Huh? Are you kidding? Would you like to come?" Mia beamed and said, "Sure." ... That's how she came to spend the first weekend with Frank in Palm Springs, which started the romance.'[17]

Kitty Kelley quotes Mia as saying at the time, 'I discovered that only in drama class could I manipulate people, amuse them, even make them notice me through this marvellous game of pretending, where I didn't have to be me.' She also said, 'I want a big career, a big man, a big life. You have to think big – that's the only way to get it ... I just couldn't stand being anonymous. I don't want to be just "one of the Farrows" third from top and fifth from bottom.'[18]

It was an amazing love match, he the bourbon and rye man's man, she a flower power child who could not stop talking about mysticism, Zen and yoga. He showered her with expensive gifts, but she said she did not care for money and talked about the inner life of the soul instead. When they married, Frank's daughter Nancy was five years older than Mia, and Dean Martin quipped, 'I've got Scotch older than Mia Farrow.'[19]

Maureen O'Sullivan said, 'Men had an instinctive desire to protect Mia. That's the secret.'[20] Frank's friend Edie Goetz was more abrupt: 'Mia was a very clever young lady and she knew exactly what she was about and what she wanted. She was crazy about Frank and she intended to marry him.'

Sinatra was amazed at Mia's tiny bare apartment which she shared with a deaf cat called Malcolm. He showered her with jewellery and mink coats but she never seemed to be much impressed with his largesse. Rumours of a pending marriage flew around as the couple spent more and more time together – once on a cruise that ended in Hyannis Port, at the home of John F. Kennedy's ailing father, Ambassador Joseph P. Kennedy. The age difference was a constant source of jokes. 'I know there's a big difference,' Mia said,' but it doesn't really matter to me. Frank is exciting and fascinating. He's the most captivating man I've ever known. I've never encountered anyone sweeter and more considerate. He's everything a girl could want.'[21]

When she was 21 and Sinatra was in his fifties, they married in Las Vegas, July 1966, a few months after Woody and Louise took the same vows in New York. 'Ha!' laughed Sinatra's former wife Ava Gardner, 'I always knew Frank would end up in bed with a little boy.'[22] Maureen O'Sullivan got a frantic phone call from one of her neighbours in New York: '"Something terrible has happened to Mia." I said, "Tell me what. Is she dead?" "No, she's married to Frank Sinatra." "Oh," I said, "Is *that* all?".'[23]

They divorced in Mexico on August 1968, not long before Woody and Louise flew to the same place to end their unhappy union. Both couples went through turbulent times, but there was an undercurrent of violence in Mia's wedded life with Sinatra which could not be described as 'sweet' or 'considerate'. In the Juarez Civil Court papers she charged Sinatra with cruelty and incompatibility. She has always denied that he hit her, but in one account producer David Susskind witnessed her once covered 'with black welts all over her body. She was bruised from head to foot, with mean red gashes and marks all over her arms and shoulders and throat as if she'd been badly beaten.'[24]

She would not give up her acting career for Sinatra, and to some it seemed she went out of her way occasionally to annoy him throughout their romance and marriage. While he served up charcoal broiled steaks for his star studded guests at the Palm Springs house, Mia would sit quietly in the corner doing her needlepoint. She once danced with his sworn enemy Robert F. Kennedy whom Sinatra blamed for ending his access to his brother Jack.

And she cut her hair so short she looked like a boy. (Salvador Dali called the hair cutting episode 'mystical suicide' but actually it was more symptomatic of how manipulative Mia Farrow can be. She wanted a break from her gruelling *Peyton Place* contract, and was annoyed when the producers would not give her one. So she presented them with no option, knowing they could not film her with such short hair and would not dare challenge 'Frankie's Girl'.) Finally she appeared near nude opposite John Cassavetes in Roman Polanski's *Rosemary's Baby*, which for that time was a daringly erotic movie about a coven of witches in modern day New York.

Sinatra was incensed but later impressed when she turned down his offer of generous alimony when they divorced, asking instead if she could keep the jewellery he had given her, some antique silver and stuffed animals from her bedroom. She did not even want the 350,000 dollar (value now, 6 million dollars) mock Tudor mansion he bought her in Los Angeles. Sinatra's friend Sidney Zion said, 'Frank ... was ready to pay a million, two million, whatever it took ... but she said I just want the rocking chair. It belonged to my grandfather.' Sinatra would say later, during her spectacular bust up with Woody Allen that, 'I haven't got a bad word to say about that kid.'

Polanski later said: 'I couldn't quite fathom the Mia–Sinatra relationship. Good host and good company though he was, Sinatra never disguised that his was a man's world. What he liked best was man talk at the bar of his Beverly Hills' home. Mia, on the other hand, was a sensitive flower child, a sucker for every conceivable cause from ecology to the rights of American Indians, and a committed opponent to the Vietnam War, which Sinatra supported. They didn't appear to have a single thing in common, yet it was apparent to all who saw them together, that this was no marriage of convenience and that Mia was deeply in love with her husband.'[25]

Mia's emotions about the marriage remain mixed. When Kitty Kelley's book about Sinatra came out in 1986, she issued a statement virulently denying the allegations of abuse, and phoned her stepdaughter Nancy to say that she still loved Frank. But she was also to say that the experience of marriage to him was not one she would wish to repeat.

The final throes of her marriage to Sinatra, and those months immediately afterwards, had been Mia's wildest flower child years, flying off to India for visits with the Maharishi Mahesh Yogi, and mixing with the up and coming new stars of the Sixties. She signed a movie contract to appear with Robert Mitchum and Elizabeth Taylor in *Secret Ceremony* which was to be made in Britain. The film immediately brought Mia into contact with the hottest Hollywood property of the time. Before long she was socialising with Liz Taylor and her heart throb husband, Richard Burton, spending time with the glamorous couple in London and Rome. Mia had flown from New York with Mike Nichols. Burton observed in

his diary, 'That M Nichols really gets the girls.' Although
he noticed Mia was so thin she was like 'a first cousin to
a matchstick'.[26]

Cast and crew of *Secret Ceremony* vividly remember the
spectacle of the waif-like child actress consorting with the
smouldering pair. On one occasion at the Dorchester
Hotel, with the Burtons and the whole crew, Mia was
wearing a child's outfit and sitting on Richard Burton's
knee in a fairly innocuous way. But Elizabeth Taylor was
less than pleased and later told cast and crew she did not
like it. 'She sat on Richard's lap in some baby doll dress
with a Peter Pan collar complaining about how she'd
broken up with Frank Sinatra,' said one of those present.
'It was sickening.'[27] That night Richard told Liz and she
was furious. She told everyone on the set about it because
she was very concerned.

At around this time a perceptive *Life* writer noted that,
'She is a cuddler – like a small forsaken animal that
snuggles its way into your lap. Once there, she may fiddle
with your earlobe – as she did with her co-star Laurence
Harvey recently. "You know, we're very alike," she
purred to him. "We smoke the same kind of cigarettes,
prefer white wine, like Bogart, and loathe each other to
the same degree." This element of surprise – claws in the
midst of soft fur – was frequently manifested during the
first several days of shooting.'[28]

This was the England of the Swinging Sixties. She was
regularly out on the town with the Burtons and the likes
of Peter Cook, David Hemmings and director of the
moment, Mike Nichols, whose *Graduate* movie had been
the spectacular hit that launched Dustin Hoffman's career. In 1968, she would agree to star in *John and Mary* with
Dustin Hoffman.

In California, on a night out with Eddie Fisher, she
jokingly suggested they drive down to Mexico and get
married, a suggestion he never took her up on. She dated
John Phillips of the Mamas and the Papas and briefly,

Peter Sellers, recovering from his own bust-up with Britt Ekland. Polanski noted they were 'true soulmates ... Like her, Peter was heavily into the whole range of crackpot folklore that flourished in the 1960s, from UFOs through astrology to extra sensory perception. They both liked dressing up as rich hippies, complete with beads, chunky costume jewellery, and Indian kaftans.'[29]

It was during this period that one model commented, 'Don't ever be taken in by Mia's act, that little boy lost routine of hers. You've only got to clock how bloody uncomfortable she is around other women to know how phony she really is.'[30] Another writer said: 'She looks innocent. She sounds innocent. But you know she can't be Shirley Temple.'[31]

She did though have a particular quality as Wally Shawn was to note years later on the set of Woody Allen's *Radio Days*. 'I feel she enjoys the fantasy of playing someone not herself and dressing up in costume the way a child or an adolescent enjoys it. She acts with a certain light touch that they have when they act, when they dress up and pretend. You can see the child enjoying it, and I felt I was seeing this in her.'[32]

Mia was turning into something of a rebel and, like practically everyone else of that generation, experimenting with everything the social revolution could offer. She even appeared in a British court once accused of telling two police officers to 'fuck off' after being hauled away from a nightclub with some friends. When the judge asked her if it was true that she had used obscene language, Mia asked that if he meant the word 'fuck', then the answer was no. That would be the nicest thing she could wish the judge, she informed him.

Her fellow rebel, although it is hard to believe now, was André Previn, the conductor and composer whom she had met years ago, but started dating during this period. He was still married to wife Dory who had entertained Mia at her house in the United States. Dory was a brilliant singer-songwriter, but a troubled woman, who was committed to a mental hospital during this fraught time. Previn had worked with dozens of celebrities as a pianist and musical arranger, and he was the official conductor of the prestigious London Symphony Orchestra. Soon the affair was an open secret. Mia and André were jetting around together and brazenly sharing hotel rooms with one another on both sides of the Atlantic while Dory read about their activities and drove herself – literally – crazy.

In their biography of Mia Farrow, Edward Epstein and Joe Morella paint an unflattering picture of Dory's views at the time. 'Dory Previn's version of events concerning the breakup of her marriage paints Mia as a calculating, selfish young woman who knew Dory was an insecure and neurotic person and knowingly took advantage of her weaknesses to steal her husband. As far as Dory was concerned, she regarded Mia as a *femme fatale* in flower child's clothing.'[33]

To be fair to Mia though, Dory later admitted that she was in no fit mental state to make objective judgements. She may very well have cast her husband and Mia in a far worse light than they deserved.

In April 1969 the biggest blow for Dory arrived when Mia announced that she was pregnant and André asked for a divorce. Dory channelled her frustration with Mia into a creative medium, and wrote a hit song: 'Beware of Young Girls'. The lyrics went: 'Beware of young girls who come to the door, wistful and pale of twenty and four, delivering daisies with delicate hands.' Almost parallel developments were happening in Woody Allen's love life. He and Louise had finished their relationship with a Mexican divorce in the spring, and his affair with Diane Keaton was blossoming while Louise suffered a breakdown.

Mia Farrow and André Previn were married in September 1969, after twin boys were delivered – Matthew and Sascha – and the family moved into a 17th century house surrounded by woods in Surrey, which they named 'Haven'. At one stage they even talked about living there for good, and appeared to relish the lifestyle of English country gentry. The grounds had an old railway van in which Mia and André sometimes camped out. He bought her a telescope. Because of Edward Heath's love of music, they became friends with the Prime Minister, and were frequent visitors to 10 Downing Street or the country home of Chequers. The family flew between London and New York, often staying at a large spread Mia had bought in the millionaire's playground of Martha's Vineyard off Cape Cod.

Mia threw herself into family life but continued her acting career, appearing in repertory in Manchester and joining the Royal Shakespeare Company in works by Shakespeare, Chekhov and Gorky for which she won critical acclaim. Maureen O'Sullivan was amazed at her daughter's stamina: 'I don't know how she did it when she was doing a play every day. She'd be up with the children, get their breakfasts, be with them until she'd go off in the car until four, do the show, come home'.[34] (A schedule that sounds a lot easier than most working mothers but was probably gruelling for someone brought up with drivers, maids and nannies.)

In 1973, Mia and André did something that she had always promised herself she would: they adopted a baby, a tiny Vietnamese child they called Kym Lark and who was later to be called Lark Song. It was the start of a trend that would define Mia Farrow's life.

After landing the plum role of Daisy in *The Great Gatsby*, opposite Robert Redford, Mia infuriated the producers by announcing that she was pregnant. In any case, the end product was not the awe-inspiring success promised by the F. Scott Fitzgerald classic, and Mia's performance was panned. But she didn't care – the end product of her more intimate labours proved to be a universally admired beautiful baby boy who took after his mother. She named him Fletcher. A year later as Vietnam crumbled, André and Mia managed to get their next adopted child out on the last plane. This Vietnamese girl called Summer Song (and later Daisy) was so malnourished and her intestinal lining so damaged that she had to be fed at first through a tube in her head.

Later, just as André and Mia were ending their marriage, the adoption papers for a Korean girl who had been abandoned by her mother came through. Mia was pleased with the new child which she called Soon Yi and decided she was aged seven. 'She's from Korea – was found abandoned on the streets of Seoul – with rickets, malnutrition – even her fingernails had fallen off, she had lice and sores everywhere. Now she speaks English and is learning to read, write, play piano, dance ballet and ride a horse. She is also learning that people can be believed in and even loved. These are golden times and I am aware of that every single second,' Mia told her stepdaughter Nancy Sinatra.[35]

The child was destined to be big trouble for Mia. When she was adopted, the authorities estimated her age at around six, a rough estimate that was to prove more contentious than anyone could ever have imagined later on when it would be revealed that she was the lover of Woody Allen. At the time, all that was known of her was that she had spent all her years in an orphanage.

Mia had set her mind on Soon-Yi, but American law prohibited American families from adopting more than two foreign children. Although the Previns lived in Britain, Mia had retained her American citizenship. So Mia launched a fully fledged campaign to change the law, which, with the help of a sympathetic Congressman, she did.

Her obsession with adopting Oriental children was a

lasting one. But her marriage to André Previn was not. Previn was highly successful during their years together and his job demanded constant travel. She was left at home with the children in 'Haven' for much of the time, and although she was enjoying a busy and satisfying stage career, Britain could not really provide her with the many openings in the film industry that she longed for. Rumours flew around about the state of their marriage, and the press hinted at infidelity on both sides.[36] The newspapers claimed that Mia was so distraught that she attempted suicide (a similar claim was to be made during the final years of her relationship with Woody Allen). But these claims were denied, and in turn she was accused of having a brief fling with Roman Polanski.

By 1977, the marriage was effectively over, and Mia set off for the South Sea island of Bora Bora to star in Dino De Laurentis's embarrassing and extremely expensive (20 million dollar) remake of the 1937 classic, *Hurricane*. The whole point of the trip, it was claimed in some quarters, was for Mia to be reunited with Roman Polanski who was to direct it. Unfortunately, having been caught having sex with a minor in Jack Nicholson's house, Polanski decided that it would be prudent to drop out of the project which produced its own share of tabloid headlines. Mia was said to have ended up fighting – literally – with her co-star Timothy Bottoms, and there was talk of romantic involvement with Sven Nykvist, the Swedish cinematographer, which magazines and other newspaper suggested caused the final end of her marriage to Previn.[37] (Nykvist became a close collaborator of Woody Allen who visited him with Mia in Sweden in 1988.) Characteristically, Mia put a brave face on the disaster-prone *Hurricane* saying that it had been a 'sense of adventure' which had led her to accept the script. Co-star Jason Robards was more blunt, claiming his only motivation was 'sheer greed'.

Strangely, the tempestuous nature of her new private life was not matched in Mia's relations with her estranged husband. The arrangements for divorce were perfectly amicable, and there was never any argument over the kids. They flew to the Dominican Republic in March 1979 to get divorced, and they had joint custody of the children. The children were perfectly happy to divide their time in America with Mia – who moved in with her mother in Manhattan and still had the place in Martha's Vineyard – and André's 'Haven'. Later, Previn moved to a large house an hour or so north of Manhattan, in Mount Kisco, a small community not unlike a British Home Counties town. Relations have remained cordial, and the two parents share costs for the children's upbringing and education. Previn's new wife, Heather, describes Mia as '... a wonderful mother. I have a great many positive things to say about Mia Farrow. She's always been a terrific mother and I don't think anybody can argue that.'[38]

After parting from André, Mia moved into her mother's big 12 roomed apartment on the Upper West Side which they divided into two. Maureen took three small rooms which had a kitchen installed, and Mia was left with the remaining eight, three of which were bedrooms for her children. For the most part, the twins Matthew and Sascha stayed in England with André until he moved to Mount Kisco, and the four younger children lived in New York. The rooms were cluttered with toys, painting crayons, musical instruments, antiques and hundreds of family pictures. Two sitting rooms looked directly over Central Park. One wall would eventually be covered completely with colour snaps of the kids.

Soon after returning to the United States, Mia adopted another Korean boy, this time a tiny child with a physical handicap. She named him Misha, Russian for Michael in honour of her dead brother. Misha wore leg braces and was weak, but the other children helped him with exercises. Mia once said, 'Catholicism is the toughest religion to live by but the greatest one to die by.'[39] But by now her views had changed. The children were all brought up respecting *every* religion – Mia reasoning that Roman Catholicism had only brought her misery. And they all loved music, playing their own instruments and listening to classical music at night. 'They choose the composer,' she said. 'One night, Matthew wanted Haydn and Sascha wanted Shostakovich. He said Shostakovich was better to jump to.'[40]

When Mia fell for Woody Allen, he was on the brink of movie immortality. Before *Annie Hall*, he had been a slightly off-beat comic turned movie maker in the Monty Python mould. He was an American Rowan Atkinson: a funny face spouting funny gags, but not destined for the sobriquet of 'genius' that respected critics would start labelling him with. But in 1977 the whimsical love story of Annie and Alvy caught the world's imagination and *Annie Hall* became a critical *and* commercial hit. The release in April 1979 of *Manhattan*, confirmed his position. Mia's friendship with him was to be revived that year.

Shortly after lunch at Lutece Woody left for Paris with his close friend Jean Doumanian and her companion Jacqui Safra, who would get small parts in *Stardust Memories* and *Radio Days*. Jean and Woody had known one another since his days as a stand-up comic in Chicago, and she was to become his closest friend although she was never a lover.[41] They were to make several trips to Paris where they would invariably check into the Hotel Crillon and bask in its rich literary heritage. Woody had formed a great affection for Paris since staying there for *What's New, Pussycat?* and he was able to enjoy the same sort of pleasures that he enjoyed in Manhattan, with the added joy of knowing the French cinemagoers were among his most ardent admirers.

The three returned to Manhattan shortly afterwards and when he got back there were many more invitations for Mia, always delivered over the phone by Woody's

devoted secretary Norma Lee Clark. His inability to use
the phone himself may have something to do with those
painful times as a teenager when he would push Jack
Victor and Jerry Epstein into making dates for him while
all their stomachs churned at the prospect of a humiliating rejection.

Nevertheless Mia happily complied with her new
suitor who took her to a variety of his favourite uptown
restaurants. First it was lunch, then it was dinner, then it
was breakfast, figuratively speaking.

Woody's disdain for the outside world was becoming a
firmly ingrained feature of his increasingly media mas-
saged ego, and he had arrived at the point where he not
only despised making movies outside Manhattan, but did
not particularly like leaving the Upper East Side. Hence
he kept his time at her West Side place to a minimum,
claiming to have never slept over for most of the years he
knew Mia. The romance was mainly conducted at his
Fifth Avenue apartment.

This may also have had something to do with the fact
that Mia's apartment was stuffed with animals that
belonged to the pet loving occupants but which were less
of an inspiration to him. At one stage the animal family
included a Wheaton terrier mutt, Mary, a Yorkshire
puppy, a parakeet, a canary, the guinea pig, a rabbit, three
hamsters, two cats, four frogs, tropical fish and a box
turtle.

The Woody and Mia myth began to unfold. Glowing
magazine profiles would picture the two celebrities
avoiding the media limelight in a spectacularly public
way. Wearing the best known disguise in the world,
Woody would walk along Madison Avenue a picture of
anxiety. With her children in tow, Mia would parade
through town keeping her private life private while the
paparazzi snapped away. It was said that when phoning
one another from their high rise apartments, the two
would wave tea towels at each other across the towering

tree tops of Central Park. Reverential reports would reveal the gruelling work habits which had made Woody the genius he was, picturing the perfectionist director pacing about his apartment in artistic angst, taking half hour showers to overcome writer's block, or labouring in monastic solitude over a prosaically battered old typewriter. To try and live a normal life like the rest of us, Woody would turn up as regular as clockwork for his jazz sessions at Michael's Pub on Monday nights which soon became one of the best known tourist attractions in town. On other days, Woody would work until around 7 p.m. when he would jump in a car and drive over to her place to pick her up for a night at the movies or the theatre and a late dinner out – invariably at Elaine's. His psyche was dissected in minute detail, his working day observed scrupulously right down to what sort of bagels and muffins he ordered during lunch breaks.

Reality, as Woody has often observed, rarely lives up to popular legend.

Anyone who has ever tried peering through the pollution soiled atmosphere of Manhattan, knows the near impossibility of spotting a tea towel waving on the other side of Central Park. And Woody has often said that he really does not work as hard as some people say. But in the Eighties, perhaps because of the preponderance of gaudy money making idols with names like Trump and Milken assaulting the headlines every day, Woody and Mia became the intellectual answer to Harry and Leona. They were the true heart and soul of New York, unsoiled by the vulgarity of conspicuous success. The reverential tone of the reporting was a bit galling, and later to be parodied wonderfully by David Blum in *New York* magazine, who imagined a memo from the publisher of the *New York Times* berating his staff for their lax Woody coverage.

National Pages: How is the recession affecting Woody Allen? Is he eating out less? Maybe National and Food could co-ordinate coverage – determine whether Elaine's and Primola are suffering revenue declines in light of Allen's fiscal cutbacks.

Metro Pages: This is where our coverage of Allen has slipped most dramatically in recent weeks. Here are just a few stories we've missed: Woody Allen and Central Park – let's travel with him as he goes from his East Side apartment to Mia's place on Central Park West. If he walks, what path does he use? If he drives, does he time his visits to coincide with the hours of the 72nd Street traverse, or does he go down to 66th Street, cross over, and drive back uptown? Is he still wearing a floppy rain hat, or has he switched to alternative headgear? (Work with Fashion on this.)[42]

As we know, Woody used to drive to Mia's, under, around or across the Park, in an expensive ivory coloured Rolls Royce, a vehicle he claimed you would not realise was a Rolls Royce on casual inspection, but would actually stick out a mile in this city of uniformly black or grey stretch Cadillacs and Lincolns. The contrast between his screen image and real life was noted by *New York Times* writer Tony Schwartz in 1980 as the Mia-Woody relationship was in its early stages and after the launch of *Stardust Memories* in which he is Sandy Bates, the successful, bright and witty film maker who is full of self-pity and cynicism.[43]

Woody's movies are full of failures – of which he is usually the most conspicuously pathetic. He has been a failed documentary maker (*Crimes and Misdemeanors*), a frustrated TV producer in *Hannah and Her Sisters*, a frustrated stand-up comic in *Annie Hall* and a failed TV writer in *Manhattan*. The women he dates in all these movies are frustrated with something or failures at something else. This is a far cry from the real Woody Allen who has been a hit at practically everything he turned his hand to, and is surrounded by the

215

super-successful of New York *and* (although he wouldn't like to admit it) Los Angeles.

Mia Farrow and Woody Allen's relationship was one which brought them mutual comforts after years of turbulence. Woody had been going out with various women since Keaton had left his life, but none of them grabbed his wholehearted attention in the way she or Louise Lasser had. Approaching 45 years old, he was at an age when most of his contemporaries and many of his friends were lapsing into the domestic pleasures of middle age and family life. Woody, the bachelor boy ever on the look out for the slightest spark of new romance, could see in Mia a refreshing change to the women he had dated over the past seven years or so. And she saw in him someone who could provide the stability she longed for, a 'soulmate' who seemed to share at least some of the aesthetic virtues she craved.

There also appeared to be promising professional prospects in the relationship for Mia. Her film career had not been particularly distinguished even though Joseph Losey, after directing her in *Secret Ceremony*, said she had the potential of becoming a great actress. It was hard to see any other cinematic quality in her other than a sort of waif-like vulnerability which was appealing for certain set roles. Mia's stage performances had been praised but certainly did not distinguish her from the rest of a hungry and equally talented crowd. She wanted to act in the movies, and preferably on projects that didn't solely rely on her perceived porcelain fragility that many directors found attractive. And she was looking for something that would set her apart from the blockbusters and sequels which Hollywood had become addicted to.

Like Woody she found meeting new people awkward and so was inevitably a nervous wreck in the initial days of shooting on a new set. Like Woody she did not want to stray far from home, preferring to stay as close as possible to her children. Many film offers came her way during her years with Woody – including the one Diane Keaton eventually played in the Steve Martin remake of *Father of the Bride*. But except for a cameo in *Supergirl* she didn't act in anyone else's films.

Generously, Woody was to acknowledge a little of his own contribution to her career, but claimed he received more in return. 'I feel I've lucked out with Diane Keaton and Mia. I'm lucky that they've made this contribution to me. My contribution is relatively minimal; I can only provide the script, and then they bail me out, they make me look good.

'People who say to them, "Oh, you're so lucky to be making films with him," don't realise the true situation. I'm the one who is lucky to be able to work with someone who can do things consistently, who's stable, pleasant to work with, who can execute my ideas, who's available to shoot my style, to reshoot. I can just call up Mia and say, "Let's go back and reshoot." When you've got someone who's got six other pictures to do, you can't have that freedom. It's this situation that goes a long way to perfecting the kind of picture I want to make. Any director knows how crucial this is.'[44]

Woody had long proved to be an imaginative and clever screen writer and director, but the financial successes of *Annie Hall* and *Manhattan*, had fine tuned his film making skills and proved he could serve up a money maker. The result was unprecedented clout in the industry where he was given virtual complete control over every aspect of his work. With that enviable control the traditional film making burdens that he despised, went out of the window. Like the out of town locations he didn't like. With that control came the opportunity to make the retrospective serious works he had been wanting to do for years, and with it came the power to hire and fire exactly who he wanted.

The camera, lighting and sound crew around Woody then is virtually the same as it is now. It has the same cinematographers and editors, and the usual cast of quietly accomplished actors, and so forms a virtual movie making repertory company. Mia once said: 'With *Midsummer* I felt like a rank amateur, with *Zelig* I felt I was getting friendlier with everyone. And now, after *Danny Rose*, it's the best it's ever been for me. Though it can disappear in a minute, I have a little more confidence than I've ever had before. I think that when you're working with people you know, you feel they're not judging you, and it makes you feel a little freer to just try stuff.'[45]

The key to Woody's total control was finance. He gets a modest budget by the industry norms so his backers know that even if disaster strikes, they are never going to lose a fortune. He knows that he can do what he wants so long as the budget is not exceeded. Which suits him and his crew fine. A modest living bunch, they rarely shoot outside New York and do not have to cough up the enormous hotel bills and location expenses which are normal for Hollywood. The furthest they go is usually Long Island or Connecticut, and when they are in town, many of the interior shots are made in their own homes. Mia Farrow's apartment features prominently in *Hannah and Her Sisters*; Woody's does in *Manhattan*. In *Manhattan* they got the spectacular firework display scene by a cameraman hanging out of the bathroom window belonging to some relatives to the crew. The crew know they will shoot at least one movie a year, and they will get paid the basic but generous pay.

It has become fashionable recently for high powered actors like Dustin Hoffman and Robin Williams to work for Actors' Equity basic rates and to take a percentage of the profits – 'points' as they say in the business. But Woody is one of the few directors who can persuade major league stars to work for a pittance with no points, no expensive hotel suites, no first class airfares. After

Husbands and Wives, Irish actor Liam Neeson admitted that his pay barely covered the cost of accommodation in New York. And Julie Kavner dropped everything to appear in *Oedipus Wrecks*. Alan Lapidus says, 'When Julie was in New York to do *Awakenings* with Robert DeNiro and Robin Williams, they put her up in the best hotel and sent a limousine around every day to pick her up. Standard fare for a movie actress. When Woody calls they don't even discuss money or perks. He phoned her in Malibu and said, "Do you want to do this little film I'm working on?" and Julie says, "Woody wants a good old Jewish girl again." For *Oedipus Wrecks* she paid her own airfare, paid her own hotel bill except when she stayed at her Long Island place – and got the cab to work. Actors will do anything to work on a Woody Allen movie. Julie adores him.'

Woody would eventually attract stars like Madonna, Daryl Hannah and Jodie Foster who would appear for next to nothing. And actors do not get emotionally mollycoddled either: when Elaine Stritch burst into tears over a trifling costume complaint during the making of *September* which had been fraught with hold ups, Woody warned her, 'Don't cry, you'll only make me madder.'[46]

In his article 'Auteur! Auteur!' for the *New York Times*, Caryn James quoted Woody as saying, 'If I had to make films without complete control from start to finish, I definitely would not do it. I'm only making films because I'm as free there as if I were writing novels. You can't create unless you're completely free.' Caryn noted: 'Few artists of his stature admit such an overwhelming need for control manifested in such a solid manner.'[47]

It was a comfortable life for Woody and Mia. Mia could deposit the kids at one of the many top schools near their homes, jump in a car to the set which would never be more than 15 minutes away, do some knitting while she awaited her scenes, and be away at 4 p.m. to pick up the children from school. There was very little reason to leave home. Mia acquired Frog Hollow Farm set in 64 lakeside acres in a beautiful part of rural Connecticut where they would spend summer and a month during Christmas. Maureen moved out when she married, but lived not far upstate. Two of her sisters live in the immediate vicinity, and her brothers and their families visited frequently from their New England homes.

Mia said: 'One of the nice things about working with him is that since he shoots in the city, we can go home after we finish for the day. You don't live on location; you can carry on your own life.'[48] He said: 'She'll come to the set and quietly do her needlepoint, and then put on her wig and dark glasses, or whatever, and just scream out the lines, and stick a knife in your nose – and then go back to sewing with her little orphan children around her.'[49]

This atmosphere of domestic urban bliss and cinema fame became the stuff of Manhattan and movie folklore as their private lives became inextricably entwined with the roles they played on the big screen. As far as Woody is concerned, the public and private were two completely different things. But observers – including some close to the director – saw a different picture. The films are not just autobiographical, but autobiographical to a painful degree. Literally painful, in the case of Louise Lasser who saw the circumstances of her mother's tragic suicide unfold before her eyes, and figuratively painful as Alan Lapidus said when he saw *Radio Days*.

With Mia, Woody embarked on a 12 year helter skelter of emotional drama spanning 13 pictures in which their lives together were laid bare across the big screen. The celluloid spewed out of his camera as rapidly as the words from a manic depressive on the doctor's couch. Like the Coney Island roller coaster, they went from the high of *Midsummer Night's Sex Comedy* to the low of *Husbands and Wives*, dragging with them a familiar cast of characters who popped in and out of this cinematic stream of consciousness with the regularity of the B.M.T. trains which had brought Allan Konigsberg across the Brooklyn Bridge to the Xanadu he dreamed of but never really seemed to find.

'My fans always make the mistake of confusing me with my screen image,'[50] says Woody, wearing for newspaper profiles the same scuffed shoes, corduroys and frayed trenchcoat that he wears as Alvy Singer, Mickey Sachs and Cliff Stern. 'If I had played the role of Michael Caine in *Hannah and Her Sisters* then I would have had an affair with my wife's sister,' he says. But when Woody walked in to Mia Farrow's West Side apartment as Mickey Sachs in *Hannah* to greet Mia Farrow and her children, there was no explanation in the script as to why the screen character's ex-wife should have two small Oriental children. We're all expected to know, because Woody's told us about his private life time and time again while continually denying that he is doing so.

Mia is already in Woody's consciousness – if not his film – when we see *Stardust Memories* which was being made in the initial stages of their courtship. Allen plays the successful film director still haunted by the tragic love affair with a 'neurotic actress named 'Dorrie', who is hooked on lithium, and ends up in an institution, where she claims 'the doctors find me beautiful and interesting'. But Allen is hooked on her because 'for two days a month she's great, the most terrific woman in the world.' The name and specifics are obviously André Previn's ex-wife Dory who Mia replaced, but the generic character is Louise Lasser (who also got a small part as a secretary in *Stardust*).

Stardust Memories was to bring Woody some of the greatest critical and personal scorn he had ever had. Besides drawing copiously from Federico Fellini's $8\frac{1}{2}$, this turgid tale of a brilliant film maker (Sandy Bates) at a crossroads in his life poured ill-disguised contempt on the friends and fans who adored him. They were portrayed as grotesque and slavish sycophants who were endlessly complaining – like Allen's ardent fans were doing – that he didn't make funny films any more. Woody's portrayal of Sandy Bates's followers and associates was so riddled with bitterness and bile that even Rollins and Joffe were stunned and began to wonder whether they had been responsible for the miserable life Woody clearly perceived himself to be leading.

Characteristically, Allen denied – contemptuously – that *Stardust Memories* was autobiographical. 'I can't always sit with people and tell them to think of it as a fictional film about a film maker going through a crisis in his life. It's hard for them to dissociate him from me.'[51] 'This is not me but it will be perceived as me,' Allen said, but as Douglas Brode demanded, 'Why should it be perceived otherwise?'[52] Sandy Bates *was* Woody Allen right down to the fact that he played stickball as a kid and hid away in his bedroom to play magic tricks. Like Woody Allen, Sandy Bates constantly casts Tony Roberts in his movies, and who should play Tony Roberts in *Stardust Memories* but – Tony Roberts!

Woody had arrived at his peak of fame and apparent undiluted praise and the backlash from those who had adored him was stinging. As a boy, Allan Konigsberg had stood outside the home of his literary hero George S Kaufman. He had approached his childhood hero, Milton Berle, and his extremely distant relative, Abe Burrows, in an effort to attract their attention. He had publicly praised Groucho Marx and Bob Hope, heaping adoration on them and imitating them. His movies had included many slavish compliments to the comics or artists he was bewitched by. In his own words he had 'degraded' himself to achieve popular success[53] in everything from appearances on TV to tacky drinks commercials. He had attracted a loyal following of fans who thought he made very funny films and were generous in their praise. But not content with being a purveyor of fine humour, he had tried to do something he was not so good at, in the form of serious drama, and when the response was little more than mildly disapproving, he viciously bit back at the hand that was feeding him.

Woody should have recalled a conversation that he had with Groucho Marx at the Pierre Hotel, New York, in 1973, when the young up and coming film maker told his hero, 'Chaplin's not funny any more. I think he had three great films [which] I think are still funny, but the others are not. The others just seem tedious to me.'[54]

He had long been praised as 'funny' but had been on a critical roller coaster since making *Annie Hall* when, as has often been said, *The New York Times* started calling him a 'genius' every day. The result was *Stardust Memories* but the backlash was so bad that he would be very careful the next time he tried to tackle drama.

Nevertheless, Woody remained the undisputed 'King of Manhattan' for the city's media élite, who would flock to Elaine's every evening to catch a glimpse of him. The fawning went on with endless complimentary magazine stories and reverential TV documentaries which he did not mind so long as they were shown in Europe or Canada. His deep seated hatred for American TV persisted, yet around this time he was influential in one of New York's most celebrated shows.

Saturday Night Live had been the brainchild of Lorne Michaels who had fostered the comic and acting talents of the likes of Dan Aykroyd, Chevy Chase and the tragic John Belushi. Michaels was a brilliant producer but believed *Saturday Night Live* had run its course and told its makers N.B.C. that he wanted to leave the show. He recommended a few people to replace him but was astonished when Jean Doumanian got the job. Comedy was not her strong suit and she had come to *Saturday Night Live* in the first place in 1976 to perform the comparatively lowly function of booking celebrities. It

was said she got there with the help of Woody,[55] his
friendship, it was hinted, was something to do with the
15,000 dollar a week appointment.

'Jean had never shown a glimmer of interest in writing,'
noted one of the show's veterans, but nevertheless Doumanian got a free rein for 10 months during which she
hired Letty Aronson, Woody's sister. She appeared to
confer with him on the phone several times every day.
His influence was endlessly speculated on, particularly as
Jean hired six cast members who were *stand-up comedians*
as opposed to the *comedy actors* who had made the show
such a success in the past. The staff she surrounded herself
with was a small circle of advisers, prompting one writer
to accuse her of relying on 'yes men' and 'sycophants'.

When the show premiered it was panned, not least for
cheap jokes about Jews, drugs and homosexuality. As the
ratings plummeted, Doumanian was sacked in a last ditch
effort to save the show. A month later Jean, Jacqui Safra
and Woody flew off to Paris for one of their homages to
the City of Light. If she did not have much to celebrate, he
did, having wrapped his next movie and the first to
include new love Mia Farrow in the cast.

Perhaps as a result of the backlash over *Stardust Memories*,
or maybe simply because Mia was now in his world, his
next movie *A Midsummer Night's Sex Comedy* arrived like
a blast of fresh air into his jaded life. Light hearted in stark
contrast to *Stardust*, it was stunningly shot in the countryside with colourful turn of the century costumes. *A
Midsummer Night's Sex Comedy* is a flight of fancy whims-
ically in contrast to the chronic despair and self-indulgent
whining of the bitter *Stardust Memories*. Actually, what
appeared as a light hearted romp in the countryside was
a nightmare for Mia who was convinced that she only got
the part as the ethereal Ariel because she was Woody's
new girl. At first awkward and unsure on the Connecticut
set, she soon settled down as his by now familiar traits

emerged. During one scene in which he had to appear as if he had fallen in a pond, Woody refused to soil himself with the real water because he is terrified of anything that might have insects and germs in it. So he had the crew splash him with bottled water.

Before long, stories of his hatred for the countryside would join the legends of their urban lifestyle as the director began spending more time at Frog Hollow Farm with Mia and the kids. On weekends, as the summer months came around, Woody would forgo his Friday evenings at Elaine's, instead stepping into a limousine or the old station wagon his film crew use, to be driven to Connecticut. It is not hard to imagine the growing disquiet in his mind as the asphalt of the F.D.R. Driveway disappeared into the distance with the familiar skyscrapers and the ominous uncertainties of rural existence reared before him in the form of hedgerows, picket fences and threatening green trees.

He would arrive at Frog Hollow two hours later a nervous guest. While Mia would plough through the grassy acres on top of a tractor, he would watch from a safe distance. When Mia, the kids and nanny would jump into her battered old truck for shopping trips to the local mall, he would stay inside the car until their confrontation with suburbia was over. He did not care for Mia's menagerie of cats, dogs, ferrets, gerbils, goldfish or chinchillas. He would never swim in the pond, speculating that it probably contained 'germs and things' and after seeing the household dogs and cats eat from plates on the table, Woody insisted on bringing his own paper plates. He also brought a special sleeping mat to lie on at night. It would be a relief when the ordeal was over on Sunday. The possibility of bumping into the Manson Family while in Connecticut was always at the forefront of his mind.

'I can see getting into the car and driving up to the country and getting out and walking around and looking at the lake and leaves and that kind of thing and then getting back in the car and coming home. That I can see. To go and spend two hours, five hours in the country, something like that. I can't see bedding down in the country overnight. I see nothing in that. I like to know that if at 2 o'clock in the morning I get a sudden urge for duck wonton soup, that I can go downstairs, find a taxicab, go to Chinatown, get it and come back home. This is important to me.'[56]

How much of this was an act, and how much was genuine neurosis we'll never know. It seems extremely unlikely that he really did not know what a shopping mall was as he claimed to *Esquire*'s William Geist. More likely than not, he was bored with the countryside like many people are, but unlike many people, managed to turn his boredom into an on-going cinematic joke for the rest of us to enjoy.

'I find it threatening too. I find that while it may be true statistically that the city is more dangerous, I feel less endangered in the city. This may be a false feeling of security but it's still psychologically helpful to me. I feel that in a crisis situation I'd at least have a chance. I know where to go and how to avoid certain things and where to seek refuge.

'In the country, as I said in *Annie Hall*, if Dick and Perry – you know the guys in *In Cold Blood* – if they show up at the house at night, I mean you've had it, that's the end of it.'[57] (Notice he says, 'as I said,' not 'as my character said'. So much for *Annie Hall* not being autobiographical.)

During *A Midsummer Night's Sex Comedy* Mia persuaded Woody to do something that he was initially uncomfortable with – pose for photographs with all the children. Her reasoning was that it would stop the paparazzi from hounding them, something Woody had his well-founded doubts about. Nevertheless he agreed, and the relationship with Mia became formally acknowledged in the popular press. In March 1991 celebrity photographer David McGough was invited to do the private shoot. 'They were a perfect couple – holding hands, constantly kissing. I could tell that Woody was still uncomfortable. They never raised their voices above a whisper.'[58]

Which is not to say that Woody minded because by now his love life with Mia was going full pelt, and after *A Midsummer Night's Sex Comedy* he started on *Zelig* (1983), the story shot in quasi-documentary style about Leonard Zelig, the human chameleon who is so insecure he uses his amazing transformational powers to 'fit in' with the rest of the world. He starts life by lying about reading *Moby Dick* in order to ingratiate himself with others who have read it, and goes through a succession of personality changes which wreak havoc on the country. It takes Dr Eudora Fletcher's love to cure Zelig who finally realises he will be happy if he just behaves as if he is himself. Alas! The discovery comes woefully late in life, and on his deathbed, Zelig laments:

'... the only annoying thing about dying was he had just begun reading *Moby Dick* and wanted to see how it came out.'

Had Woody finally got to the stage in his life where he could admit that he had only ever started reading Kant and Kierkegaard to meet the right women? And had he found the right woman, after successfully assimilating himself into the intellectual culture he adored? Of course it was unlikely that he would ever have found love in the arms of the real Eudora Fletcher, but it was beginning to look like he had found it in Mia Farrow.

She was central to his next three films starting with *Broadway Danny Rose* (1984), a bittersweet Damon Runyonesque fable in which she is the blowzy blond Tina Vitale, girlfriend of seedy club singer Lou Canova. It is clear that by now Mia is having a major impact on his work, having suggested the character herself after spotting a similar woman at a restaurant one night. She told Woody she would love to play a role like that because it was so different from what she was really like. She made tapes of women with similar accents and watched Robert DeNiro in *Raging Bull* to get the accent exactly right. She even binged on pasta to put on weight. The result was one of Woody's most endearing movies with all the fun and slapstick comedy of *Sleeper*, plenty of the poignancy and heartstring pulling of *Annie Hall*, but none of the introspective drivel of *September* or *Interiors*. He was to describe it as 'largely entertaining,' but his fans loved it and Vincent Canby called it a 'love letter not only to American comedy stars and to all those pushy hopefuls who never quite made it to the top in showbiz, but also to the kind of comedy that nourished the particular genius of Woody Allen.'[59]

Broadway Danny Rose was also part tribute and part apology to Woody's old manager Harvey Meltzer. The central character is a good natured and big hearted theatrical manager who tirelessly works for his clients, including balloon bending acts and water glass virtuosos who rarely get further than the Borscht Belt summer camps. Danny's big problem is that when he does find a client who makes the big time, they always end up betraying him and finding high-powered representation. Danny Rose is clearly a portrait of Harvey Meltzer whom Woody left in favour of Rollins and Joffe. Like Danny Rose, Harvey Meltzer, who lives in Florida today, says lines like, 'might I just interject one concept at this juncture?' In the movie, Danny is in a booking agent's office trying to get some Memorial Day appearances for his acts, all of whom the agent is not interested in – except Sonny Chase 'the best act you've got,' but Danny doesn't handle Sonny any more...

'I discovered the kid, he slept on my sofa. I supported

him. I don't want to bad mouth the kid, but he's a horrible, dishonest, immoral louse. And I say that with due respect.'

In 1992, Harvey said, 'In all fairness to him, he's obviously a peculiar individual. Maybe because of the type of work he does, I give him the benefit of the doubt. He's a very deceptive individual and I'm sorry to say that because I don't want to speak ill of anybody.'[60]

Is Woody mellowing under Mia's influence? Around this time he would often comment that when his cousin Rita used to show him the movie star magazines all those years ago, he would never have dreamt that he would date the ex-wife of Frank Sinatra. It was unimaginable, even for a precocious kid like Allan Konigsberg.

He was not the father of her children yet, but that new found delight lay just around the corner on his next project which was in a way a tribute to Rita. His cousin was depicted as Cecilia in the touching cinema fantasy *The Purple Rose of Cairo* (1985), a character incidentally, in whom Woody said that he saw bits of himself.

Cecilia is a Depression-era New Jersey housewife with an unemployed and abusive husband. She has nothing to look forward to except movies and their colourful characters whom she dreams about all day. To her amazement one day, one of her heart-throbs Tom Baxter (Jeff Daniels) jumps out of the imprisonment of his remorseless and repetitive screen life. In doing so he releases her – albeit temporarily – from the imprisonment of her real life.

Woody and Mia were so comfortable on the set together that Daniels could not help but contrast her calm with his uptightness at being offered his first role on an Allen movie. 'For me it was a make or break film. I really needed to come through ... and Mia made me relax ... she would sit there and knit and her kids would sometimes visit the set, and it was clear that there were things more important to her than whether this was a good career move.'[61]

In the same interview, Daniels noted Mia's acting qualities which Polanski had first realised existed behind her porcelain facade. These qualities had begun to bloom under Woody who was transforming her from a type-casting into the major American film presence she is today. For a crucial scene, he needed her to cry repeatedly for several takes. 'Mia just put down her knitting and she comes over and sits down, and she does it. And then she does it again. She did it maybe ten times ... She nailed it every time. It wasn't the usual, "Could you give me a little more glycerin?" or whatever the stuff is that they put in your eyes to make you cry. She'd just wait about five seconds and sure enough then would come the tears. Woody says, "Ok, I think we've got it," and she goes back to her knitting.'[62]

In a newspaper interview at the time, Woody revealed that he had big plans for his new woman. 'I'd like to do a broad comedy with her, a really broad comedy. And I'd like to do a very, very serious kind of thing where she gets a chance to go through a lot of things in an hour and a half. It would be fun to explore these things together – I haven't scratched the surface for her yet.'[63]

Around then, Woody bumped into his old flame Bryna Goldstein in Michael's Pub where he was playing the clarinet at his regular Monday night gig. They talked about children. She had had a miscarriage years ago and he had been very supportive at the time. Now he told her he was 'indifferent' to the idea of children, mentioning the fact that the woman he was with had dozens of them. 'They took up too much time and interrupted his schedule, was his attitude,' Bryna says. In fact Woody was fond of the Korean born boy Misha, who had had cerebral palsy when Mia adopted him. With his encouragement she changed Misha's name to Moses after the Philadelphia basketball star Moses Malone. But otherwise, he was distant from her gaggle of kids.

Mia had expressed a desire to have a child with Woody in 1984, but he had resisted, fearing a young child would reduce the time they had available together. Woody finally relented after Mia assured him the child would live with her, and he need not be involved with the child's care or upbringing. After six months of unsuccessful attempts to become pregnant with Woody's 'lukewarm' support, Mia decided to adopt a child, and on July 11, 1985, the newborn Texan child, Dylan, joined the Farrow household.[64]

In effect, it became his child too, although he did not officially become its adoptive parent until several years later. Bryna said: 'Mia's genius was that she threw Dylan at him to show what it was like to have a child. It was an essay in expert teaching. He'd said he was indifferent to the idea to me, maybe because he's such a kind guy he didn't want to upset me because of my own miscarriage experience.'

The portents for parenthood had been ominous. Woody may very well have wanted kids when he first went out with Louise Lasser but by late middle age, the prospect of screaming children wrecking the harmony of his hard earned daily ritual was not a pleasant one. Woody was probably being truthful when he told Bryna Goldstein that he was 'indifferent' to the idea. He certainly told other friends that he felt Mia already had enough kids and he was annoyed sometimes by the amount of time she spent on them.

But Mia was absolutely and irrevocably dedicated to her mission in life, and observing how Woody had become fond of Moses, more or less assuming the role of parent to him, she was convinced that he could adapt to parenthood with a younger child.

Strangely Mia was right – despite all the past evidence to the contrary, Woody soon found that he loved being a dad to Dylan. Ironically though, far from increasing the bond between him and Mia, the arrival of Dylan was to be the beginning of the end for their relationship. Woody had a new girl in his life.

Manhattan Movie Maestro

Alice: 'Mother Teresa. She's my idol.'
Douglas: 'Alice. People are starving and you fill the nursery with every conceivable toy.'

Alice

Dylan changed Woody's perspective of parenthood – far more than the biological child he was later to have with Mia. Dylan was a little girl and he had always adored little girls even while trying to avoid having anything directly to do with them or with Mia's children. He had loved his sister Letty from the first day she arrived in his life, aged eight, and he had told Louise Lasser that he wanted to have, 'lots and lots of baby girls'. Louise had been like his first baby, and he loved spoiling and mollycoddling her. He had been disappointed when Letty's first child had been a boy. He told *Playboy* in 1967 that he wanted, 'eight or twelve little blonde girls ... I love blonde girls,'[1] and two decades later he was rewarded with one of them. One friend of the family said that Mia soon started complaining that Woody was treating Dylan like he used to treat her. Dylan was the one to get presents, and Dylan was to get the cuddles and kisses.

Now in 1985, his reaction to Dylan took time to develop, from the moment he looked upon the baby with ill-disguised dispassion when he went to the airport to pick mother and child up. He went out of his way to make sure he didn't form any sort of emotional attachment to Dylan which would distract him from Mia and his work. But as the months passed by he became besotted with the child. And he discovered Dylan *was* distracting him from Mia

and his work, whether he liked it or not. In the past he had
spent very little time at Mia's apartment. Now he'd get up
at five in the morning just to be over at Mia's place to see
Dylan wake up and have breakfast with her before
rushing off to start work which he would finish as soon
as possible so he could see the girl to bed.

Woody's attitude to Dylan changed so much that he
began spending some mornings and evenings at Mia's
apartment in order to be with Dylan. He even visited
Mia's country house more often and took extended
holidays in Europe with the whole family although he
remained aloof from the other children except Moses,
with whom he was cordial.[2]

He was mesmerised by the little child in a way which
he had not been with any of the other children who did
not 'belong' to him, but in a way that was similar to the
way he had heaped attention on Letty when she was a
child. Friends noticed how on entering a room full of
people, Woody would home in on Dylan straightaway,
his eyes ignoring everyone else but never leaving her. He
was, a friend said, 'infatuated' with Dylan. Even when
Dylan grew to be school age, Woody was reluctant to
leave her alone. Other parents thought it was odd that he
stationed himself on a sofa in the waiting room of her
nursery school, the Episcopal, until she was finished. And
once, at Park Avenue Christian Nursery, while other
parents waited outside, he sat Dylan on his lap in the
classroom, until he was asked to leave.[3] But this, friends
said, was evidence of his overwhelming concern for
Dylan.

By his own account given to Eric Lax at the time,
Woody was obsessed with Dylan to a degree that would
be unusual in most other parents. The perennially anhedonic Allen had never really thought such joy was
possible. Something he said to Eric Lax at this time is very
telling. Woody attended a lunch in the spring of 1987 with
top *New York Times* editors to talk about his objections to

the 'colourisation' of old black and white movies, and afterwards commented on the fact that he had sat through the whole discussion with a rubber child pacifier (dummy) in his pocket. 'I remember sitting at that lunch with all these accomplished journalists in business suits and hoping that they don't frisk me and find it.'[4] A remarkable statement. Why would anyone frisk a lunch guest? And why would anyone be shocked, stunned or otherwise surprised to find a father had a child's dummy in his pocket? Fatherhood for Woody, was clearly an amazing thing.

Whenever possible, he got Mia or one of the nannies to bring the kid on to his movie set or the studio where they were filming. In late 1991, he transported his whole crew to East Hampton, Long Island for some shooting on *Husbands and Wives*. At the clapboard beach house just off Dune Road, it was a breezy but bright day with perfect blue skies – picture postcard weather conditions calculated to send the director into a deep depression. Which they did. All day long as dozens of extras and crew froze, Woody appeared increasingly glum as the weather showed no signs of worsening, and he showed no inclination of rolling the cameras. Then, suddenly, his eyes lit up! The nanny had arrived with Dylan and Satchel. He ran out of the house to meet them and for 20 minutes the delighted father played with his kids on the beach while 200,000 dollars of film shooting time wasted away. Most of the crew had been with Woody since the late Seventies, when this sort of behaviour from the quiet and reserved movie maestro, who had rarely been known to express any great emotions on the set, would have been unthinkable. Since Dylan arrived it had been an everyday occurrence.

It was as if Woody had rediscovered his childhood. A constant refrain from childhood friends was that Woody was never the glum and morose man that he became later. He may have been as he said, 'visited by the bluebird of anxiety at a very early age', but he coped with it by looking on the bright side of life. Jack, Jerry, Elliott and Mickey remember that he was a trickster and japester. Bryna Goldstein's mother remembers her house was always full of laughter when Woody was around. Woody's marriage to Louise Lasser had been full of youthful fun and exuberance. Something had certainly turned him sour late in life when he descended into the morbidity of films like *Interiors*, but Dylan had turned the tables for him.

As his interest in Dylan increased, his attention to Mia began to wane. First imperceptibly, then so rapidly that Mia almost became jealous of the child as if she were another woman. 'Everything was fine between us until Dylan came along. Then you stopped getting me presents and started getting her presents.'[5] She began to see him as a 'cold' lover, and even 'cruel'. For a long time she had been thinking about calling an end to the relationship but told friends she 'didn't have the guts'.[6]

The conflicting emotions of their lives surfaced in his next movie, *Hannah and Her Sisters*, which would prove to be as big a popular hit as *Annie Hall*, and *Manhattan*. It is a sweet and poignant portrait of Hannah (Mia) and her extended but disjointed family. Hannah is the central Madonna-like sister in the middle of this familial chaos who is unreservedly giving. So giving in fact, that her husband Elliott (Michael Caine) finds it incomprehensible and escapes the suffocating environment of her all-consuming love by having an affair with Hannah's sister. Woody is Mickey Sachs, Hannah's ex-husband who is pessimistic about his chances of love until he finds it with another of Hannah's sisters played by Dianne Wiest. 'The heart is a resilient little muscle.'

Woody's Mickey is the usual hypochondriac trying to make sense of a senseless universe. He used to be married to Hannah but their union broke up under the strain of his infertility, a problem she suggests might be caused by 'excessive masturbation', a theme that crops up again in Woody's movies.

'Hey, you gonna start knocking my hobbies!'
Mickey Sachs, *Hannah and Her Sisters*

A close friend of Mia's was later to say that *Hannah and Her Sisters* was a portrait of Mia and her children. At the time Maureen O'Sullivan said Mia was Hannah, the only cohesive force in a disparate family where the real mother (played by Maureen) is too lost in booze and the past to care. (Maureen refused Woody's first offer to appear in the movie because the description of her character that he outlined for her was a 'boozy old flirt with a filthy mouth'.) Maureen said: 'I felt it was a complete exposure of herself. She wasn't being anything – she was being Mia.'[7]

Mia angrily denied that assertion but since Allen described the role of Hannah as a 'romanticised view of Mia' it appears that he not only thought he was describing his lover, but was portraying her in a generous light. What was striking about the fictitious Hannah character, is what many would see is striking about Mia. She appears to be genuinely loving and amazingly kind, going to excessive lengths for her own extended family. But is she too good, as Woody's friends would later hint Mia was, just as Elliot believes for a time in *Hannah and Her Sisters*? Is she just too overwhelmingly *giving* that she either cannot be genuine, or must she have a superiority complex? The ambiguity of Hannah is as exact a portrait of Mia as Annie Hall was of Diane Keaton.

No matter how much Woody was beginning to like being father to Dylan, his feelings about Mia's burgeoning children and the innate sense of superiority it seemed to give her remained ambivalent, and a coolness had crept into their relationship.

On the one hand he seemed impressed. 'I've noticed in

recent months that a lot of people I know are having babies. Women friends will say that the biological clock is ticking and I tell them not to bother to get pregnant – just adopt. When I first met Mia and she was telling me about all the children she had adopted, I said, "Oh, what a nice gesture" and she said, "No, I had it all wrong; it's not what she had done for them, it was what they'd done for her." Now I know how she felt.'

On the other hand, he was frightened that he would be introducing into the world innocent children, who would fall victim to the myriad of problems that beset society. The issues of drugs, crime, cruelty of man to his fellow man, hatred and violence, were, for Woody, heightened by the innocence of children. Here they are, pure as driven snow, and who knows what they will be turned into in years to come?

Unfortunately also, the intimacy of his scenes with Dianne Wiest in *Hannah and Her Sisters* brought gossip that Woody had fallen for the actress. 'The scenes in the film between Woody and Dianne Wiest were at times intensely intimate and tender, and Woody watchers speculated that a new romance might be on the horizon.'[8]

The cooling of his relationship with Mia was immediately obvious after *Hannah* when *Radio Days* was being made. In it Woody was to revisit his past, but the production was also haunted by Mia's past. The crooning voice of Frank Sinatra was heard in the background over one sequence, and a nightclub scene was shot in the St Regis Hotel where Mia had met Salvador Dali. Despite the fact that it was Woody's biggest budget to date, Mia played a less than sympathetic role as the two-bit cigarette girl who would do anything for radio stardom, including sleeping with the man she thinks will make it happen for her. She does get radio stardom – but only for a fleeting moment as her show is taken off the air when war breaks out.

The stress free inner calm noted by Jeff Daniels on

Purple Rose of Cairo had disappeared to be replaced by occasional displays of fraught tension. There were hints of trouble on the set. 'He can be very devastating. I think I saw her [Mia] tear up once; maybe I'm wrong and it was for something else, but she's a very emotional young lady. They have an understanding. There is with Woody a slight intimidation factor. He's very precise in everything that he does, very tough but in a way that's not verbal, not emotional, very quiet. He will scold, but in this quiet way. His screen persona is meek, but he's not that way at all. And he's no different with me than with Mia.'[9]

He had been different with Mia once, and his attitude had noticeably hardened throughout 1986 as he began to bond more and more with Dylan. In January 1987 *Radio Days* came out which was a disappointment at the box office, but his ardent fans loved it. Woody immediately started his next movie, *September*, a bleak drama about six people trying to come to terms with their pasts. The shooting was even bleaker with half the original cast – including Maureen O'Sullivan – being dropped in a highly tense atmosphere not helped by the director's usual unhappy scowl.

Then something happened which had Woody wearing a different expression. Despite his concern at the size of Mia's family, when Mia suggested adopting another child, he was enthusiastic – because of his developing affection for Dylan. It was yet another example of the contradictions in Woody's world, and can only be put down to the fact that he presumed the new child would be 'his'. But before another adoption could be arranged, Mia became pregnant with Satchel.[10]

A wide-eyed Woody was pictured leaving his apartment building, a look of perplexed disbelief written across his face. 'This was an accident and, once it occurred, Mia would never think of having an abortion. And I don't think that I would either. We were both surprised. It was nothing that we were planning particularly. It was just a sudden surprise and were both sort of happy about it.'[11]

He added that there were no plans to marry or move in with the mother. 'We only live five minutes from one another and we're constantly at each other's house and constantly working together. We have no plans that I know about to alter our extremely comfortable and viable situation.'

Mia was old to have a child – she would be 41. But Maureen O'Sullivan said that it was not too old to have a baby – she had been 40 after all when Tisa came along. The child would be Maureen's twentieth grandchild. Asked how the news had leaked out, Maureen said she presumed someone from the Queens sound stage had leaked it to the press.

Woody told Eric Lax his own mother's reaction to Mia's pregnancy. 'By you?' she demanded. 'This after seven years!' Woody had to pause for thought before saying uncertainly, 'I guess so'.[12]

'I think I'll be profoundly wise and generous, liberal, understanding. I'd be surprised if I'd be less than perfect as a father. The thing hasn't really sunk into me. But I think that at some point when I'm actually confronted with the issue – with offspring – then I think I'll be delighted.

'I feel pleasant about it. I think it will be a good experience for me. I think it will deepen me. I hope so. Either that, or it will put me in a crazy house.'[13]

It did.

Satchel O'Sullivan Farrow was born in December 1987, was named after Satchel Paige, a favourite baseball hero of Woody's and – according to him – looked like Edward G Robinson, a favourite movie hero. Otherwise the 4lb 4oz baby delivered by Caesarean section was fine. His arrival though illustrates the many paradoxes that accompany everything Woody does. On the one hand they called him 'Farrow' rather than 'Allen' because Woody did not want the child to be left out in a crowd of Previns and Farrows. On the other he was annoyed when *his* name was left off the birth certificate by Mia who was responding to his coldness, like for like. Woody got lawyers to reinstate it, but from then onwards he would seem to put great psychological distance between himself and both Dylan and Satchel by often referring to them as 'bastards'. He later explained it was meant to be in the literal sense not the pejorative, but it's an odd way for a loving father to behave.

On the one hand Woody was worried at the size of Mia's family. On the other, he had been 'enthusiastic' about possibly adopting another. But then, when he was presented with a natural child, Woody withdrew. During the pregnancy, Woody didn't indulge in any of the affectionate habits that expectant fathers are expected to do. He didn't touch her stomach, listen to the foetus, or try to feel it kick. Mia at first believed that Woody was simply squeamish about the details of pregnancy and the delivery process. But the two of them began to withdraw from one another.[14]

He remained closer to his adopted girl Dylan than his biological boy Satchel, but the thought that he had produced a child stunned him. Satchel was not left out but Mia rapidly was. The arrival of the boy completed the process begun when Dylan was adopted, acclimatising Woody to parenthood, but not to the woman who accidentally made him a parent. He said that sex stopped between the two after Satchel arrived but other reports claim that he said it was over before the baby was born, and Mia herself complained to him while she was pregnant, 'You've been cold and cruel and I want a more conventional relationship.'[15] (To confuse matters, Mia would later say it wasn't true that they never had sex after Satchel.)

He later said: '[I didn't adopt Dylan, she did] ... but a month after she was there, I found myself bonding with her. She was just the greatest little girl. Suddenly I got

241

tuned into the joys of parenthood. When Mia said, "it would be nice if she had someone else, I think I'll adopt another child," I said, "great". And coincidentally she got pregnant shortly after that. I was delighted.' But he added: 'The relationship was starting to wane anyhow. Dylan's arrival sort of resuscitated it for a while; we had something in common, co-parenting the kids. But when Satchel came along, it drifted down to a polite and cordial end.'[16]

He told Roger Ebert: 'My feelings about the baby are very complicated. You know Mia and I adopted a baby, Dylan, before she got pregnant, and there is absolutely no difference in the love that I will feel for the new child and the love I feel for Dylan. In fact I love Dylan so much that I would be pleasantly surprised if I love the baby we are having together as much as the one we adopted.'

After Satchel arrived Woody and Mia may have ceased sleeping together but they remained on cordial terms as many estranged parents would do, especially people who lived so close to one another, and the two continued to be involved in making movies together. He had cast Louise Lasser and Diane Keaton in movies after he had broken up with them, and he did not see any reason why he should not do the same with Mia. He would still be around at Mia's place every day to see the kids get up, and he would make sure he was there at night to tuck them in. Mia and Woody also continued to dine out together, and to many of their friends and relations, they did not appear to be any different than they had ever been.

The days continued much as before on the surface but emotionally, Woody was always on a different wavelength to Mia. (In all his movies, characters rarely display fits of passion or even small displays of emotion. When Tracy cries in *Manhattan*, it's one of the few times anyone in his movies is seen to do so. Bitter-sweet memories surface all the time, but rarely tears.) Whereas Woody came from a strong family unit which remains close to this day, and he had had clear objectives throughout his life, Mia had come from a chronically disturbed family and had pursued an erratic stage and screen career. She had sacrificed her career for love, something Woody would never have dreamt of, and she often found herself at a loss as to what to do. Woody had always striven for the very best in everything, not least emotional self-satisfaction. He was generous in the sense that money would be no object if a friend or good cause needed it, and he was ceaselessly generous to his mother and father who wanted for nothing when he made money.

He was also incredibly generous with help towards artists and colleagues in the film business trying to make it. Diane Keaton would not be where *she* is today without Woody Allen's help. Dianne Wiest and Danny Aiello owe a great deal to him. Other actors like Alan Alda and Martin Landau, who initially displayed promising sparks of great acting talent before descending into the dramatically empty depths of television, were 'rescued' by Woody under whose guidance they both turned out masterful performances in *Crimes and Misdemeanors*.

But Mia Farrow's style of generosity was as incomprehensible to him as Hannah's had been to Mickey Sachs and Elliot who couldn't understand *why* she felt obliged to *give* all the time without any consideration for her own welfare. 'Why this constant need for infants and little ones?' Allen's friend and costume designer Jeffrey Kurland would demand, 'Get on with your life!'[17] Woody was someone who believed in a remorseless and rational drive to self-improvement, and if you could help somebody along the way, then great! But Mia seemed to have inherited something of the kindly but 'irrational' Roman Catholic tradition of faith, hope and charity.

Her family was an all-consuming passion, with rarely a day going by without at least one of the children visiting her mother on the set. Mia's dressing room at the Kaufman-Astoria Studios in Queens began to resemble a nursery. 'I've never known anyone who cared so self-lessly about children, and who put so much of herself into them ... They always came first,'[18] said Soon-Yi's godmother Rose Styron. Woody has observed, 'Mia has a talent for mothering the way some people have a green thumb for gardening or an ear for music or a talent for medicine.'[19] It was what Mia's sister Tisa described as her 'mission in life', a vocation to take care of as many disadvantaged kids as she possibly could. And Mia's good friend Leonard Gershe said: 'Mia told me long ago, when she was adopting the fifth or sixth child, "Lenny, I was so lucky to find out fairly young that pink palazzos and swimming pools were never going to fulfil me. They don't do it for me. I'm not interested in fashion, I'm not interested in jewellery. I'm interested in giving a life to someone whose life would not exist if it weren't for me." What's so terrible about this? It's absolutely sincere.'[20]

For her children, Mia always boasted that they were given sufficient pocket money allowances enough so that they could order pizzas for 'three playmates', so that they would all have friends, a throwback perhaps to her own isolation in the children's polio ward. André Previn's wife gets to see the family often when they visit her Mount Kisco home. 'Mia is a wonderful mother. I've adopted a child and it's a very fulfilling experience. I don't know what prompts someone like Mia to adopt one or two or three or four. I have no idea what is behind that except I can only assume it's an enormous heart and a love for children and a need and a wanting to share her home and her heart with children. Her day is spent with children, her night is spent with children. She has children all over her all day long.

'I know the children that she's had with André, and if they are a reflection of the way Mia has brought them up, then I wish my children the same because they are unfailingly polite, unfailingly courteous, they are unfailingly well behaved and they are extremely funny and nice to be with. The children are a reflection of the parents and if the children are unfailingly all of these things then it must be a reflection of their mum and their dad and I think in this case their mum has a very important input into their lives and I think she has done an astonishing good job.'[21]

Mia was remarkably good at bringing her children up in the circumstances. News stories began to leak about some of them getting into trouble, such as the night Lark jumped a subway turnstile when she ran out of money, after spending half the night at a party she had not told her mum about. A year or so later, Lark and Daisy were picked up for shoplifting with a couple of friends. They had been pinching some underwear from a mall in Connecticut. And on another occasion Daisy had not received her monthly allowance from André Previn so she forged a signature on Soon-Yi's but was made to pay it back when Soon-Yi came home from school and found out. Daisy also skipped five days at school when Mia was in Vietnam.

Given the size of the family and the fact that they live in a city where kids – even well-to-do ones – go around with knives and guns in their school bags, the occasional misfortunes of the Previn–Farrow clan can realistically be classed as misdemeanours rather than crimes. And Mia's attentiveness was certainly more than Woody's who could rarely remember details such as the birthdays of his children, the names of their friends or their pets.

A woman who had been tutoring the children for 12 years, Audrey Sieger, said, 'Most of my students are New York City kids. Many have parents who are glamorous and famous, and most of these kids are very troubled and neglected and grow up very fast … Mia's family is very unusual. She – at any time in these 12 years – has been able to tell me in detail about every one of her kids. These kids travel on buses with bus passes. They cook dinner for each other. They do their own laundry. Different kids over the years have been assigned the job of going to the supermarket. They have not been raised by nannies.' Mia according to Sieger, was 'warm, loving and sincere, and throughout all my years of working with the kids, having them at my office, calling at home, they were happy kids, giggling and laughing and involved with each other.'[22]

But there were persistent rumours that Mia consciously or unconsciously treated her biological children better than the adopted ones, even relegating the latter to the role of 'servants'. Letty Aronson noticed the difference when she visited Mia's apartment with her own child Erika after Satchel had been born. 'Afterward, my daughter kept talking about how the maid did this, the maid did that. I said, "What maid?" She meant Lark. 'We always joked that Lark would be the one to get out of the house and write the "Mommie Dearest" book.'[23]

In 1993 though, when Woody and Mia faced one another in court over custody of three of her children, it was clearly stated in the summing up, that Mia had not treated her adopted children any differently from the biological children, although she acknowledged 'problems' that she had had with Dylan, Satchel and Soon-Yi.

Woody had often voiced concern to friends about the sheer scale of Mia's chosen mission, and his worries were underscored when scandals about Korean 'babies for sale' rackets began to hit the headlines. Since 1957, nearly 35,000 Korean babies were adopted in the United States. In 1988, when the Olympic Games were held in Seoul, N.B.C. television exposed how the babies were almost treated as a national export with large sums of money changing hands. It was a mutually beneficial procedure: the Korean families would get much needed hard currency, sometimes as much as 50,000 dollars; and Americans desperate for a child could cut through the red tape they met at home. There was never any question that Mia did anything wrong, and the agencies she used were perfectly reputable, but Woody was concerned never-theless.

The self-styled portrait of Mia as a latter day saint is a disingenous one. There is a vivid streak of virtue about the actress, much of it inherited from Maureen. In 1980 Maureen's old co-star Johnny Weissmuller was on his death bed in Los Angeles's Motion Picture Home where he had been through a long illness. They had not seen one another for 20 years but Johnny's family contacted Maureen to tell her that he would like to see her once more before he died. She didn't think twice about it, flying out to Los Angeles where veteran entertainment reporter Tony Brenna was waiting to meet her and take her to the hospital. 'The moment Maureen entered his hospital room and approached his bedside, Johnny's face just lit up in a huge smile. Maureen went up to him and gave him a big hug, took his hand and said, "Me Jane, you Tarzan". They both laughed. Johnny was just beaming. Maureen and Johnny spent hours together talking and reminiscing.'[24]

Brenna revealed that Maureen said to him, 'You never give up on the people you care about. When you're a friend, you're a friend for life. That is something I believe and that I have passed on to all my children and grandchildren. I know that they believe it too.'

But that episode of unadulterated kindness is tinged with the theatricality of Maureen's gesture, a character-istic of every family steeped in the grandiloquent tradi-tions of a superficial and fickle business. The atmosphere that reigned at Maureen and Mia's bustling West Side abode was already evident in 1969, shortly before her divorce from André Previn. A writer was allowed into Maureen's apartment where she witnessed first hand the bizarre lifestyle. 'At the stately apartment of Mia's mother, a welcome atmosphere of banal normality sets in. It lasts about five minutes. Doug is Tisa's boyfriend. Tisa is Mia's younger sister. It is Doug's birthday. Everyone is glad he is having another birthday because, not so long ago, while getting over a "bad period", Doug would wander from window to window – on outdoor ledges 11 flights above the pavement.

'Disconcertingly, bouncy Mia Farrow has a habit of adopting her mother's exact voice and manner when she addresses her – theatrically elegant, cautiously refined, words strung carefully out like pearls. She becomes her mother, then returns to herself.

'Someone has just turned up a small printed card that says "GO AWAY THOU BALD HEAD". Everyone laughs uncontrollably. Why not hang it inside the elevator to scare bald tenants? More white wine. "The new generation is just an orgasm," confides young Doug. "We're the dirties, the weirdies," says lovely Tisa. "Ten thousand people march to get a paragraph in the paper," frets Mia, "but I get pages – an inane actress girl talking about her great ideas on life. It bothers me, it offends me."'[25]

Mia's kind image has to be tempered by the observations of many in her building who have observed her to be 'imperious' and 'unfriendly'. As for the earth mother image of getting the children to do the shopping, residents of 135 Central Park West used to notice Woody's car at her beck and call for grocery shopping trips. Time and time again, the notion that Mia 'isn't as nice as she seems' cropped up. 'I know about her and not the sweetheart she claims,' said one. 'She's a bad, bad girl.'

Mia sent some of her children to the Ethical Culture School just around the corner from her apartment. It's an expensive college that attracts an eclectic collection of kids from middle income families and the children of neighbourhood celebrities like Sean Lennon who's also a friend of the Farrow clan. One day a mother from downtown went to pick up her daughter and a friend's Oriental daughter. 'Mia actually was surprised and she gave me a look as if to say "Oh, there's another one like me", and it looked like she was interested in talking to me.

But she wouldn't deign to speak to me because I was on a different level of society evidently, to her. None of those people are really all that friendly.'

Woody admired Mia's dedication and spirit although he was concerned that she may have been taking on more than she could handle. But it was her vocation, not his, and if she thought having children would woo him back, she was wrong. He was being wooed by someone else by now – not a woman but a film studio. Impressed by his consistently high standard of work produced at minimal cost, Disney were anxious to have the director working for them and offered him the backing for a couple of projects. Woody had received many other such offers in the past but none of them had been as good as his unprecedented deal with Orion, headed by his old friend Arthur Krim, which gave him virtual total control.

However, in the late Eighties Orion was on the brink of financial extinction, and Woody was anxious to find a suitable alternative backer. He eagerly accepted Disney's offer and the collaboration produced two movies. The second, *Scenes From a Mall*, was instantly forgotten, not because it was such a bad film, but because Woody's fans could not cope with the idea of their hero wearing a pony tail and tortoiseshell glasses, or being an executive who shops in a Los Angeles mall. Observers sensed too that Woody did not like being quite so overwhelmed by his boisterous co-star, Bette Midler.

The first Disney movie, on the other hand, became a favourite of his fans. At only 41 minutes long, it's the shortest he's ever made, yet ironically may say more about what was going on in his mind at the time than all the others put together.

Oedipus Wrecks (which he started shooting in spring 1988) is his vignette in the series of three *New York Stories*, made with Francis Ford Coppola and Martin Scorsese. It is the story of lawyer Sheldon Mills who hasn't yet resolved his relationship with his overbearing Jewish mother, despite being 50 years old. *Oedipus Wrecks* includes all the Woody Allen themes of guilt, assimilation, food, magic, sex, spiritualism, truth and reality. He also managed to cast his old teacher from P.S. 99 in the movie, as a friend of his worried mother.

Sheldon's real name is Millstein but he changed it to assimilate, a fact his mother Sadie loudly reminds him of all the time. His fiancée is Lisa (Mia Farrow) a *shiksa* goddess with lots of kids not approved of by Sadie who would rather Sheldon marry a nice Jewish girl. Sadie is so overbearing Sheldon seeks psychiatric advice and laments to his doctor, 'I love her, but I wish she would disappear'. Which she does, in a magic act, a miraculous event that temporarily has Sheldon feeling much better – until she reappears over the skies of Manhattan hectoring Sheldon about Lisa and revealing to the whole city her son's most intimate childhood memories. His life becomes unbearable, until Lisa walks out and Sheldon falls in love with Treva, played by Julie Kavner. Miraculously his mother returns to the earth.

The ending soundtrack is: 'I Wanna Girl (Just Like the Girl That Married Dear Old Dad).'

When Alan Lapidus saw *Oedipus Wrecks*, he laughed when Sadie called Lisa a 'korva'. 'What's a "korva?"' demanded the Mia Farrow character. (Answer: it's Yiddish for 'whore'.) *Variety* observed: 'For whatever his students will make of it, *Oedipus Wrecks* marks the first time Allen has ended up with a Jewish woman since the earliest days of his film career.'[26] Doug Brode said: 'This is the most Jewish of Allen's movies, the only one in which he ever suggested, that remaining within the culture might not be so bad, as compared to the endless allegories of assimilation he's shared with his audience over the years.'[27]

'Woody is acknowledging that maybe his mum was right in the first place,' says Alan Lapidus who has no doubt through his own experience and knowledge of Woody, that the film maker had laid his life bare in his work. Certainly *Oedipus Wrecks* was the first time Woody had allowed an image of his mother to be shown uncluttered with Groucho Marx disguises.

When Woody and Mia first started seeing one another, his contact with the children was minimal, they, perhaps, spending a Saturday afternoon over at his apartment. He did not like pets, so rarely visited Mia's West Side place. But the two parties would often meet midway in Central Park, where they would all go for a walk often ending up at the Russian Tea Room for lunch. The press once noticed Woody and the kids feasting on oysters which set him back a grand total of 1,000 dollars one Saturday lunchtime.

As Woody increasingly took on the role of parenthood to Dylan, Satchel and Moses, he began to spend more time over at their mother's apartment. But paradoxically, he was actually becoming more distant from most of the other children, because his presence in their midst was purely and simply for the benefit of his own charges. Correspondingly, he was also becoming more distant from Mia.

It was in this somewhat illusory atmosphere that the whole family set off for Europe in the summer of 1988. Woody took nine of the children, Mia and his close friend Jane Martin to Scandinavia, Italy and Russia. The Russian leg was to be short lived, Woody demanding to leave within hours of arriving in Leningrad and finding himself unable to cope with the lack of service. In Sweden the family visited Sven Nykvist, Allen's long-time cinematographic collaborator and the man Mia had allegedly fallen in love with 10 years earlier on the set of *Hurricane*. The children and Mia had a great time but for the most part he stayed indoors, writing on hotel notepaper the script which was to become *Crimes and Misdemeanors*.

While Mia, seven of the kids and Jane Martin enjoyed the pleasures of Stockholm, Helsinki, Venice and Rome, he scribbled away in their hotel suite the beginning of the script that was to become one of his greatest movie achievements. Jane took some photographs of the happy travellers on their trans-continental trek, but Woody looked like a sulking school child who would rather be somewhere else.

Woody loves living in Manhattan and avoids travelling outside it, but he leaves town more often than he cares to admit. The European vacation with Mia's children was becoming a regular fixture, and it is odd that he once said he hadn't been out of New York for seven years when Jack Victor arrived in Ireland to find himself treading in Woody and Mia's footsteps. 'My wife and I got in a horse-drawn cart in Phoenix Park and the driver, without any prompting, said, "I had that Woody Allen and his wife in the back the other day!",' recalls Jack. But traipsing around holiday spots with a gaggle of giggling kids was not his forte.

It was on one of these European vacations, that Mia noticed the intensity of Woody's obsession with Dylan. She was soon becoming concerned that the relationship had sexual undertones. During a trip to Paris when Dylan was between two and three years old, Mia told Woody: 'You look at her in a sexual way. You fondled her. It's not natural. You're all over her. You don't give her any breathing room. You look at her when she's naked.' Her apprehension was fuelled by the intensity of the attention Woody lavished on Dylan, and by his spending play time in bed with her. He would read to her in bed dressed only in undershorts, and would permit her to suck his thumb.[28]

Crimes and Misdemeanors, which he started shooting in the autumn of 1988, explores all his usual questions of love, death, good and evil, God and logic, reality and illusion. It did so more masterfully than any other movie that he had directed to date and came out to universal applause. But it also has some of the best one-liners in any of his films:

Barbara: 'Once the sex goes, it all goes.'
Cliff: 'It's true. The last time I was inside a woman was when I visited the Statue of Liberty.'

Cliff: 'When you see Lester later be careful. Because if this guy tells you he wants to exchange ideas, what he wants is to exchange fluids.'

Cliff, (lecturing his niece about show business): 'It's worse than dog eat dog. It's dog doesn't return other dog's phone calls.'

And for those who believe that Woody Allen has too often displayed a flagrant disregard for other people's feelings, he ridicules himself in *Crimes and Misdemeanors* as much as anyone else. Woody is Cliff, the pretentious little film maker who self-righteously believes he's morally superior to everyone else, but is really racked with envy, jealousy and guilt; a pathetic little man incapable of adjusting to normal relations with the rest of society. In reality Cliff is trying to have an extra-marital affair – *trying* – not even succeeding! He fantasises about Halley (Mia) and is racked with bitterness and jealousy about Lester (Alan Alda) the rich and successful TV producer who sweeps Halley off her feet.

Rich in religious thought and imagery, *Crimes and Misdemeanors* is full of minor deceit and major treachery, appropriately enough for the era of junk bond kings and property crooks in the late Eighties when the film came out. It is the petty liars and cheats who suffer while the big time criminals get off scot-free.

Cliff's documentary attempt to parody Lester is funny like much of Woody's own films, but in the end it's totally ineffectual as far as its maker is concerned. It achieves nothing. In the end, the only hero Cliff has, the obscure Professor Louis Levy, in whose philosophy Cliff has invested such faith, commits suicide. Professor Levy's words trail off towards the end, leaving at least the possibility of hope ...

> 'Human happiness does not seem to have been included in the design of creation. It is only we, with our capacity to love, that give meaning to the indifferent universe. And yet, most human beings seem to have the ability to keep trying, even to find joy from simple things, their family, their work – and from the hope, that future generations might understand more ...'
>
> Louis Levy, *Crimes and Misdeameanors*

The Mia character is the one who claims to agree with Cliff's worthy and altruistic aims initially, but nevertheless ends up in the arms of the Philistine but much more attractive Lester.

Crimes and Misdemeanors also had a very brief role for Daryl Hannah, the leggy blonde girlfriend of John F Kennedy Jnr. She was Lester's date in one of the scenes and was hardly noticeable, but *New York Post* writer Jami Bernard claimed Daryl's part originally reared much more prominently in Woody's mind. 'Rumour had it that Woody cast Daryl Hannah ... just so he could stage a few love scenes with her. They did retake after retake, but she appears just briefly in the final version.'[28]

The idea was laughed off by Hannah. 'Woody was looking for a Daryl Hannah type, and I'm a Daryl Hannah type,' she said. Other co-stars like the Australian actress Judy Davis have vigorously denied any romantic liaisons. And once Woody also shrugged off a question about whether one of the thrills of being an all-powerful director was casting beautiful girls in his movies.

But the fact is Woody *was* beginning to cast many of the profession's most attractive and desirable starlets in his movies. Long before Sharon Stone sent temperatures soaring with her cross legging antics in *Basic Instinct* she had a reputation as one of Hollywood's hottest and sexiest young stars – and Woody gave her a part in *Stardust Memories*. Barbara Hershey is a brilliant and talented actress, and no doubt a classic leading lady for Woody Allen films as she proved in *Hannah and Her Sisters*. But Barbara had made something of a sensation when she hinted that her love scenes in *Boxcar Bertha* may have been more real than imagined.

His crew speculated about his intentions with actresses such as the accomplished Jodie Foster, and the un-accomplished Madonna, both of whom appeared in *Shadows and Fog*. Madonna's performance in *Shadows and Fog* caused speculation in newspaper stories which suggested that huge sequences with the Material Girl in had to be cut because they were so bad. Woody went to the extraordinary length of issuing a written denial of the claims, a bizarre move for a man who rarely comments on press reports. Bizarre in view of the facts too. Madonna has been in several movies but has never received the critical applause she wants. And while shooting *Husbands and Wives* at a beach house on Long Island, one of his crew commented off the record, 'Madonna was wooden in *Shadows*. She was a nice enough girl, and obviously *wants* to be a great actress and she may have great potential, but she just didn't have it for us especially compared to that English chick who was a dream – totally professional and a joy to work with.'

That 'English chick' was Emily Lloyd, the talented *Wish You Were Here* actress bursting with youthful exuberance and blossoming sex appeal. Woody chose her for the part of the teenage English student who falls for her Manhattan college professor in *Husbands and Wives*. A few weeks after the Long Island shoot, Emily abruptly left the production when Allen spotted 19-year-old Juliette Lewis in that spring's huge hit, *Cape Fear*. Juliette's performance opposite Robert DeNiro won unanimous acclaim for her adolescent seductiveness and understated sensuality. Allen went to see the movie and immediately decided she was the girl for his film. Emily Lloyd, who had originally been overwhelmed to be in a Woody Allen movie, left on 'amicable' terms.

The list goes on. Sean Young, whose sexy backseat limousine scenes with Kevin Costner in *No Way Out* caught the public's imagination, was offered a part by Woody in *Crimes and Misdemeanors* but found herself on the cutting room floor. The Australian supermodel Elle Macpherson was given a brief part in *Alice* as the beautiful girl Joe Mantegna gets to ogle undressing after Joe has taken some of Alice's disappearing herbs. There is no question about the acting abilities or otherwise of many of these actresses, but what is strange is that a director who had prided himself on shunning Hollywood should fall for so many of its greatest female stars.

There was also something perverse about this trend to hire glamorous Hollywood girls, and it began to show itself in the subtext of his movies. Various strands have run through Woody's work which have been well documented – his obsession with his mother, a desire to explore sexual taboos, the element of crime and criminality. Douglas Brode was the first to pinpoint Woody's use of food as a metaphor for sex. But when *Oedipus Wrecks* came out in 1989 the image of a 'whore' emerged. In *Alice* – if it was there at all – it was in the more subtle form of Alice's bright red coat. But in *Shadows and Fog*, the theme reached its conspicuous climax when the action centred around a whorehouse and a cast representing some of the best talent in Hollywood. Madonna, Kathy Bates, Kate Nelligan, Lily Tomlin, Julie Kavner, Jodie Foster, John Malkovich and John Cusack all agreed to appear in *Shadows* for the normal union-agreed daily acting rate. Is he taking some sort of perverse pleasure in tempting all these high-priced stars to come and work for 'scale' in a movie about whores? Allen insists that there is little or no commercial advantage to him in getting these names on cinema marquees. So why does he do it? Isn't he the director who believes in good acting first and star billing second?

Woody needed publicity for *Crimes and Misdemeanors* but it's hard to explain why he and Mia would entertain celebrity writer Glenn Plaskin at her home. Mia told him: 'Living together would be too disruptive. I like the idea of seeing one another in our prime time. When it becomes too much for him, he goes home. When we want to. Particularly as I get older I appreciate that freedom. If I want to hang a picture I hang it. It's *my* house. It sounds petty, but it's great. All my life, it seems I lived with a man and it was always *his* house.'[29]

The following year, despite his continuing coolness towards her, Woody paid Mia a tremendous cinematic tribute by casting her in the title role of *Alice*. The advertising hoardings for *Alice* in Christmas 1990 featured a startling, red picture of Mia – and nothing else – no words or text besides the title. He'd delivered her a present any actress would kill for.

In *Alice* a rich Roman Catholic woman realises she has been living her life with a twisted set of values, but gets a chance to change after visiting a Chinese acupuncturist, Dr Yang, who prescribes for her some herbs. She discovers that her distant and cold husband has been cheating on her, but Alice finds solace in India where she works for a while with Mother Teresa before returning to New York – not to be the Upper East Side, but to a grubby part of downtown Manhattan where she takes care of children.

'Playing what is, in effect, the Woody Allen role, that of someone who is both fearful and determined, both romantic and pragmatic, Ms Farrow gives the kind of performance that, if there is any justice, will win her an

Oscar nomination this year, maybe even an award,' wrote Vincent Canby in *The New York Times*.[30] There was always a sour note to Woody's mentorship though, as David Denby once noted, describing Mia as 'one of Woody's meek and fluttering women.' 'There's something creepy about Allen's love for dithering women. Diane Keaton had to get away from him and work for other directors before some iron came into her voice.'

In 1991 Mia set off for Cambodia to adopt more children.

But Mia flew to the Far East concerned about the relationship between Dylan and Woody. The previous autumn, Mia had expressed concern to Satchel's therapist, Dr Susan Coates, about Woody's behaviour with Dylan which she thought was 'not appropriate'. Dr Coates agreed that it was inappropriate, and she started to work with Woody to make him understand this and modify his behaviour. But Dr Coates was adamant that it was not a sexual problem. She observed, 'I understood why she was worried, because it was intense. I did not see it as sexual, but I saw it was inappropriately intense because it excluded everybody else, and it placed a demand on a child for a kind of acknowledgement that I felt should not be placed on a child.' Dr Coates also recommended that Dylan enter therapy with Dr Nancy Schultz which the child did in April 1991.[31]

About this time, another of Mia's adoptees was becoming close to Woody. The child was Soon-Yi, the little girl Mia had broken her back over to get her into the United States and who was about to break her heart. Mia would testify that she was 'racked with guilt' about bringing the little girl into the family – because it allowed Woody to victimise her – but others believe that the beautiful young girl was as capable of seducing Woody as he was of her.

Soon-Yi had been found by an orphanage abandoned in the streets of Seoul. The orphanage learnt that her mother had left her there a few days earlier, promising to return but in fact never coming back. Soon-Yi's mother was a prostitute who had subjected the frail girl to degrading and debilitating punishments. She would force Soon-Yi to kneel on a doorstep and continually slam the door against her head.

Mia decided to adopt Soon-Yi in 1977 in the midst of her marital difficulties with André Previn, but immediately came across the hurdle of American federal law banning more than two adopted foreign children per family. She went to great lengths to get the law changed, first by getting the Justice Department to grant the girl 'parole status' which allowed Mia to bring her into the States. Then she persuaded Massachusetts Representative, Michael Harrington, to sponsor a special bill which Congress passed, repealing the old law.

When Mia flew to Seoul she had to wait 10 days for bureaucracy to work its way through before becoming Soon-Yi's mother. She washed pots in the orphanage kitchen every day until the papers came through. When they did, she said: 'There are many people like me who thrive on children, who love them so, and the need for adoptive parents is so great worldwide, that the law had to be changed. I'm pleased it was. But I am mostly pleased for me because I have my beautiful Soon-Yi with me.'[32]

It was not easy at first when the traumatised child, who could only speak gibberish, had to get used to this new white mother who was going to take her away from the home she had known most of her life. Mia had brought her a doll which Soon-Yi was terrified of because she thought it was an animal. She also brought her a pretty dress, but when the little child saw herself in it, she wanted to kick the mirror in.[33]

Soon-Yi's initial reaction to her new life was intense but she was soon in the swing of things as the daughter of an international celebrity. Mia was in the middle of her break-up from André Previn and having put her career on the back burner for several years, needed cash quickly not least for the upkeep of the children. She did Robert Altman's instantly forgettable *A Wedding* in Chicago and immediately flew off to Cairo with Fletcher and Soon-Yi in tow to shoot *Death on the Nile* with David Niven and Peter Ustinov. Taking the children went against the advice of her doctor who feared problems with the heat, diet and injections. But Mia's response was to complain about the fact that she could only take the children who she felt needed her most. In the end it was she who suffered through bugs and fleas and dirty water. On her next trip to Bora Bora for *Hurricane*, she left all the children at home.

Soon-Yi was the eldest child Mia had adopted at the time (although she subsequently adopted Tam), and it's possible that this could be why she grew up isolated from the rest. From the beginning they noticed she did not assimilate into the bustling household as well as the rest of them. For the first three years she called Mia 'Good Mama' (as opposed to her natural parent 'Bad Mama') before adopting 'Mia' which all the other children used. But some noticed she never seemed to be as close to her new mother as the others were, despite Mia's greatest efforts. She cherished a picture of Fred Astaire which she kept by her bedside, and the others noticed she seemed to live in a dream world. She shared a bedroom with Lark and Daisy but was never as outgoing as they were. They presumed she wanted to be a nun because she was so moral and disapproving of bad behaviour such as cheating at school.[34]

That was what Woody thought when he first noticed Soon-Yi who seemed to disapprove of him. He had little to do with any of the family at first, and it was not until Dylan and Satchel came along that he started to spend so much time over at Central Park West and have closer contact with the others. In fact Woody used to pay Soon-

Yi and Lark 70 dollars to babysit Dylan and Satchel on alternate weekends.

By now Mia's brood included four natural and five adopted children. Her twins by André Previn, Sacha and Matthew, were 21 and in their final years at Fordham University in New York, and Yale, respectively. Their sister, adopted Vietnamese orphan Lark, was almost 20 and studying at nursing school. Their natural brother Fletcher was 17 and at the Collegiate School, and Daisy, 17, was at prep school in the city. Moses had had cerebral palsy and Woody had taken special care of him, Dylan and Satchel were all going to good schools. Amazingly, with these nine children on her hands, Mia was in the midst of negotiating to bring three further children into her home. But it was a home in which, for one reason or another, Soon-Yi had never felt very comfortable.

Her relationship with Woody began to get closer in the last six months of high school. She told him she was interested in being a model so he taught her how to dress properly and had professional photographs taken which made her look very glamorous. When she had earlier expressed an interest in acting, Woody had arranged for her to get a bit part in *Scenes From a Mall*. One summer's evening he asked if anyone fancied going along to a basketball game and Soon-Yi surprisingly said 'yes'. Mia may regret her own reaction to that now, but at the time it was encouraging, telling Woody it would get them both over any negative feelings they had towards one another. The date went well, and Woody was to take her to more basketball matches later on and the other children noticed that Soon-Yi increasingly began to doll herself up for him.

Woody said: 'Just fortuitously, I was over at Mia's and I had no one to go to the basketball game with. And Soon-Yi said, "I'll go" and so I took her, and I found her interesting and delightful. Mia had encouraged me to get to know her. She would say "Take a walk with Soon-Yi, do something with her. Try and make friends with her, she's not really as hostile to you as you might think." Mia thought it was fine so I took her to the game.

'I took her to a game again, maybe a month later. And this happened on a few occasions. And we struck up a relationship. It was strictly – I don't want to say an intellectual relationship, because I'm not saying we were discussing Kant or anything, but we chatted about different things.'[35]

'We'd chat when I came over to Mia's house. It started to become hotter and heavier late last year [1991]. We had a number of conversations, saw a couple of movies, and you know it just – well, I can't say there was any cataclysmic moment.'

In September 1991, Soon-Yi entered Drew College in New Jersey, naive, socially inexperienced and vulnerable. She was, said Woody later, lonely and unhappy at school and began to phone him daily. But she was also spending weekends at home with Mia, and didn't convey these thoughts to her, or that she was in daily communication with Woody.[36]

In the months that Woody and Soon-Yi had become intimate, he would later say that it had only crossed his mind for a fleeting moment that maybe there was something odd about the relationship. But he consistently claimed that it would really be no different had he had an affair with a secretary. It is easier to understand his claim that he never saw anything incestuous in the arrangement, because time and time again both he and Mia had insisted that the six elder children were André Previn's, and in any case, at anything between 18 and 21, Soon-Yi was an adult. She was, after all, the same age as the young English rose Woody had cast for the role of sexy seductress in *Husbands and Wives*, Emily Lloyd. Soon-Yi was, Woody insisted, 'a grown, sophisticated person. She was raised in New York.'[37]

Woody would later claim that Soon-Yi began to make

complaints about Mia and her household of children. Soon-Yi also started opening up about her relationship with Mia, expanding on rumours that the adopted children had been treated differently to the natural born kids. This was to be categorically denied in court. These were never substantiated by the other children or hard evidence made public, but Woody claimed what Soon-Yi told him was enough to take her complaints seriously.

'She told me things that were surprising about the family, and that it was not exactly as happy as I thought it was. She and other kids had problems with their mother. Soon-Yi did not have a good relationship with her, and we spoke about that … She was impatient with her for having trouble learning the language. There were many other things.

'[I believed it] because I made it my business to find out. She was worse to Soon-Yi because she stood up to her. And there was a definite difference in the way she treated the adopted children and her own children.'[38]

But how much of this was accurate, and how much was down to Woody's over-active imagination, will probably never be known. During his bitter custody battle with Mia, the court found that it had been Woody who had attempted to turn Mia's children against one another. The court found that his efforts were so inciteful and ill-judged, that they warranted a 'careful monitoring' of his future contact with the children.[39]

Soon-Yi was a psychology major, with 'B' average grades and because she had been so old when Mia adopted her she had always had difficulties learning to read. There were some reports that her mother had written words on her hand, in a bid to get her to learn the language, something that humiliated her in front of classmates. Soon-Yi may have been resentful of Mia and maybe her turning to Woody was a way of getting back at her mother. But Mia was probably woefully unaware of any of these feelings, her time pre-occupied with

Woody's forthcoming adoption of Dylan and Moses. The couple had been planning to do this for some time, and papers had to be presented to the local courts.

'I had dinner with them on October 28,' said Leonard Gershe, the playwright and lyricist who is a close friend of Mia's. 'Everything was just the same. Woody spent the whole night talking about the adoption – that he was willing to move hell and high water to get it through. Would you be so anxious to adopt a child with a woman you're not going to see any more? And would she have allowed it? Maybe it was over in his mind. It certainly wasn't in hers. But if it were over, then it makes his eagerness to adopt Dylan even more sinister.'[40]

By then only Woody and Soon-Yi knew of the depth of their relationship although his crew were aware that he had a new companion to take to Knicks games – if not her real identity – and were talking about it openly. Matthew and his girlfriend Priscilla Gilman had already arrived at the conclusion that Soon-Yi had someone in her life. That summer she chose to remain in Manhattan rather than go to Connecticut with Mia, and every so often she would slip out in the evening all dressed up. The family knew she had a crush on Woody because she always dressed up before going out to ball games with him, but Matthew and Priscilla had no idea it was Woody that she was sneaking out to see. Priscilla suggested they follow her one day, but Matthew respected Soon-Yi's privacy.[41] Other reports had Woody and Soon-Yi taking his limousine together that summer, up to Connecticut every Friday to spend the weekend with Mia.

Husbands and Wives continued apace. The story about the screwed up and disintegrating relationships of a group of Manhattan friends, it revolves around the Woody and Mia characters. Woody is Gabe and Mia is Judy, living in a hell-hole of an unhappy marriage in its final throes. She wants another child but Gabe does not. Gabe is tempted to have an affair with his 19-year-old

student Rain (Juliette Lewis). Rain goes on a date with
Gabe – to a basketball game.

'Do you hide things from me?'
Judy to Gabe, *Husbands and Wives*

Allen finished writing the script in the summer of 1991
just as he was becoming closer to Soon-Yi. The shooting
started in November and it wrapped on January 20, seven
days after Mia discovered nude pictures of Soon-Yi which
convinced her that Woody had been having an affair with
the young woman.

Woody has said that there was no 'cataclysmic event'
leading to his love for Soon-Yi, but according to Mia's
lawyers, it was his 56th birthday on December 1, 1991
when her lawyers claim that the two began sleeping
together. It would not seem unlikely. As friends of Mia
point out, you have to be very, very close to someone
indeed, to strip naked and pose for nude photographs.
Since Mia discovered nude pictures on December 13, it
does not take a tremendous stretch of the imagination to
believe that Soon-Yi and Woody must have been intimate
for a long time before then. Mia's side alleged they had
been sleeping together for many weeks before then. The
exact start of the sexual affair became crucial in a later
court battle, after the custody hearing which Mia was to
win. The adoptions of Dylan and Moses were finalised in
mid December. It was Mia's contention that they should
subsequently be nullified, because when the adoption
papers were being signed, Woody had fraudulently concealed his relationship with their sister Soon-Yi. Woody's
lawyers would contend 'there is no proof of fraud ...'
Regardless of these later events, the adoption of Dylan
and Moses was as rich in irony as many of Woody's
scripts.

Yet never before had two single people been permitted
to adopt a child in New York. It was only because of their

265

good standing that their lawyers were able to get the papers pushed through court. Their lawyer, Paul Martin Weltz, said, 'To have a second parent of the intellectual ability and the financial ability of a Woody Allen – how could anybody at that point think of a single negative?'[42]

Mia was not thinking of anything at that stage but her work and the three other children she was planning to adopt. They were Tam, a blind Vietnamese girl, and Isaiah, a crack addicted baby. She had also set her heart on another child. Pre-occupied with this, and the children already in the family, and overwhelmed with work on *Husbands and Wives*, Mia was blissfully unaware of the timebomb ticking beneath her nose. *Husbands and Wives*, was possibly, as *New York* magazine later pointed out, the first movie made about a scandal before the scandal had broken out.

Mia began to have her suspicions and on December 13, in a panic, went over to his apartment in search of proof while Woody was out filming. There, on the mantelpiece, she discovered a set of Polaroid pictures of Soon-Yi in the nude, tucked into a Kleenex box. He would later call them 'erotic'; she called them 'pornographic', a description verified by the later court description of the six photographs: 'She is posed reclining on a couch with her legs spread apart'. Mia was utterly shocked, not expecting to find anything as bad as this. She was later to believe he had placed the pictures there deliberately as a way of getting her to end the relationship. By this time he had legally adopted Dylan and Moses, and Mia was convinced this was a ploy to finally end it with her. She was furious with herself for signing papers which described him as 'far more of a father [to Dylan] than most natural fathers are or choose to be.'[43] Mia was rapidly coming to believe Woody had behaved cruelly to her.

In a state of blind fury she burst into tears and phoned a friend before calling Soon-Yi who slammed the phone down on her. Immediately afterwards she phoned

Woody Allen and told him to stay away from her children. Mia raced across Central Park to her own apartment. Woody was putting in the last few days' shooting on *Husbands and Wives*. It was a critical juncture but he closed the set for the remainder of the day and rushed over to Mia's place where a screaming match ensued.

The exact sequence of events after this may never be known and were probably too frenzied for the participants to remember correctly, but Mia's friend Leonard Gershe was struck by how Woody appeared unmoved by the moral implications of what he had done. 'I don't think he really understands what everybody's excited about,'[44] said Gersche. It's a failing Woody *has* acknowledged in the past – an inability to distinguish between what is moral and what is not. He told Eric Lax of an instance when he tried to con his grandfather out of a few small cents with no guilt about the moral implications.[45] Even those friends of his who do not believe Mia's worst accusations conceded that the relationship with Soon-Yi was 'abusive' in the sense only that he was a worldly adult taking advantage of an unworldly young woman who had not even had a date before. But time and time again, since the incident hit the headlines, Woody has appeared generally unmoved by any calls to morality.

A close associate of André Previn says, 'His morality flew out of the window when he concealed the fact that he was having an affair with the sister of his two children before they were adopted – that was immoral. It was wrong and he should never have done that and that was a dishonest thing to do. Which makes me wonder whether this man has many morals because in the good old days if one was faced with a moral dilemma and you knew you were doing something that was incorrect, you would say "I may not do this".

'When he purportedly fell in love with Soon-Yi he should have had more self control and said that even if I am going to finish my relationship with her mother, I should not have an affair with this child. It's as simple as that.'[46]

Mia's own recollections of Woody's behaviour on the day she discovered the pictures, paint a picture of a man unmoved by his actions. When he first came around to her apartment, she begged him to leave. Then: 'He came back less than an hour later, and I was sitting at the table. By then, all of our children were there ... and it was a rather silent meal. The little ones were chatting and he walked right in and he sat right down at the table as if nothing had happened. He started chatting with the two little ones, said 'hi' to everybody, and one by one the children took their plates and left. And I didn't know what to do. And then I went out.'

For the next few days Mia was in a state of jealous rage towards Soon-Yi and bitterness towards Woody. She confronted the girl when she was on the telephone, and thrusting the nude pictures in her face, demanded to know how Soon-Yi could have interfered in her relationship with Woody. The young girl taunted her, 'the person sleeping with the person is the one with the relationship.' Her mother, in tears of rage, pounced on her, kicking the phone on to her leg and slapping Soon-Yi across the face. Soon-Yi fought back and had to see a doctor after the struggle. Mia was so distraught she wrapped a photocopied picture of her nude daughter around a carving knife and plunged it into a picture of herself. Yet she went on working on *Husbands and Wives*. Much was to be made later of her washed out looks in the movie which depicted a similarly disintegrating family situation, but in fact those scenes had been completed long before Mia knew about Soon-Yi.

Mia's friend Casey Pascal says Soon-Yi insisted to her that she had never realised Mia would find out. The following weekend there was a big confrontation with the rest of the family at Frog Hollow. Dylan and Satchel watched the television, the other children – including Priscilla Gilman – had a meeting with Soon-Yi. They gave her the choice of staying if she promised it would never happen again, but she just stormed out.

Not long after Mia finished her last two days of shooting on *Husbands and Wives* Tisa Farrow said: 'She was in denial obviously. He made her feel like she couldn't live without him. She took a long time to get pissed off. She's no less vulnerable just because she's an actress and has money.'[47] She was annoyed enough to send her ex-lover an elaborate Valentine's Day card with pictures of her children pierced with turkey skewers. And he was cruel enough to send her a red satin box with an antique heart inside it.

It was astonishing in view of the circumstances that both of them managed to carry on something approaching a normal life while the wreckage of their relationship bobbed around them. In February, the 11-year-old Vietnamese girl Tam arrived and not long after the crack addicted baby Isaiah whom Woody went to the airport to pick up. They also dealt with a six-year-old Vietnamese boy recovering from polio, the two of them had been going to adopt. In fact it turned out he had cerebral palsy and was retarded which Mia couldn't cope with so she sent him to a New Mexico family who already had older retarded children and wanted him.

Her version is that Woody wanted to come back. She sought a psychologist's help for the first time in her adult life, and was given an antidepressant which provoked a bad reaction. Her mind was in a confused and bewildered state and she wrote a suicide note which she subsequently ripped up. She suffered so many panic attacks, Mia decided to give up the therapy and pills. But remarkably she continued seeing Woody – once at Elaine's and once elsewhere, where she says he suggested making it up together and ripping up the pictures of nude Soon-Yi.

One of Mia's problems was that in addition to being

emotionally tied to Woody, she had become dependent on the work he gave her, to the exclusion of every other director and movie opportunity. She had invested 12 years of her life in him. Through nobody's fault in particular she had cut herself off from the film community. Although Woody's sister Letty would disparagingly describe her as a 'second rate actress', that was hardly fair. Her acting in his movies had certainly been on a par with many of the biggest names in Hollywood. But she had turned down dozens of other requests to appear in films. Partly because Woody persuaded her to stick with him, but also because she wanted the comfort and security of working in Manhattan, where she could earn a living and at the same time take care of her children.

Woody used to make films cheaply but that was no longer necessarily the case. In 1992 *Variety* reported that 'Woody Allen makes expensive pictures and demands a rich deal.' And hands on the set of *Husbands and Wives* noted that there was no shortage of cash available then. One day the whole crew transported itself to Long Island where a beach scene was due to be shot but due to beautiful blue skies, the crew was moved back to Manhattan. Woody doesn't like blue skies. 'That's 200,000 dollars down the drain!' laughed one crew member.

Yet Mia was only being paid 200,000 dollars a movie by then, a pathetic amount even for a 'second rate actress' who, in most of Woody's films, was the leading character. It was less even, than the sort of money she was being paid in the late Seventies for *Hurricane*, *The Wedding*, and *Death on the Nile*. Since Woody was only making an average of one movie a year, that effectively meant Mia was bringing up a colossal family on around 200,000 dollars a year – the sort of salary which would not be uncommon for medium level executives in Manhattan. But Woody would later say he often gave her cash – as much as 1 million dollars – if she was ever short of money.

'Mia told me he was always telling her she had no talent at all,' said Leonard Gershe[48]. 'She was only good in his pictures, not in anybody else's. Nobody would ever hire her again.' *Vanity Fair* also claimed that she would suffer blistering put-downs from Woody. He lit up on her once because she was four degrees out on the weather in the Russian Tea Room, and she didn't know how many types of pasta there were in the world.

Soon-Yi had been taken out of the family situation. Having graduated from high school, she got a job as a counsellor at a summer camp in Maine. It was a situation which Mia thought gave her an opportunity to try and patch things up with Woody. Then she received a letter from the summer camp management which informed her that Soon-Yi had been fired because she did not get on with the children and had been receiving strange phone calls from someone called 'Mr Simon'. The letter advised her: 'Throughout the entire orientation period and continuing during camp, Soon-Yi was constantly involved with telephone calls. Phone calls from a gentleman whose name was Mr Simon seemed to be her primary focus and this definitely detracted from her concentration on being a counsellor.' Mia was plunged into frenzy once more. At first Woody denied that he was 'Mr Simon' then admitted he was.[49]

Then the story hit the headlines knocking the Royal scandals of the Princess of Wales and the Duchess of York out of the news. André Previn told reporters he thought Allen's behaviour towards his daughter was despicable. A source close to Previn emphasised that there were no feelings of ill will against Allen personally, merely the thought of a young girl sleeping with a man so much older. 'André's very distressed about the whole thing and he finds the whole thing unbearable. He was very very distraught about his daughter. It was one of the most distressing things that he had to undergo recently. It was a dreadful situation and not one I would recommend for any father who loves his daughter. It could have been any other father who behaves towards his daughter and her mother. One simply doesn't do that.'

The news broke coincidentally with the run up to the launch of *Husbands and Wives*. TriStar Pictures immediately brought the launch forward to capitalise on the publicity. It is a well-known fact in the industry that Woody Allen pictures do not make money so TriStar can hardly be blamed. (To save Woody publicity, they sympathetically excused him from interview junkets to promote the film.)

Instead of opening in just eight cities as the original plan had been, TriStar decided to screen it at an unprecedented 800 movie houses across America. Already, bootleg copies of *Husbands and Wives* were circulating for 200 dollars a go. Never before had life and art intermingled as much as this. On August 25 a special screening was held for the press which proved to be an uncomfortable feeling of *déjà vu* for those watching the director's private life unfold on the screen.

This story of people falling apart as they find they can no longer talk to one another or make love was enough to strain the credibility of Woody Allen's claims that his films are not autobiographical. When Juliette Lewis pulls away from kissing her English professor she asks him 'Do you seduce all your students?' a ripple of sniggering broke out in the theatre.

David Denby, the *New York* magazine film critic observed, 'Did Woody Allen create his own disasters as a kind of neurotic's delight – immolating himself as a longed-for and utterly satisfying revenge against himself?'

Scenes From A Marriage

'"No! No! Don't tell André about it!" He was rolling on the floor. "My stomach hurts, my stomach hurts." André said, "What's that?" I said, "That's Woody, rolling on the floor."'

Mia Farrow (Court testimony, March 29, 1992)

This, according to Mia's sworn testimony, was the moment Woody was forced to face the truth about his relationship with her adopted daughter Soon-Yi. She was arguing with him in her Central Park West apartment, when André Previn called on the phone. What followed was to delight Woody fans who could barely stifle their giggles, while the director's detractors regarded the thought of a grown man behaving like a bad little boy with stern rebuke. Mia *did* tell André, and the news stunned her ex-husband who was widely reported the next day saying Woody's behaviour was 'despicable' and that he wished better for his daughter. From that moment on, Soon-Yi occupied André Previn's mind day and night.

His wife Heather, was a great admirer of Woody's work, and emphasised that André had not been attacking Woody personally, merely the idea of such an older man taking up with such a young girl. She said, 'The comment was not a reflection on Mr Allen, whom my husband doesn't know at all. I think it was a fairly natural reaction that any father might have had. André felt that the man had behaved with a certain lack of discretion *vis-à-vis* André's daughter.

'André's very distressed about the whole thing and he

273

finds it unbearable. He was very, very distraught about his daughter. It was one of the most distressing things that he has had to undergo recently. It was a dreadful situation and not one I would recommend for any father who loves his daughter.' Soon-Yi became estranged from both Mia and André, refusing their entreaties to return home, and staying on the campus of her New Jersey college when she was not with Woody in Manhattan. But it would soon become apparent that the blossoming young woman who had sparked the scandal, was not going to be centre stage over the months of wranglings that followed. That role was handed to Woody's adopted child Dylan, the girl he readily admitted to being obsessed with, and whom he now tried to keep custody of to the exclusion – if necessary – of Soon-Yi from his life.

The scandal and court case which followed Mia and Woody's public bust-up, will go down in movie world folklore just as surely as those that toppled his hero Charlie Chaplin and her old friend Roman Polanski. The relationship with Soon-Yi was sensational enough, but when Woody was alleged to have abused Dylan at Frog Hollow farm, the tabloid press had a field day. The accusations dated back to August 4, 1992 when Woody had travelled to Connecticut to spend time with his children. Mia, still trying to recover from his behaviour with Soon-Yi, and cope with his over-indulgence of Dylan, had warned her baby sitter Kristie Groteke, not to allow the two to be alone together. What then happened is still a source of bitter dispute, but the result was that Mia took Dylan to a local paediatrician and the little girl eventually accused her father of molesting her. The Connecticut State Police were brought in and Woody initiated an action to gain custody of Satchel, Dylan and Moses. This up until now private couple appeared in court to air their dirty laundry in public. But for months beforehand, interspersed with comical episodes, they exchanged insults in a farrago of allegations and counter allegations in the press and on television.

Mia at first seemed to claim that Woody had abused their daughter Dylan in circumstances which even his detractors found hard to believe. Mia made the notorious video of Dylan making the accusations. It was alleged that he had whisked the seven-year-old girl into a small attic at Mia's Frog Hollow farm, and had been caught behaving in a dubious manner with the child by a baby sitter. Mia, who was in the habit of recording the children's activities on a portable video camera, subsequently taped Dylan who, it was claimed, repeated verbal allegations that she had already made against Woody. The tape recording was to become the subject of some debate. Woody's side argued that it was a strange way for a concerned mother to behave when confronted with serious allegations of child abuse. And his side also claimed the tape showed signs of being 'doctored' while Mia's questions to Dylan appeared to be 'coaching' the little girl. Mia stood by the video, but it proved to be a liability rather than a help. While nobody – except Woody – doubted her good intentions in making the film, it added credence to the image of her as an 'hysterical' woman, and a team of specialists which viewed the video were able ultimately to dismiss it although there was certainly no proof that Mia had doctored the tape or coached the child.

'Allegedly, I took her to the attic, according to what the child protection agency told me was the allegation, and did unspeakable things to her. But nothing at all happened. Nothing. In light years I wouldn't go into an attic, I wouldn't even know how to find Mia's attic. I'm a famous claustrophobic.'[1] Woody pointed out that on the eve of hammering out a child custody agreement, he was hardly likely to drive to Connecticut and molest a child in broad daylight.[2]

Woody told legendary New York writer Pete Hamill (brother of Brian, the photographer who has worked with Woody for many years) that before the child abuse charges surfaced, Mia had called him and said she had a nasty shock in store for him. '"What are you planning to do, shoot me?" She said, "No, I'm not going to shoot you, but it's pretty nasty..."'[3] Hamill claimed 75 per cent of child abuse charges turn out to be unsubstantiated. On TV and in print, Woody was to claim repeatedly that Mia had threatened him with violence, but when it came to the court case, Mia denied ever making any threats of violence against her ex-lover although she did concede that an allusion to 'putting his eyes out' had been a 'misunderstanding'.[4]

Woody was later shown to be less than straightforward in his dealings with Mia, and it's possible that his claims of her threats were engineered to assist his case. But even if Mia did issue warnings, veiled or otherwise, it would hardly be the first time that a bust-up between two lovers had resulted in threats of bodily violence.

The video fell into the hands of Rupert Murdoch's Fox Five network in New York. They refused to show it and would not reveal where they had acquired it from. But soon details of the accusations leaked. Woody's side claimed that the video had clearly been doctored and Dylan had been prompted to make the charges. Mia cooperated with a 'picture spread' in *Hello!* and the widely read magazine *Vanity Fair* splashed a huge exposé of Woody across its glossy pages. Claiming to be 'Mia's Story' and quoting Tisa Farrow and Maureen O'Sullivan as well as other sources named and anonymous, *Vanity Fair* painted an unappetising portrait of the director of whom, it was said, there was an 'unwritten rule' not to allow him to be alone with Dylan. Both magazines pictured Mia with a little boy lost look which did not go down too well in all quarters. 'For a *Hello!* photo spread, she chose to appear as Little Lord Fauntleroy in knee socks and cord knickerbockers and Fair Isle. For her *Vanity Fair* exclusive she engaged the manipulative lens of Annie Leibowitz. Here she goes one step too far. She has one knee sock pulled up and the other bagging down around her ankles. The hobnail boot is *de rigueur*. How can knee socks be taken seriously on anyone over eight, let alone 48? It's like knitting an angora sweater for a boa constrictor. And wasn't Dory Previn all too prophetic when she wrote a song *Beware Of Little Girls* soon after Mia had stolen her husband.'[5] Woody vowed to sue immediately and Mia disclaimed responsibility for the story, finally telling a TV station: 'I never accused Woody of child molestation.'[6] Her sister Tisa, also appeared to cast doubt on the molestation charges.

A close friend of them both loyally said: 'She never did say he molested her. It was never her who said it. It was the paediatrician in Connecticut. He felt that the child may have been molested and it was his duty to report it to the powers that be. An enormous machine started that neither Woody nor Mia or anybody could stop. From that instant on it was taken out of Mia Farrow's hands.' But these disclaimers were disingenuous to say the least. If Mia had not actually said publicly that Woody had molested Dylan, she and her friends and family had certainly fuelled the charges and at first did nothing to stop the wilder allegations.

Money, as ever, became an issue with Mia initially failing in a bid to get Woody to pick up her 300,000 dollar legal bills after he successfully proved she was hardly poor. For his part, he was to hire seven lawyers and spend more than 2 million dollars on the case during which it emerged that his net worth was 'a mere 16 million dollars' which by Manhattan and showbiz standards is woefully low. Mia claimed it was actually in excess of 20 million dollars, which is roughly what Arnold Schwarzenegger was reportedly paid for just one film several years ago. It was revealed that Mia was worth some 4 million dollars, mainly in stocks, bonds and cash. Her 70-acre Connecticut farm, Frog Hollow was valued at a modest 500,000 dollars and the public were dismayed to read that her enormous

New York apartment was rent-stabilised at around 1,200 dollars a month: less than what some one-bedroomed downtown hovels cost. Soon she was to sign a 3 million dollar deal to write her autobiography. She also agreed to appear in John Irvin's *Widow's Peak*, due to be made in Ireland. Her fee was not disclosed, but given the size of star salaries and the likely box office potential her new-found notoriety guaranteed, it would not be surprising if she eventually gets more money for one film than Woody ever paid her for all his.

Woody's side claimed Mia's representatives had demanded a 8 million dollar payment in return for 'stone-walling' the child molestation probe.[7] One of Mia's attorneys was the flamboyant Harvard law professor Alan Dershowitz who had earned fame from a string of celebrity cases, notably when he won an acquittal for Claus von Bulow on charges of trying to murder his wife. More recently, Dershowitz represented disgraced hotel queen Leona Helmsley, and heavyweight champ Mike Tyson. Mia had spotted Dershowitz's book *Chutzpah* on Woody's bedside table, and telephoned him as soon as the crisis struck. Dershowitz was also accused of offering Woody a 'down and dirty' agreement of 5 million dollars. But Mia's side cast scorn on both 'blackmail' claims, saying the figures were a reference to an informal discussion about the cost of child support trust funds. In any case, tabloid newspaper readers were soon titillated to see a photograph of a Chase Manhattan cheque written out to Mia for 1 million dollars from Woody.[8] He had written it in September 1990 to cover Moses, Dylan and Satchel's education and health expenses before the imbroglio had arisen.

More titillation at Woody's expense was going on in the privacy of Mia's home where, in court documents, Woody claimed that the actress had shown guests the home movie video she had taken of Dylan 'over drinks for their entertainment'. Woody demanded a copy for himself. *The Daily News* quoted a source saying, 'If you didn't get invited to watch this at the house, she would frequently send them home with their own cassette.' Woody's court petition claimed hilariously: 'Everyone in the states of New York and Connecticut has seen it, why can't [Allen]?' Mia's attorneys agreed that at least three friends had seen the tape but it had not been for entertainment. They were the singer Carly Simon who is a close friend and neighbour of Mia; Rose Styron, wife of the author William Styron, and author George Plimpton who said he was a 'little bit surprised' when Farrow fetched the tape. 'There wasn't anything frivolous about it. I think she wanted to share her anguish,' he said.[9]

In happier times it had been common practice for Mia to film the activities of her children, so the tape playing incident was not as bizarre as it appeared. It was, perhaps, only natural that a mother in the heat of the media limelight, which was sometimes hostile toward her, would want to prove her sincerity by showing friends the tape of Dylan.

One of the most important precepts of Dershowitz's 'campaign strategy' when faced with a public battle is to present the best possible image for his client, particularly when that image has been tarnished. 'In America, you cannot win your cases unless you win them first in the court of public opinion.'[10] He immediately set about presenting Mia as a good and loving mother. Meanwhile Woody was working on his own public image, allowing photographers to picture him without hiding under his hat and performing conspicuously noble acts. At one stage he was spotted donating 160 dollars to a charity for infants with AIDS. Woody has always been a strong supporter of charities, and friends speak about his generosity to people in need. But before it had always been in private. In another story headlined, 'Woody to the Rescue', it was described how he valiantly saved Jean Doumanian from choking on a piece of Italian bread at the Primola restaurant by heroically deploying the 'Heimlich Manoeuvre'. He eventually granted an interview to the glossy celebrity magazine, *Hello!*, a publication that Mia had already appeared in at the start.

Woody had already granted two interviews to *Newsweek* and *Time*, whose executives had been under the mistaken impression they were getting an exclusive, and were somewhat miffed when each ran almost identical stories simultaneously. Now Woody invited CBS's popular news magazine show *60 Minutes* into the very same penthouse apartment where he had entertained the print journalists. 'On many, many occasions, over the phone and in person, Mia had said to me, "You took my daughter, and I'm going to take yours,"' he told correspondent Steve Kroft. 'She threatened to have me killed and kill me. And then to stick my eyes out, to blind me. Because she became obsessed with Greek tragedy and felt that that would be a fitting, you know, vengeance … When you get a phone call at four in the morning saying that you're going to be killed and that your eyes are going to be put out, you get scared because it's the middle of the night and your heart's beating.'[11] Later, in court, Mia was to deny ever making such threats, although she agreed she had compared herself to a character from the book *The Trojan Woman* named Hecuba, who puts out a man's eyes. But she pointed out that if Woody had sincerely been scared, he would have hired 'a hundred' bodyguards,[12] echoing Alan Dershowitz's claim after the '60 Minutes' TV appearance that Woody was such an insecure soul he would have called the police if he thought his life was really threatened. André Previn was quoted as saying, 'Mr Allen has acted with complete disregard for morality and ethics. He is laughable.'[13]

When the scandal had first broken, some of Mia's children turned up at newspaper offices and one appeared on CNN, prompting Woody to accuse the actress of parading her kids in front of the cameras for her own ends. In fact, Mia's children appeared to be acting independently of their mother, and it was really only Moses who made an early and ill-advised appearance before the cameras outside Frog Hollow. The rest of the time, given the press scrutiny, she could hardly help being pictured coming and going with the boys and girls. But now she kept a dignified silence over his TV appearance much to the annoyance of her friend and public relations consultant John Springer. Dershowitz scoffed, 'He claims all he cares about are the children. But if he really did care about them, he would be shielding them from this media feeding frenzy.'[14]

From the serious accusations of child abuse, the case descended into petty farce with Woody and Mia behaving like two spoilt children squabbling over toys. Indeed, on Satchel's fifth birthday, just before Christmas, these two adults did squabble over toys. Woody sent his driver Donald Harris to Mia's laden with presents from the upmarket Fifth Avenue kids' store, F.A.O. Schwartz, for Satchel *and* Dylan with hand-written notes saying, 'I love you, daddy'. It was a tradition that both children got presents on each other's birthdays. But in an affidavit Harris said Mia tore the notes off the gifts. But Mia's attorney said Dylan had become upset when she learn the presents were from Allen.

Gossips on the set of his movie *Manhattan Murder Mystery* claimed that Woody conducted a quick straw poll asking who they would prefer to be marooned on a desert island with: Mia Farrow or Diane Keaton. The winner, apparently, was Mia, although Woody's office said the whole story was 'absurd'. In the meantime, Mia was winning the heart of private detective Tom Mullen staking out her building. Mullen was on the trail of somebody else, but Mia thought he was after her. Spotting him in his car, she confronted Mullen but he assured her he was only performing some surveillance work on someone else. 'Are you sure you're not spying on me?' she demanded. He assured her that he wasn't. 'Do you swear to God on the Holy Bible?' He did. 'Do you swear on my kids?' she demanded. Mullen went one better and pulled out a snapshot of his two sons. He said, 'She held my hand, looked into my eyes and made me swear. She seemed to believe me then.'[15]

Every conceivable person with a link to the battling duo, was drawn into the controversy. Woody and Mia's respective doormen and driver had their say on the matter. Woody's, Nick Shkneli, described the director as a 'a very nice guy, a genius and a great tipper.' While a 68-year-old doorman at Mia's place says: 'Mia and her mother are great people, they don't make them like that anymore.'[16] Now it was the battle of the nannies. Nannies and baby sitters took sides in a series of claims and counter claims, none of which were ever to have any real impact on the final court case.

When Woody and Mia's day in court finally came, they were before Justice Elliott Wilk in the mundane Room 341 of Manhattan's State Supreme Court, an impressive neo-Roman structure in the city's administrative downtown district. The trial began on March 19, 1993 after a team of child-abuse experts at Connecticut's Yale-New Haven Hospital had cast serious doubt on the allegations about Woody. He appeared at the court house arriving in the old station wagon he often used to get to his movie sets and wearing a tweed jacket. The arrivals and departures of the two celebrities and their cohorts of advisers and attorneys became a great spectacle for the crowds of lesser known litigants, defendants and workers who crowded the dingy interior halls.

Mia, whose performance before the trial Woody had sarcastically described as hardly Oscar-winning, actually won some sympathy during the hearings despite an apparently contrived effort to look like a demure Catholic convent girl. 'She's in the courtroom hurling accusations at Woody Allen to do with emotional incest and child abusing, and she's coming on like an abused child,' noted one writer. 'Her garb is flat shoes, Peter Pan collars and pleated skirts.'[17]

Newspaper reporters covering the hearing noticed that her most frequent reply to questions was, 'I don't recall', and many of her responses were delivered with a 'touch of dramatic flair'.[18] At one stage she testified that she believed Woody 'might' be gay, prompting his lawyer to ask her outright if she believed that to be true. The *Daily News* reporter noticed how she waited a long, long time – with considerable dramatic impact before saying, 'No'.[19]

Despite an effort to paint a malicious and vengeful portrait of Mia, the actress came across as a woman who had been drawn into a devastating emotional trauma by a man who appeared totally unaware of the hurt he had caused. If she had behaved strangely, Mia had not behaved any differently from what many women would have done. Her appearance on the witness stand was a success and it left the audience leaning towards her depiction of Woody as 'cruel and cold.'[20]

A close confidante of André Previn understood Mia's reaction. She said, 'Mia's behaviour can hardly be condoned but is entirely understandable. Don't you think that when a woman has put her trust in somebody for so many years and it transpires he's been having an affair with her daughter under her nose, do you not think that that colours the whole of the preceding 11 years? You cannot then look back with any feeling of equanimity on the entire relationship. I'm sure he can't and am sure she can't.' She was echoing Mia's own words in a letter her friend Maria Roach released in the middle of the scandal. Mia had written to her friend at the height of her distress over Woody's affair with Soon-Yi. She said Woody had left Soon-Yi 'morally bankrupt' and had 'demolished' any bond that may have existed between herself and him. Mia bewailed the loss, not just of a lover – but a child too.

But even though Woody's side acknowledged the pain

caused by his behaviour with Soon-Yi, they painted a picture of Mia hiding behind her children. His lawyer Elkan Abramowitz said that Mia had 'an absolute right' to hit the roof over Soon-Yi, but the situation should have been resolved in private without dragging the children into a public battle. 'It is vile, because she is trying to get them to fight her battle.'[21] Other aspects of Mia's behaviour which emerged during the court hearing appeared perplexing. She said that she was concerned at Woody's 'inappropriate' behaviour with Dylan, which sometimes left the child 'aroused'. She was concerned enough to raise the matter with two psychologists who told her not to worry. Days later, in an affidavit to support Woody's legal adoption of Dylan, she swore, he was 'far more of a father to [Dylan] than most natural fathers are or choose to be.'[22]

Other testimony which didn't help Mia, was the reading of a letter from Moses to Woody in which his adopted son disowned the director as a father, and hoped that Woody would become so humiliated – he would commit suicide. The letter was widely reported in huge headlines the following day.[23] Moses was a subject of Woody's attempt to secure custody, so his views mattered. But the appearance tended to lend credence to Woody's claim that Mia had 'coached' the children to say what she wanted. Despite this set-back, Woody came across as amoral and self-obsessed, genuinely puzzled as to why anyone should find it strange that he had had an affair with Soon-Yi. Questioned about his role as a dutiful father, he was incapable of answering simple questions about the children's lives, their birthdays, their friends' names and whether or not Moses liked baseball. 'I'm willing to say it, I don't know,' he confessed.[24] He recalled taking them to lots of places, but not exactly where. When shown some holiday snaps, and asked to identify where they were taken, he replied: 'Some place in Europe'.[25] He even acknowledged calling Satchel 'a little bastard',[26] but in the literal, not pejorative sense.

There were moments of humour which could have come straight out of Woody Allen movies. After Mia had discovered his affair with Soon-Yi, he claimed to have agreed to sexual trysts with Mia at the Hotel Carlyle 'to soft pedal things.'[27] It was also claimed in court that Woody had once argued that his affair with Soon-Yi was good for the young woman's shaky self-image, provoking laughter from spectators.[28] And there was positive hilarity when it was revealed that one of Mia's ex-husbands had offered to break Woody's legs. 'Miss Farrow, did you tell Dr Schultz (a family therapist) that one of your former husbands had offered to break Mr Allen's legs?' demanded Allen's lawyer, Elkan Abramowitz, as Mia visibly blushed, and spectators swapped knowing grins. Abramowitz pressed on, 'Between your two prior husbands, Mr Previn and Mr Sinatra ...' But he was stopped by a cry of 'Objection!' from Mia's lawyer, and 'Sustained!' from the judge. So we will never know whether it was the conductor from the Royal Philharmonic, or the singer from Hoboken, New Jersey, who threatened to break Woody's legs. 'It was a joke,' explained Mia meekly.[29]

It was apparent to all that the sympathies of Justice Wilk did not lie with Woody by the time his sister Letty Aronson turned up to testify on his behalf. She said Mia had behaved the worst by trying to divide the family, but admitted he had made an 'error of judgement' in beginning a sexual relationship with Soon-Yi.[30] In the midst of this on-going real life soap opera, it was this girl who had sparked the crisis and who seemed to have sunk into insignificance. For paparazzi photographers staking out Woody's apartment, Soon-Yi Previn wore the glowing smile of a newly-found actress when they snapped her coming and going in the director's car. She seemed to enjoy every minute of the attention, and the two of them were pictured strolling through the park, wandering around stores. But gradually she seemed to fall into the background, and Woody was seen lunching with his old girlfriend Diane Keaton, the star of his latest movie, *Manhattan Murder Mystery*. Jean Doumanian appeared by his side at restaurants and Knicks' games. People began to forget about the young Korean girl who Woody had said only a few months ago, that he might possibly marry.

'Regarding my love for Soon-Yi: it's real and happily all true,' Woody admitted when rumours of their affair were no more than that. 'She's a lovely, intelligent, sensitive woman who has and continues to turn my life around in a positive way.'[31] He gave glowing accounts of their life together saying that they more or less did the same things he'd done with all his women – watch Bergman films, go to ball games, get take in pizza and walk in the Park. He angrily denied reports that Soon-Yi was in some way retarded and that he had taken advantage of that. Soon-Yi had some reading difficulties, but otherwise was a perfectly average student at a good school.

The relationship he insisted, was 'serious', and could very well lead to marriage. 'I see it as a major, major situation. I see no limit for it at the moment.'[32] Soon-Yi herself said that the 'terrific' relationship with Woody was 'full of dramatic overtones' but was essentially quite simple. 'It revolves around conversations, film talk, sports talk, books and art.'[33] Woody appeared less afraid of the Press than he once had been, and was pictured walking along Fifth Avenue with his possible future bride. Delivery men were shown delivering pizzas to his apartment where the lovers were sharing a quiet night in. They were even spotted looking at rings in Tiffany's one day, and the supermarket tabloids speculated he was soon going to propose to her. But always in the background was Jean Doumanian and occasionally other women from his past like Diane Keaton.

Later his ardour for Soon-Yi seemed to have faded. Woody rarely granted television interviews, and even sued a Canadian journalist for selling an interview with him to an American network. American TV, he insisted, had persistently failed to take his movies seriously, and he didn't want to appear on the small screen in his own country. Now, in the heat of Mia Farrow's accusations, he invited CBS's *60 Minutes* to talk to him in his private sanctuary high above Fifth Avenue.

Woody's responses to *60 Minutes* correspondent Steve Kroft were terse and to the point. But he seemed to flutter a little when Kroft asked whether the relationship with Soon-Yi was still 'long term.' Woody explained Soon-Yi still had a few years to go before she graduated and was away at school where she lived. She didn't live at his apartment, which was strange for two ardent lovers, since her school in New Jersey was only a drive away from Manhattan. Kroft asked if Woody saw Soon-Yi at the weekends. He replied, 'Yeah, I see her when she get's off school, when she's off for the holiday or something ...'[34]

After seeing the show, Mia's sister Tisa scornfully pronounced that Woody already seemed bored with Soon-Yi. 'This is the "woman who turned his life around?" Now, it's "Oh, I see her on weekends and holidays." He doesn't seem so hot and heavy on her now. It sounds like he's already bored with her.' One report even claimed that Woody had proposed to Soon-Yi over the previous Thanksgiving Weekend and they would marry in the spring. But the alleged wedding date came and went without incident.

Soon-Yi was still engagement ring-less and looking somewhat forlorn and friendless in the bare room of her college in New Jersey when a reporter tracked her down. The inside of the room showed little sign of her being anything other than a young student at a typical college where, it was reported, other students tired of what they thought were Soon-Yi's delusions of grandeur. It was revealed nobody wanted to room with her, and fellow students were dismissive of the lonely girl who was not accorded the celebrity status of her lover.[35]

New York Post writer Daphne Barak discovered a girl less controlled and sure of herself than the one who had appeared in interviews with *Time* and *Newsweek* magazines which some cynics said appeared 'coached'. She asked Soon-Yi if it was true her boyfriend was losing interest in her...

'That's not true. That's not true at all that he's less interested in me ... He loves me. It's the first time in my life that someone really cares for me,' she said studiously ignoring the fact that Mia had rescued her from the streets of Seoul. 'And I don't care what people say about the age difference ... It's just pure jealousy. And you shouldn't believe anything you hear. She – Mia again – is very different from what people think ... She's just mad he never married her.'[36] For the most part though, Soon-Yi's plight went unnoticed, provoking one adoption agency to express concern at what appeared to be a racist response. If Soon-Yi had been a 'freckle-faced, all-American type,' claimed *New York Daily News* writer Betty Liu Ebron, wouldn't the public have been quicker to condemn Woody Allen's behaviour? As it is, Asian girls were branded with an 'exotic-slut stereotype,'[37] she said.

Then came the bombshell André Previn had feared. Letty Aronson indicated that her brother would break off the relationship with Soon-Yi if it helped win custody of the children.[38]

It had been the situation André Previn feared most. Mia Farrow's lawyer, Eleanor Alter, expressed her client's fears on the subject too. 'Mia feels Soon-Yi was victimised, and the horror is that she brought the person who victimised Soon-Yi into the house. She cries about Soon-Yi a lot in private. She worries what will happen to her when Woody dumps her.'[39] André Previn's wife Heather had privately expressed exactly those fears several months before.

'André is worried that the relationship is not going to

continue and he's worried for Soon-Yi because the poor little girl was swept of her feet by this older fellow and I think that if he does set her down on the other side of this and say "Thankyou but no thankyou", there will be one extremely unhappy and sad young lady. André doesn't blame Soon-Yi at all. He feels that Mr Allen took terrible advantage of a situation and he should not have done that.

'Then of course who will deal with that – it will have to be Mia and André who will deal with that again. That's where I get a little upset with Woody because he's not thinking. You know he's going to add insult to injury if he does drop Soon-Yi.

'If Soon-Yi is in love with Woody then for her this is the all-time wonderful relationship and it will be an absolutely devastating thing if Woody then says to her, "It's over". And then what happens to her – she's burnt her bridges, she's cut off her relationship with her mum, she's virtually made it clear to all and sundry that she's not interested in them as a family anymore. But if it finally ends, then what will poor Soon-Yi do?

'I would not be pleased and I don't think any mother would be pleased if their daughter's heart was broken, especially by the man that she was encouraged to run away from home with.'

The court judgement which was finally made public on June 7, 1993, was devastating to Woody although he and his lawyers tried to put a brave face on it. Contained in a 32-page summary of the trial's findings and conclusion by State Supreme Court Acting Justice Elliott Wilk was a savage indictment of Woody as a father and a man. He was described as having 'serious parental inadequacies', of being 'self-absorbed, untrustworthy, insensitive', and lacking judgement. Woody had inflicted serious damage on the children, and healing was necessary. Wilk acknowledged that Mia Farrow was not faultless, and that although she was generally a good mother, there had been problems with her relationship with Soon-Yi, Dylan and Satchel. But Wilk added: 'We do not however, demand perfection as a qualification for parenting. Ironically, Ms Farrow's principal shortcoming with respect to responsible parenting appears to have been her continued relationship with Mr. Allen.'[40]

Mia retained custody of all three children, and the only concession Woody won on visitation rights, was an extra two hours a week of supervised visitation with Satchel. He was denied visitation with Moses unless the young man agreed to it. He was denied visitation to Dylan until the girl's therapist thought conditions were right for father and daughter to be reunited. Wilk instructed that that should happen 'within six months'. The Justice branded Woody's custody action 'frivolous' and ordered the director to pay all Mia's legal bills – estimated to be in excess of 1 million dollars. He had already acknowledged spending 2 million dollars on his own lawyers. Immediately after the judgement was delivered, Woody and his lawyer Elkan Abramowitz held a press conference during which they tried to put the best spin on the result. Looking – unusually – tanned and rested, wearing a blue blazer and open neck white shirt, Woody peered wide-eyed from behind his spectacles, talking as if he had won the court battle.

But worst than Justice Wilk's verdict, were the withering words contained in the findings and summary. Wilk acknowledged that it was unlikely Woody could ever be successfully prosecuted for sexual abuse of Dylan, but he added: 'I am less certain, however, than is the Yale-New Haven team, that the evidence proves conclusively that there was no sexual abuse.'

Wilk said Woody had demonstrated no parenting skills that would qualify him as an adequate custodian for Moses, Dylan or Satchel, and that none of the witnesses who had testified on his behalf provided credible evidence in favour of giving him custody. His only response to a question of why he should be given custody, was characterised by Wilk as a 'rambling *non sequitur*' which consumed 11 pages of transcript, but supplied little credible reasoning. His deficiencies as a custodial parent were magnified by his affair with Soon-Yi, and the fact that Woody had ignored her for 10 years was no excuse for believing he was a father-figure in the Farrow household. Indeed, what seemed to be utterly perplexing to Wilk, was Woody's persistent failure to comprehend that he had done anything wrong. While Woody throughout the trial had insisted Mia had been attempting to divide her children and turn them against him, Justice Wilk found the opposite, and that Woody had not only tried to turn her biological children against the adopted ones, but even 'incited' household employees against each other.

By comparison, and despite the fact that Wilk said Mia was not without her faults, *she* emerged as almost saintly. 'It is evident that she loves her children and has devoted a significant portion of her emotional and material wealth to their upbringing. When she is not working she attends to her children. Her weekends and summers are spent in Connecticut with her children. She does not take extended vacations unaccompanied by her children. She is sensitive to the needs of her children, respectful of their opinions, honest with them and quick to address their problems.' Wilk said there was no credible evidence to support court testimony on Woody's side which claimed she favoured her biological children over her natural ones; he did not believe Mia had 'coached' Dylan on the videotape; and he dismissed Mia's notorious Valentine's Day card, her destruction of photographs, and emotional notes, as understandable anger. 'Mr Allen's resort to the stereotypical "woman scorned" defence is an injudicious attempt to divert attention from his failure to act as a responsible parent and adult.' He described Mia's determination to protect Dylan as 'commendable' and her reaction to Woody's behaviour as appropriately cautious and flexible. It was prudent, he said, for Mia to deny Woody access to Dylan after August 4, 1992.

As for Dylan, not only did Wilk question the results of the Yale-New Haven Team, who had destroyed notes and supplied a 'sanitised', and therefore 'less credible' report, he also pointed out that two doctors who had expressed doubts that Woody had sexually abused the girl, were not experts in the field, and their opinions may have been coloured by their loyalty to Woody. He also dismissed the testimony of a retired New York City police officer called by Woody's side. He claimed to have 'an intuitive ability to know if a person is truthful or not' and had concluded Dylan lacked credibility. 'I did not find [this] testimony to be insightful,' wrote Wilk, who added that although nobody would probably ever know what occurred on August 4, 1992, Woody's behaviour toward Dylan was grossly inappropriate and that measures must be taken to protect her.

Woody's relationship with Moses was superficial, opined Wilk, and he would not require the 15-year-old to visit Woody although he hoped Mia would try to promote some sort of interaction. 'I hope that Moses will come to understand that the fear of demons often cannot be dispelled without first confronting them.' Noting that Woody's relationship with his own natural son Satchel, had been 'strained', Wilk nevertheless said it was commendable that he wanted to spend more time with him – if sincere. He had restricted visitation rights to the boy, not because he feared for Satchel's safety, but because of Woody's '...demonstrated inability to understand the impact that his words and deeds have upon the emotional well being of his children.' He added, 'I believe that Mr Allen will use Satchel in an attempt to gain information about Dylan and insinuate himself into her good graces.'

Louise Lasser had been right when, on a freezing cold day during the previous February, she had said: 'This whole thing is nothing to do with Soon-Yi. It's about Dylan. Mia would have recovered from the affair with Soon-Yi. But Mia never recovered from the realisation that Dylan replaced her in Woody's affections.'

Louise Lasser has just finished giving her regular acting classes at Carnegie Hall. She takes the brisk, mile long walk through Central Park to her 20th storey home in an apartment block on the Upper East Side. On the left in the distance as she follows the ice encrusted footpath, is Mia Farrow's West Side apartment from where, in happier days, she would wave to Woody in his penthouse on the East Side. A bit further down from Mia's place peeking over the bare trees, is the eyrie with panoramic views which Diane Keaton had decorated in stark white.

Louise walks her 14-year-old dog Pushky across the cycle tracks and under the roadways of the Park, arriving on Fifth Avenue at the busy intersection with 72nd Street where honking Yellow Cabs and whistling cops vie for attention.

'I've lived here all my life,' she says looking through the rising steam at the solid bank of concrete wealth towering over the avenue. 'We lived on 77th. Woody lives over there in a penthouse – it's beautiful – and my parents lived where the terraces are ... Then we lived just there – where I think Dick Cavett lives now – and now I live just around the corner a house-and-a-half away from someone I was deeply involved with a couple of years ago.'

Woody's world is a small one, concentrated on a select number of city blocks in Manhattan's Upper East Side, and rarely having anything to do with the outside world. Not unlike his films, his thoughts and his obsessions rarely stray outside the town and its incestuous intellectual community. His near neighbourhood in Manhattan is home to many of the people who have played a role in Woody's life, and who have been fictionalised as characters in his work with immense success. It's a world insulated from the uncertainties and fears that appear to have overwhelmed Woody for all his life. And just as he has sought refuge in familiar surroundings with a familiar cast of characters real, fictional and imagined, Woody's life, both on and off camera, has woven a thread which returns repeatedly to similar passions, fears and longings invariably dating back to his childhood.

To all intents and purposes, Woody Allen is a movie mogul. His films may gross less than most, but he has more control over them than any other actor or director in the business. He may live modestly in a New York flat with none of the usual star trappings of beach homes and country estates. But he's a multi-millionaire capable of painlessly writing out a cheque for 1 million dollars to Mia Farrow. 'When she said, "I'm short of money" I gave her 1 million dollars, I gave her 100,000 dollars,' he testified.[41]

Yet despite all this, which would surely make most people feel secure, Woody still appears to be the insecure little boy who is frightened of the dark, and who gets stomach ache when he doesn't want to do something. Old enough to be a grandfather, he was still chasing girls in the best traditions of those silver screen rakes he admired as a boy, and not unlike his heroes Groucho Marx and Charlie Chaplin. How many other 57-year-old men could sit down with a reporter, looking every bit the little boy lost, and talking, in a peculiarly teenage way, about 'dating' girls and getting 'hot and heavy'.

Just as he never seems to have left his boyhood behind, either wilfully or subconsciously, the same themes that first emerged then crop up time and time again in his later life. Great and lasting friendships inspiring loyalty and trust from people he has not spoken to in years. But also doomed and broken relationships, sexual failure and experimentation, endless guilt over affairs with his best friends' women.

Time and time again Woody would insist he was not the character depicted in his films. Repeatedly he would deny that his movies were based more than loosely on any form of reality. The denials come with an unblinkering conviction – yet they fly in the face of every shred of evidence. Woody Allen has absorbed every detail of his life and poured it into his work, sometimes producing startlingly original movies, and more often than not rehashing old and familiar ideas into new and equally entertaining forms.

His writing and the first movies were littered with references to his parents, childhood friends and sweethearts: Jerry Epstein was the Dr Epstein in *Take the Money and Run* and in the same movie, Virgil's wife was 'Louise'; Sid Caesar's TV family were the Victors; his mother and father were relentlessly parodied as Groucho Marx lookalikes intermittently on the screen and in stand-up comic routines. He has bared his private life for all to see, from inconsequential details like his birth date on the blackboard, and his old head teacher Eudora Fletcher, to more personal revelations; like Mia Farrow's adopted children in *Hannah and Her Sisters* and in *Annie Hall* he even publicised the pseudonym 'Max' which he used privately, supposedly to escape the limelight.

Much of his nightclub routine was devoted to real life boyhood experiences, and jokes about his first wife Harlene which he, presumably, laughed off, but which she sued him over because they were so cruel. Louise Lasser recognises herself in several different movies, and *Interiors* is acknowledged by her and Jack Victor to be an accurate portrait of her family. Vicky Tiel and Bryna Goldstein both recognise parts of themselves in movies. *Annie Hall* was one long – and affectionate – joke about Diane Keaton, and the series of movies he made with Mia Farrow came so close to their real life experiences that it's absurd to pretend their remarkable cinematic collaboration was *only* fiction. Audiences were stunned – literally – by *Husbands and Wives* which was greeted with an eerie and uncomfortable silence at early private press screenings, and stifled laughter later when the general public flocked in unusual numbers to see the film. The characters, the plot, the emotions, were all so close to reality that it seemed implausible to have been based on anything *other* than reality.

But friends have observed in Woody an ability to deny reality. Perhaps it's an ability we all share, but Woody seems to have turned it into a fine art, eradicating any fact or event which doesn't fit into his perfectly envisioned scheme of things, or which may cast him in a less than satisfactory light. As friends were surprised how he could ignore the obvious anti-Semitism of his youth, Woody displays a tendency to shoo unpleasantry out of his life.

And always his denials come with a wide-eyed and almost consciously unblinkered innocence of somebody who cannot take the accusations seriously. When Martin Konigsberg saw before his very eyes Louise Lasser's furniture being moved out of Woody's flat as their relationship reached its end, his son's only response was to deny anything was afoot. 'Nothing's happening, dad. Are you crazy? What do you mean?' he said at the time.

Nothing ever seems to change in Woody's world – real or imagined. Despite five counsellors and countless hours of analysis, and despite years of searching for some hidden meaning to life, Woody remains as perplexed and bewildered as ever. He will protest that each of his movies explores different territory to the last, but practically all of them peddle the same themes with what some believe is monotonous regularity.

What has changed dramatically is Woody's own circumstances and professional confidence. Years ago as a struggling entertainer Harlene caught him showing nude pictures of her to a friend. He turned as red as a beetroot and was lost for words, his friend observed. In 1991, a similar set of nude pictures were to escalate an argument with Mia Farrow. But when he was caught in the unwelcome glare of the press in the ensuing imbroglio, he confronted the crisis in the same masterful manner he had used to win himself unprecedented artistic control over his work. Like a seasoned public relations man, he stepped confidently on to a podium at the Plaza Hotel and issued a terse public statement, quipping with newsmen on the way out as he was to do with many of them over the next few months.

And there was one more crucial difference between the Harlene and Soon-Yi pictures: on the latter occasion Mia suspected Woody had left the intimate Polaroids of her daughter in a deliberate attempt to provoke a row. Woody, the guileless intellectual had become Woody the calculating manipulator who knew how to inflict as much emotional damage as possible. It's a long way from the 'scared little rabbit' his old friend Len Maxwell once described, or the Woody who told Nora Ephron that he had 'an inordinate amount of difficulty coping with situations others don't find trying'.

But the image of the hapless little man, hopelessly at odds with the world, was always the most disengenuous of Woody's fictions. That quote in particular which he gave to Ephron smacks of a familiar pretence shared by would-be highbrows, who like to think that their minds are so full of the important questions in life, they really can't cope with mundane matters like telephones and cars.

Friends speak of how Woody was, unlikely as it may seem, always in charge of their small group. They remember how he would drive Nettie to distraction by deliberately provoking her, playing with the emotions of a mother who found her son too hard to handle. Louise Lasser was attracted to this very element of control. 'Women are looking for a man to be in control,' she says. 'And movie directors are the ultimate controllers. That's what they do: direct.'

'He's a control freak,' says veteran film expert Doug Brode. 'He's notorious for suing and he wants to make sure everything that's written about him is the way he wants it written.' Brode recalled the experience of an exceptionally talented and widely admired Canadian TV movie journalist who earned Woody's wrath after selling an interview with the director to an American TV network. Brode is the author of a totally uncontroversial book on Woody's work. But since it was published, Woody has failed to respond to any of Brode's letters.

Brode has an interesting reflection on Woody's current plight. 'Think for a moment about the scandal and the fact that Woody Allen has lost control of his popular image – completely – more so than any other celebrity ever has. Imagine being a control freak who would sue a very nice guy because his interview appears on the wrong channel, and then think how he must feel today when all his control has been taken away.'

Control permeates every aspect of Woody Allen's life. From the cab driver who once picked him up in New York and was subjected to a barrage of instructions as to which precise route to take and which exact lane to drive in, to the unprecedented control he has over his movies, a contract envied by every other director in the business.

His desire to be in charge is no better illustrated than in his relationship with women from whom he demands, and usually gets, unswerving loyalty. Louise Lasser has little or nothing to do with Woody today, but she freely admits that he dominated her life from the moment they met until many years after their break-up. So much so, that when she was a television star and was offered a lucrative book contract, Woody persuaded her not to sign it for fear that she would be obliged to discuss their private life. He was no longer her husband at this stage, yet she agreed to his request.

Stacey Nelkin became close to Woody during the shooting of *Annie Hall* and later admitted the director had based Mariel Hemingway's character in *Manhattan* on her. But despite claims by friends that he had manipulated her, Stacey rushed to the defence of her ex-lover when confronted by the Press.

The women in Woody's movies are invariably neurotic or vulnerable in some way. And more often than not, the women Woody associates with in private display similar characteristics. Mia Farrow has been painted by many as a scheming and manipulative woman. But there is much about her which genuinely is vulnerable. Louise Lasser is the first to admit that for many years her relationship with Woody was a father-daughter or even a doctor-patient one. It's grossly unfair to charge, as many have, that Diane Keaton owes her whole acting career to Woody Allen. In fact, the actress was a bigger 'star' than him when they met, and she subsequently struck out on her own in a number of highly-praised roles. But her best work was with Woody, she is invariably associated with him, and her immediate agreement to step in for Mia Farrow on *Manhattan Murder Mystery* demonstrated how close she is to him, and how confident in him she is.

Woody has employed some of the most attractive and talented actresses in his films including Madonna who must surely have reminded him of the pouting Marilyn Monroe he fantasised about in Greenwich Village years ago. He has hired the sexually alluring Daryl Hannah, and the brainy and beautiful Jodie Foster. These women are at the top of their careers and, for one reason or another, have achieved professional respect independently of Woody Allen. The director who says he's not motivated by box office success, invited these strong willed women to take part in his movies, often for performances which were ultimately indifferent, or could have been fulfilled by less well-known actresses. In one case the actress's scenes were left on the cutting room floor. Woody had these Hollywood goddesses within his orbit – but the relationship never progressed beyond the professional to romance. They are his peers, yet there is no evidence he has ever had any romance with any of them. Is it because, as Vicky Tiel claims, he wants the women Warren Beatty would want, but he knows he can't dominate in the same way Beatty does?

Woody is used to getting what he wants, but if he *is* attracted to compliant women, he doesn't always get exactly that. Mia complained about the power he exerts. Ironically though, thanks to the court case, its allegations of child abuse and attendant revelations about his private life, Mia may eventually have punished Woody more than he was ever capable of doing to her. Regardless of whether or not the police report cleared Woody, and even though both Mia and her sister Tisa have publicly backtracked on their accusations, the director has been delivered a blow it will be hard to recover from. In this respect Mia shares with Woody's first wife Harlene Rosen an unusual distinction. They both hit back hard.

And since they did the effusive praise Woody tends to heap on his other women has diminished somewhat. Harlene, he says ambiguously, is a 'formidable' woman; Mia the loving mother becomes Mia the 'hysterical' woman. But effusive praise is generally the order of the day for women on Woody's right side. In much the same way that Woody became obsessed with what was the 'best', be it the best part of town to live in, the best restaurants, Woody is rarely satisfied with attributing to his lovers or friends, anything but the most extravagant praise.

Before falling out with Harlene he would boast to Bryna about Harlene's achievements, and he would tell Bryna her artistic efforts represented 'real beauty'. Louise Lasser, he would tell friends, was the funniest person in the world; Diane Keaton, he would tell Louise, was the greatest American actress of her generation. And each one of them would be praised for their 'sophistication'. These women were not the mindless products of America's crass commercialism. They were sophisticated intellects who knew all about Kierkegaard and Kafka.

But as the movie writer Joe Queenan succinctly observed, 'The humorous but superficial conversations involving Kierkegaard, Schopenhauer, Nietzsche, McLuhan, etc, that occur again and again in Allen's films are not really the way that grown-up pretentious people talk in New York, but rather the way pretentious college kids talk everywhere.' He added: 'There is no evidence that Allen has ever read the philosophers he cites, but even if he has, he certainly doesn't attempt to incorporate any of their theories into what are fundamentally commercial films.'[42]

Which of course, is the whole point. This overwhelming 'sophistication' to which Woody aspires started as nothing more than a pretence (to which he has readily admitted) to win women. It started all those years ago when he was a stand-up comic and fell for a certain sort of Greenwich Village girl who liked to litter small talk with meaningless literary nuggets and phoney philosophical thoughts. He says it developed into a genuine interest in literature and philosophy, and he certainly seems to possess an extensive vocabulary of his subject. But sometimes the idea of 'sophistication' to him seems to have become a ruse – and fairly transparent one at that – to justify what many see as unbridled sexuality.

When Stacey Nelkin was asked about her romance with Woody when she was only 17, she characterised the relationship as a 'sophisticated' one and talked about visiting museums and art galleries. Woody told reporters his relationship with Soon-Yi was a 'sophisticated' one. It's almost as if he identifies sex and sophistication with one another. They were both, when he was a boy, two of the things he aspired to: Manhattan, which he deemed sophisticated, compared to his own suburban background, and sex, which was absent from his life in Brooklyn from where all his troubles and neurosis seemed to stem.

This is stranger still, because the recollections of his

friends from that era, are of a happy time, and a happy
boy. They never remember a Woody overwhelmed with
the preoccupations and dilemmas which seem to hound
him today. Bryna Goldstein's mother Sadie could always
tell when Woody was in her house because it would be
ringing with laughter. Jack Victor, Mickey Rose and
Elliott Mills all remember how Woody could turn even
the worst childhood experiences into a joke. Yet as he
outgrew those youthful setbacks and irritations, and
achieved the success he craved, everything unravelled for
Woody.

During Woody's progress through life, as he gradually
realised those dreams and aspirations which pushed him
since going to the movies for the first time, as he began to
acquire wealth beyond his imagination, and as he became
one of the most powerful players in the most glamorous
business in the world ... did he also realise that it's all
pretty futile at the end of the day? Has he realised that the
girls he loved as a boy, and the women he loved as a
young man, are gone forever? That it's impossible to
rekindle romances which were in his heart but not theirs?
That the romances he seems to be able to attract as a
successful man, are not as fulfilling as he imagined they
would be? Is it as he's often said, that the meaning of life
is that there's no meaning to life?

Epilogue

'It was women like my sister Letty, my friend Jean Doumanian, and Soon-Yi, who helped me get through this.'[1]

Woody lost his case, along with the privacy and reputation he had so jealously coveted, not to mention much of the fortune he had less zealously accumulated. Mia walked from the courthouse victorious. Her triumph was topped the following year with a commendable performance in *Widow's Peak*, a high spirited Irish comedy. *Widow's Peak* gave the lie to Letty Aronson's claims that Mia was a 'second rate actress' who had only prospered thanks to Woody Allen's patronage.

The actor Jim Broadbent, who was to co-star as Clancy, an incorrigibly romantic country dentist, arrived on the set apprehensive. Broadbent already knew that his next job would be in New York with Woody Allen, who was preparing a film about 1920s' Broadway. He wanted to avoid mentioning the fact to Mia. 'I eventually plucked up the courage to tell her and she was very good about it,' he recalled. 'She told me, "He's a great director, just don't have children by him."'[2]

She was less generous with others. 'I regret the day I ever met him,' she told visitors who cared to listen.[3] Mia no longer refers to Woody by name. By the time *Widow's Peak* was released in spring 1994, the eradication of his role in her life was almost complete, with Dylan renamed Eliza (after Doolittle) and Satchel now called Seamus. She had never been happy with the name Dylan, which she always thought was a boy's name. It was never made clear whether the children themselves had asked to change their names, or whether it was Mia's decision. But the name Seamus was a hark back to Mia's Irish roots which she spoke fondly of. She even spoke of giving up her Manhattan apartment, and moving to Ireland for good. Mia had been a frequent visitor to Ireland since the age of three, when Maureen O'Sullivan brought her back to Boyle, in Roscommon, where her grandfather had been a major.

Widow's Peak had been especially written for Maureen and Mia by Hugh Leonard who envisaged the mother and daughter team recreating their relationship for the big screen. As it was, 10 years had elapsed since Leonard penned the script. At 82, Maureen considered herself much too old, so Mia played the mother, with Natasha Richardson as her glamorous daughter.

Mia was to claim that she never had great confidence in herself. Far from encouraging her, Woody had, she insisted, constantly knocked her self-esteem. Now, in Ireland she believed herself even less capable. For the first time in 13 years she was working for another director, on location a million miles from her familiar stamping grounds of Manhattan and Connecticut, and she had a growing family to care for. But if she felt isolated, at least *Widow's Peak* afforded Mia a glimpse of the carefree world she once knew before her family came along. She became friends with her co-star Joan Plowright and the poet and playwright Brendan Kennelly, professor of English at Trinity College. Ruddy faced and corpulent, Brendan was once a notorious boozer around Dublin, well known for charming the girls. It was claimed Mia had even gone on a pub crawl with Brendan, downing several pints of Guinness on one evening. Known for his feminist adaptations of the Greek tragedies, Brendan once wrote a version of the Euripidean tragedy *Medea*, in which the Queen avenges herself on her errant husband by killing their children.

Mia talked with trepidation about her future, constantly worrying whether there would be enough work to support her family. As well she might. Her monthly outgoings amounted to almost 20,000 dollars according to former nanny Kristie Groteke. (Included in this figure was 3,000 dollars a month which Mia still spends on therapy for Satchel/Seamus, Moses and Dylan/Eliza despite dismissing therapy as 'useless'). Kristie was the nanny hired by Woody who had found herself in the uncomfortable position of perhaps having to testify against her employer in the child-abuse hearings. Now she was cashing in on her own brush with fame. While Mia was enjoying her first movie in a decade without Woody, Kristie's story about the bust up was hitting the book shelves.[4]

This insider's story confirmed that Woody was the controlling, even manipulative person he had been depicted by Mia. But equally he could be surprisingly lacking in confidence. He was almost as dependent on Mia as she had been on him. When Mia told Woody to get the hell out of her apartment with Soon-Yi, Kristie claims that he replied: 'No, no, no, I don't want to be with her, I want to be with you.'[5] She quoted him as pleading: 'I'm in love with you. Please Mia, let's use this incident to find a deeper relationship between us. I want to be with you. I want to marry you. Let's work it out.'

The image is a forlorn one, and Woody certainly began to look increasingly vulnerable after his court defeat. Mia was ensconced in a huge mansion on the outskirts of Dublin with five of the children. Soon after filming began, Woody arrived – incongruously, on board a private jet – with Letty Aronson, Soon-Yi, and bags full of toys for Dylan and Satchel. But Mia refused to let him see the children. Woody was left in an uncomfortable limbo, waiting to see whether she would change her mind. He shared a 300 dollar a night room at the Shelbourne Hotel with Soon-Yi while he waited. He dined with Soon-Yi at The Commons restaurant, a short stroll away from their hotel. The following morning, guests were surprised to see the familiar floppy-hatted figure sitting alone in the foyer, reading a book while waiting for an answer from Mia.

While Woody was in Ireland, a private tape was leaked to the press. It was of a telephone conversation between Mia and Woody in which the former graphically described the latter's sexual inadequacies. There were only a handful of people who could have known of the tape's existence. The full details were splashed over New York's tabloids – and later London's – as Woody waited to see his children.

Eventually Mia allowed him a few hours with the children. He took Satchel to the zoo in a limousine complete with walkie-talkie toting chauffeur. They headed to Pets' Corner where Satchel licked an ice-lolly while gazing happily at the rabbits, guinea pigs and budgerigars. In the eyes of the Fleet Street reporters who converged on Dublin by the dozen, Woody was a pathetic spectacle. A bewildered and isolated man. 'It has become fairly common place to make accusations of child molestation,' he told one reporter.[6] 'I have been able to disprove these claims because of who I am. But I've had letters from men across America who haven't been in the same position. They can't defend their good name.' But the sad fact of the matter was that Woody, with all his millions, had been unable to clear his name fully too.

If Mia did intend to exact revenge on the man she once venerated, she was succeeding, and Woody's public persona was changing for good. From now on, newspaper editors looking for stock pictures of the movie maestro would invariably choose those which made Woody look a little odd: his hat pulled down as if to conceal something, his blood-shot eyes staring at the camera like those of a startled rabbit caught in the glare of car headlights. Mia was emerging as a latter day Madonna, with angelic features bathed in an evanescent glow.

After the fiasco in Dublin, Woody flew on to London to promote *Manhattan Murder Mystery* amid farcical security arrangements. Journalists were struck by the cloak-and-dagger secrecy surrounding their interviews at the Regent Hotel. They were sworn to secrecy over the hotel venue; they were led to his suite flanked by security guards. In one comical moment, Woody materialised from the darkness of a room as if from thin air.

He gave several interviews remaining, characteristically, a bundle of contradictions throughout. He had always insisted that he found it difficult to cast American men in his movies. This was for purely artistic reasons, he asserted. The reason was that most American male actors become 'stars' while their European counterparts remained unadulterated 'actors'. The Michael Caine part in *Hannah and Her Sisters* was a case in point, he had often said. Now at the Regent he told a different story. In fact he had hoped Robert DeNiro would have taken Caine's role – but he demanded too much money.

In New York, before flying to Britain, he told *Rolling Stone* magazine that he would go on making movies as long as people gave him the money to do so. Once in London he had another idea when asked what he would do if he could lead his life again. 'Gee. I probably would not have been a film maker. I probably would have gone to college. I would not have dropped out of school ... Believe it or not, and it sounds so silly to hear myself say it, I would like to have gone into a more physical profession. I think I could have been a ballet dancer. Seriously, I was very athletic.'[7]

Manhattan Murder Myster was being released in New York as Woody spoke. He habitually leaves town when his movies come out. 'It's not that I brace myself for a blow or anything. It's just that it's better not to read about your work from other people.'[8] But he came across, resolutely, and reassuringly, as someone who genuinely doesn't give a damn about what other people think of him. 'My life has not changed much at all. I pretty much do the same dull things as I always did. I get up in the morning and write, and practise my clarinet, and go into Michael's Pub on Monday night ...

'I walk down the street, and people say "hello," and I try to avoid it. People ask for autographs and I give them. But then I wouldn't know because I never, or rarely have any real contact with the public. People never come up and say, "I saw your movie and I didn't like it." They just walk past. That's all a performer really knows – generally nice things.'[9]

The accusations of child abuse must have hurt Woody more than anything else. He was cleared of them, but not unconditionally. One New York official accused his superiors of 'covering up' for Woody. The charge was dismissed. But then, a Connecticut official was also to cast doubt on Woody's innocence. Strangely, Woody was able to extract a little comfort from Kristie Groteke. Potentially Kristie could have been a potent witness against her former employer had the child abuse charges gone ahead. As it was, her insider's account hinted that Mia's use of the word 'abusive' may have been misunderstood. Kristie wrote that Mia often over-reacted to minor problems. Mia changed all the locks at Frog Hollow after Dylan's videotaped description of Woody's actions. But Kristie said Mia always ran to the locksmith when she had an argument with Woody. In June 1992, Mia first told Kristie that Woody had 'sexually abused one of the kids' – but the 'kid' was Soon-Yi.[10] To use the phrase 'sexual abuse' smacked of hysterical hyperbole.

Perhaps the whole affair was not such a bad thing for Woody. The reverential tone of reporting which once greeted his every new movie (no matter how good or bad) and his every action (no matter how absurd) was galling even to those who admired him. He had been placed on a pedestal which was not necessarily of his own making. More often than not – ironically – he was placed there by the very sort of pseudo-intellectual he had routinely panned in his work. The media circus which followed his affair with Soon-Yi, and his public humiliation, at least revealed he was not quite the omnipotent icon some had regarded him to be.

Manhattan Murder Mystery opened to generous applause from critics and cinema audiences alike. It was generally agreed that this light-hearted comedy was Woody at his best. It was the Woody Allen of old with good gags, no high philosophy and a straight story line. The chemistry between himself, as a middle-aged book editor, and Keaton as a superannuated Nancy Drew obsessed with a neighbour she suspects of murder, was palpable. 'It's like an old marriage, or like I'm a kid sister,' she said.[11]

Angelica Huston earned plaudits as Woody's seductive author. It was left to Huston, Keaton and the other co-star, Alan Alda, to promote the movie with interviews. Woody had to be kept off American television screens in the pre-movie promotion. He avoided newspaper and magazine junkets in New York where he had faced a hostile press. Instead, he spoke to writers in a friendlier but less influential Chicago. The strategy was a response to the disastrous marketing campaign of his previous movie. Figures showed *Husbands and Wives* had lost a significant amount of money in America, despite TriStar's marketing campaign which had tried to cash in on the adverse publicity of the case. But the strategy backfired and *Husbands and Wives* made less money at the box office than it cost to shoot. The film is thought to have lost 10 million dollars. There was a row and Woody left TriStar.

The setback may have had a silver lining since it forced Woody into the arms of his closest friend Jean Doumanian. Jean established Sweetland Films to make movies with Letty Aronson and Woody. TriStar let him off the hook of the final picture he was due to make, and Woody immediately signed a three-picture deal with

Sweetland. Both TriStar and Woody denied that his departure had anything to do with his personal problems or the potential of a public backlash against him. Others disagreed.

'Spielberg he ain't,' the influential money magazine *Business Week* said. 'The 57 year old filmmaker hasn't scored at the box office for years. Now ... Allen is a bona fide nightmare for marketeers.'[12] Publicly, TriStar, which paid an estimated 20 million dollars to make *Manhattan Murder Mystery* and another 5 million dollars for promotion, is playing it cool. It's only making 250 prints of the film, less than a third the number it released of Allen's 1992 *Husbands and Wives*. 'His films have always had a small audience of mostly urban intellectuals,' says box office follower Jack Krier, president of Exhibitor Relations Co. 'And now he's losing them as well.'[13]

Despite everything the cast and crew of *Manhattan Murder Mystery* had noticed how unmoved Woody appeared to be by the tumult around him. 'If anything,' said one of the assistant directors, 'Woody was more relaxed on this set than he's ever been. He was laughing and joking more than I've ever seen him before.' Diane said, 'I think humour is a beautiful way of dealing with these real big problems.'[14]

Woody was equally generous. 'It's a pleasure to work with her,' he told *Rolling Stone* magazine.[15] Adding, less convincingly, 'I think, along with Judy Holliday, she's the best screen comedienne we've ever had.' (He also compared acting with Diane to dancing with Fred Astaire.)

Throughout the making of the movie, Woody was unusually tanned. He had increased a rigorous regime of exercises on equipment built into a special room of his Fifth Avenue apartment. He practised alone on his clarinet for at least an hour a day. And he never missed a Monday evening at Michael's Pub playing. In December 1993, he made his thousandth appearance at the club where he had performed – give or take the odd night off through illness or because he was out of town – since 1971.

'It was not hard to get through the year,' he told friends later sitting in his screening room in an old Park Avenue Hotel not far from his Fifth Avenue apartment. 'When all these personal problems began, I was determined it wouldn't become the entire focus of my life. I wasn't going to stop work and get obsessed over a court appearance. I went into work every morning, and it was an easy picture. We finished it nicely, on schedule and under budget.'[16] 'God, I know several people who died of AIDs during the year,' he once said in exasperation after a solicitous friend asked how he was coping. 'That's a problem. What I went through? It's a pain in the ass.'[17]

According to Woody the worst time in his life was actually after the movie *Manhattan* when he thought he was suffering from a brain tumour. He sounded less convincing when he claimed to have coped with the Mia situation by reasoning it was about the kids not him. He said, 'When I saw a father on the street with his child, it sent a pang through me. Physical pain.'[18] This is the man who apparently couldn't remember which bedrooms his children slept in. Allegedly he knew little about Moses except that he had cerebral palsy; nor did he know the name of Eliza's and Seamus's paediatrician, or the names of the children's friends, or even know the names of the pets that so annoyed him.

Time and time again in interviews with magazines from the star-gazing *Hello*, to *Rolling Stone*, Woody returned to Holocaust imagery. 'People who were in concentration camps learned that it was possible for them to shave every day and be disciplined, eat their food. Certain things were important under those ridiculously horrible conditions for keeping their sanity and health and best chance of survival. I felt that this was true here. Even though I was going through terrible things, I wanted to keep a focus.'[20]

Woody has started talking of leaving New York and

living in Paris. He has always had a soft spot for Europe. Possibly because his movies have always been received better there. (*Alice* made more money in Paris alone – never mind the whole of France – than the whole of the United States.) Some of his friends say talk of him leaving Manhattan is 'just Woody being Woody'. Others believe he may be forced to go if he's continued to be hounded by bad publicity over Mia and Soon-Yi. All agree he would never give up his base in the city he loves.

Nothing has altered his melancholy perception of the world. 'The real world is a place that I've never felt comfortable in,' he said.[20] 'I think that my generation grew up with a value system heavily marked by films. You know, there was no television, we didn't read books. Your values and everything you thought about life you got from this overwhelmingly powerful image of the movies ... My tendency, like when I made *Manhattan,* was to portray things very romantically. People are always telling me that they just don't know the New York that I write about, that they don't know that it really ever existed. I think it did. It may only have existed in movies, I don't know. But for me that's all derived from a childhood of movie-going. My ideas of romance come from the movies. I mean, I speak to adults my age, and they're constantly telling me that they still are hurt in life because they can't get their minds around the fact that things are not the way they were led to believe when they were growing up.'

If Woody's view of the world remained bleak, at least his children's prospects appeared to have improved. By late 1993, Dylan and Satchel were doing better psychologically, emotionally and intellectually. Dylan's school has said that her grades were up. Court papers stated that she had blossomed, was less shy and more open.

The development did not go unnoticed by the *New York Post*'s caustic gossip columnist, Cindy Adams. A longtime supporter of Mia, Cindy noted: 'Once labelled this "seriously troubled child", Dylan used to lock herself up. She'd pretend to be an animal. She'd bark like a dog. She'd run around screaming, "Hide me, hide me." No more. Dylan, who wants not to see "daddy" *at all*, has done better this year than ever before. No instance of her previously regressive behaviour has been manifested.' Satchel improved too. The boy, who often resisted seeing his father on the supervised visits, even skipped a grade.[21]

Cindy's bosses were more sympathetic to Woody when Connecticut State Attorney Frank Maco – after conducting a 13 month probe – announced he would not prosecute Woody Allen on charges of molesting his eight-year-old daughter Dylan, but felt there was 'probable cause' to believe Allen was guilty. He then said he wouldn't attempt to try the case because Dylan was 'fragile' and shouldn't have to testify in court.

'Just because show business celebrities don't always behave well, there's no excuse for high ranking government officials to engage in conduct that violates basic standards of fairness,' thundered an editorial.[22] In response, Woody asked for disciplinary action to be taken against the state attorney, and has filed complaints against the prosecutor with the Connecticut Bar Council and the state Criminal Justice Commission.

Throughout her stay in Ireland, Mia tried to avoid mentioning Woody. But despite that, and despite her bitterness, she couldn't help but reflect wistfully once: 'Watching your own movies is a form of masochism. But I do have the movies we made together. He is a good film-maker.'[23] In fact, Mia normally finds watching her own movies excruciating, and says she has never been pleased with any she has made. She admits though, to having enjoyed making *Rosemary's Baby*, *The Purple Rose of Cairo* and *Broadway Danny Rose*.

Mia developed a contempt for 'therapy' and claimed

Woody simply used it to give him *carte blanche* to do exactly as he pleased without reproach. 'He had two psychotherapists he saw at least twice a week,' she said, 'and that certainly didn't make him a better person.' In one of the most revealing interviews ever of Mia, she conceded she had always fallen for powerful people. Her explanation sounded convincing: 'If they liked me, I would be so grateful I would love them back with all my heart.'[24]

Chrissy Iley, the *Sunday Times* magazine's star writer who interviewed Mia was not known to be soft on subjects. She at first thought her – literally – mad. But she quickly became impressed by her. 'Mia's apartment is not a madhouse and she is not mad and three days after meeting her I determined never to laugh at a Woody Allen film again.'[25]

Mia dismissed claims that her huge family was in some way a recreation of her own unhappy past. 'As well as the obvious negatives about children from big families not getting enough attention from their parents, there are a lot of positives because they get a lot of attention from each other. I remember how comforting it was for me as a child to return home and find each of my siblings doing their thing. It was a whole little community. There is such a lot of safety in being a large family. Each one looks out for the other. The younger ones have fabulous older brothers as male role models; and the older children are devoted to their younger siblings.'[26]

Taking her own children with her wherever she goes, she recalled as a child being taught to be seen but not heard. How she would be summoned down to say goodnight to her parents and their guests when they had dinner parties. Of being introduced to John Wayne who perched her on a high chair then promptly forgot about her and left her there. It was too high to get off but Mia had been brought up not to say anything, so she sat there and waited.

Mia said, 'Certain things are not forgivable. Of course a person can promise to change, a person can promise to be contrite. But some things are unforgivable because they are unrepeatable.'[27] Woody was more forgiving of Mia. While she went out of her way to avoid mentioning him, he quickly introduced her name into any conversation. 'Mia is great at telling jokes, and if I wrote a joke for her she delivered it very beautifully. Diane can't even deliver a joke – she ruins them.'[28] They continue to talk through lawyers, but he predicts they will soon be back on first name terms.

Woody also reflected on his relationship with Mia. 'I wish she would come to me with an open heart and say: "Let's put an end to this." But I watched her today and she was furious at the outcome. Bitter. You would think any mother would be relieved that a three-member panel, two of them women, found that her daughter had not been molested. But so deep is her venom that she actually sees this as a loss. That is terribly sad. She knows I never molested Dylan.'[29]

When Woody was a young man who didn't mix with the 'in crowd', he and his friends analysed the behaviour and motivations of those who did, and their appraisal was invariably an uncomplimentary one. Success and popularity generally had more to do with a superficial glamour and an easy charm which Woody found lacking in integrity. He and his friends rejected conformity. They became a close cadre of companions pledged to eschewing the temptations of 'image'. They aimed to explore higher levels of emotion and intellect. Pretentious perhaps, but at least original.

But as success multiplied his fame Woody began to believe the myths about him. The *New York Times* didn't actually call him a 'genius' every day. But enough people did. And the predictable consequence was a man who believed he could do no wrong. Woody Allen became the willing victim of the popularity he claimed not to crave. Ultimately the result was a sex scandal and messy court battle which obscured much of the artistic, intellectual and personal integrity he had ever fought for. A lifetime of genuine achievement disappeared in a welter of tabloid headlines.

Like everyone else, Woody Allen is a multi-dimensional character. His life can probably be as mundane as anyone's. Much of the time he moves in a world beyond that which the rest of us can hope for. He's made at least one howling error of judgement in the full glare of an unforgiving public. Perhaps there have been many more which never made the headlines. His detractors would have it believed so. But his life has included greater success than the rest of us can imagine. If we dub someone who can find his way around the Cross Bronx Expressway a 'genius', then a man who's made one movie every year of his professional career, must also be entitled to that over-used compliment. Woody Allen will be remembered for the hours of enjoyment that he has brought his fans. His memory will be bathed in the magical neon glow of a Manhattan skyline reaching ever heavenwards to the music of George Gershwin.

Appendix

----------------------------------- x

WOODY ALLEN,

                 Petitioner,   Index No.

         -against-   68738/92

MARIA VILLIERS FARROW, also known as
MIA FARROW,

                Respondent.
----------------------------------- x

ELLIOTT WILK, J.*:

INTRODUCTION

On August 13, 1992, seven days after he learned that his
seven-year-old daughter Dylan had accused him of sexual
abuse, Woody Allen began this action against Mia Farrow to
obtain custody of Dylan, their five-year-old son Satchel, and
their fifteen-year-old son Moses.

As mandated by law, Dr. V. Kavirajan, the Connecticut
pediatrician to whom Dylan repeated her accusation, reported
the charge to the Connecticut State Police. In furtherance of
their investigation to determine if a criminal prosecution
should be pursued against Mr. Allen, the Connecticut State
Police referred Dylan to the Child Sexual Abuse Clinic of Yale–
New Haven Hospital. According to Yale–New Haven, the two

---

*I acknowledge the assistance of Analisa Torres in the prepara-
tion of this opinion.

major questions posed to them were: 'Is Dylan telling the truth, and did we think that she was sexually abused?' On March 17, 1993, Yale–New Haven issued a report which concluded that Mr. Allen had not sexually abused Dylan.

This trial began on March 19, 1993. Among the witnesses called by petitioner were Mr. Allen; Ms Farrow; Dr. Susan Coates, a clinical psychologist who treated Satchel; Dr. Nancy Schultz, a clinical psychologist who treated Dylan; and Dr. David Brodzinsky, a clinical psychologist who spoke with Dylan and Moses pursuant to his assignment in a related Surrogate's Court proceeding. Dr. John Leventhal, a pediatrician who was part of the three-member Yale–New Haven team, testified by deposition. Ms. Farrow called Dr. Stephen Herman, a clinical psychiatrist, who commented on the YaleNew Haven report.

What follows are my findings of fact. Where statements or observations are attributed to witnesses, they are adopted by me as findings of fact.

FINDINGS OF FACT

Mr. Allen is a fifty-seven year old film maker. He has been divorced twice. Both marriages were childless.

Ms. Farrow is forty-eight years old. She is an actress who has performed in many of Mr. Allen's movies. Her first marriage, at age twenty-one, ended in divorce two years later. Shortly thereafter, she married André Previn, with whom she had six children, three biological and three adopted.

Matthew and Sascha Previn, twenty-three years old, were born on February 26, 1970. The birth year of Soon-Yi Previn is believed to be 1970 or 1972. She was born in Korea and was adopted in 1977. Lark Previn, twenty years old, was born on February 15, 1973. Fletcher Previn, nineteen years old, was born on March 14, 1974. Daisy Previn, eighteen years old, was born on October 6, 1974.

After eight years of marriage, Ms. Farrow and Mr. Previn were divorced. Ms. Farrow retained custody of the children.

Mr. Allen and Ms. Farrow met in 1980, a few months after Ms. Farrow had adopted Moses Farrow, who was born on January 27, 1978. Mr. Allen preferred that Ms. Farrow's children not be a part of their lives together. Until 1985, Mr. Allen had 'virtually a single person's relationship' with Ms. Farrow and viewed her children as an encumbrance. He had no involvement with them and no interest in them. Throughout their relationship, Mr. Allen has maintained his residence on the east side of Manhattan and Ms. Farrow has lived with her children on the west side of Manhattan.

In 1984, Ms. Farrow expressed a desire to have a child with Mr. Allen. He resisted, fearing that a young child would reduce the time that they had available for each other. Only after Ms. Farrow promised that the child would live with her and that Mr. Allen need not be involved with the child's care or upbringing, did he agree.

After six months of unsuccessful attempts to become pregnant, and with Mr. Allen's lukewarm support, Ms. Farrow decided to adopt a child. Mr. Allen chose not to participate in the adoption and Ms. Farrow was the sole adoptive parent. On July 11, 1985, the newborn Dylan joined the Farrow household.

Mr. Allen's attitude toward Dylan changed a few months after the adoption. He began to spend some mornings and evenings at Ms. Farrow's apartment in order to be with Dylan. He visited at Ms. Farrow's country home in Connecticut and accompanied the Farrow-Previn family on extended vacations to Europe in 1987, 1988 and 1989. He remained aloof from Ms. Farrow's other children except for Moses, to whom he was cordial.

In 1986, Ms. Farrow suggested the adoption of another child. Mr. Allen, buoyed by his developing affection for Dylan, was enthusiastic. Before another adoption could be arranged, Ms. Farrow became pregnant with Satchel.

During Ms. Farrow's pregnancy, Mr. Allen did not touch her stomach, listen to the fetus, or try to feel it kick. Because Mr. Allen had shown no interest in her pregnancy and because Ms. Farrow believed him to be squeamish about the delivery process, her friend Casey Pascal acted as her Lamaze coach.

A few months into the pregnancy, Ms. Farrow began to withdraw from Mr. Allen. After Satchel's birth, which occurred on December 19, 1987, she grew more distant from Mr. Allen. Ms. Farrow's attention to Satchel also reduced the time she had available for Dylan. Mr. Allen began to spend more time with Dylan and to intensify his relationship with her.

By then, Ms. Farrow had become concerned with Mr. Allen's behavior toward Dylan. During a trip to Paris, when Dylan was between two and three years old, Ms. Farrow told Mr. Allen that '[y]ou look at her [Dylan] in a sexual way. You fondled her. It's not natural. You're all over her. You don't give her any breathing room. You look at her when she's naked.' Her apprehension was fueled by the intensity of the attention Mr. Allen lavished on Dylan, and by his spending play-time in bed with her, by his reading to her in his bed while dressed in his undershorts, and by his permitting her to suck on his thumb.

Ms. Farrow testified that Mr. Allen was overly attentive and demanding of Dylan's time and attention. He was aggressively affectionate, providing her with little space of her own and with no respect for the integrity of her body. Ms. Farrow, Casey Pascal, Sophie Raven (Dylan's French tutor), and Dr. Coates testified that Mr. Allen focused on Dylan to the exclusion of her siblings, even when Satchel and Moses were present.

In June 1990, the parties became concerned with Satchel's behavior and took him to see Dr. Coates, with whom he then began treatment. At Dr. Coates' request, both parents participated in Satchel's treatment.

In the fall of 1990, the parties asked Dr. Coates to evaluate Dylan to determine if she needed therapy. During the course of the evaluation, Ms. Farrow expressed her concern to Dr. Coates that Mr. Allen's behavior with Dylan was not appropriate. Dr. Coates observed:

> I understood why she was worried, because it [Mr. Allen's relationship with Dylan] was intense, ... I did not see it as sexual, but I saw it as inappropriately intense because it excluded everybody else, and it placed a demand on a child for a kind of acknowledgment that I felt should not be placed on a child....

She testified that she worked with Mr. Allen to help him to understand that his behavior with Dylan was inappropriate and that it had to be modified. Dr. Coates also recommended that Dylan enter therapy with Dr. Schultz, with whom Dylan began treatment in April 1991.

In 1991, Ms. Farrow expressed a desire to adopt another child. Mr. Allen, who had begun to believe that Ms. Farrow was growing more remote from him and that she might discontinue his access to Dylan, said that he would not take 'a lousy attitude

320

towards it' if, in return, Ms. Farrow would sponsor his adoption of Dylan and Moses. She said that she agreed after Mr. Allen assured her that 'he would not take Dylan for sleep-overs ... unless I was there. And that if, God forbid, anything should happen to our relationship, that he would never seek custody.' The adoptions were concluded in December 1991.

Until 1990, although he had had little contact with any of the Previn children, Mr. Allen had the least to do with Soon-Yi. 'She was someone who didn't like me. I had no interest in her, none whatsoever. She was a quiet person who did her work. I never spoke to her.' In 1990, Mr. Allen, who had four season tickets to the New York Knicks basketball games, was asked by Soon-Yi if she could go to a game. Mr. Allen agreed.

During the following weeks, when Mr. Allen visited Ms. Farrow's home, he would say hello to Soon-Yi, 'which is something I never did in the years prior, but no conversations with her or anything.'

Soon-Yi attended more basketball games with Mr. Allen. He testified that 'gradually, after the basketball association, we became more friendly. She opened up to me more.' By 1991 they were discussing her interests in modeling, art and psychology. She spoke of her hopes and other aspects of her life.

In September 1991, Soon-Yi entered Drew College in New Jersey. She was naive, socially inexperienced and vulnerable. Mr. Allen testified that she was lonely and unhappy at school, and that she began to speak daily with him by telephone. She spent most weekends at home with Ms. Farrow. There is no evidence that Soon-Yi told Ms. Farrow either that she was lonely or that she had been in daily communication with Mr. Allen.

On January 13, 1992, while in Mr. Allen's apartment, Ms. Farrow discovered six nude photographs of Soon-Yi which had been left on a mantelpiece. She is posed reclining on a couch with her legs spread apart. Ms. Farrow telephoned Mr. Allen to confront him with her discovery of the photographs.

Ms. Farrow returned home, showed the photographs to Soon-Yi and said, 'What have you done?' She left the room before Soon-Yi answered. During the following weekend, Ms. Farrow hugged Soon-Yi and said that she loved her and did not blame her. Shortly thereafter, Ms. Farrow asked Soon-Yi how long she had been seeing Mr. Allen. When Soon-Yi referred to her sexual relationship with Mr. Allen, Ms. Farrow hit her on the side of the face and on the shoulders.[1] Ms. Farrow also told her older children what she had learned.

After receiving Ms. Farrow's telephone call, Mr. Allen went to her apartment where, he said, he found her to be 'ragingly angry'. She begged him to leave. She testified that:

> [w]hen he finally left, he came back less than an hour later, and I was sitting at the table. By then, all of the children were there ... and it was a rather silent meal. The little ones were chatting and he walked right in and he sat down at the table as if nothing had happened and starts chatting with ... the two little ones, said hi to everybody. And one by one the children (Lark, Daisy, Fletcher, Moses and Sascha] took their plates and left. And I'd, I didn't know what to do. And then I went out.

Within the month, both parties retained counsel and attempted to negotiate a settlement of their differences. In an effort to pacify Ms. Farrow, Mr. Allen told her that he was no longer seeing Soon-Yi. This was untrue. A temporary arrangement enabled Mr. Allen to visit regularly with Dylan and Satchel but they were not permitted to visit at his residence. In addition, Ms. Farrow asked for his assurance that he would not seek custody of Moses, Dylan or Satchel.

On February 3, 1992, both parties signed documents in which it was agreed that Mr. Allen would waive custodial rights to Moses, Dylan and Satchel if Ms. Farrow predeceased him. On the same day, Mr. Allen signed a second document, which he did not reveal to Ms. Farrow, in which he disavowed the waiver, claiming that it was a product of duress and coercion and stating that 'I have no intention of abiding by it and have been advised that it will not hold up legally and that at worst I can revoke it unilaterally at will.'

---

[1]Ms. Farrow has commenced an action in the Surrogate's Court to vacate Mr. Allen's adoption of Dylan and Moses. In that proceeding, she contends that Mr. Allen began a secret affair with Soon-Yi prior to the date of the adoption. This issue has been reserved for consideration by the Surrogate and has not been addressed by me.

In February 1992, Ms. Farrow gave Mr. Allen a family picture Valentine with skewers through the hearts of the children and a knife through the heart of Ms. Farrow. She also defaced and destroyed several photographs of Mr. Allen and of Soon-Yi.

In July 1992, Ms. Farrow had a birthday party for Dylan at her Connecticut home. Mr. Allen came and monopolized Dylan's time and attention. After Mr. Allen retired to the guest room for the night, Ms. Farrow affixed to his bathroom door, a note which called Mr. Allen a child molester. The reference was to his affair with Soon-Yi.

In the summer of 1992, Soon-Yi was employed as a camp counselor. During the third week of July, she telephoned Ms. Farrow to tell her that she had quit her job. She refused to tell Ms. Farrow where she was staying. A few days later, Ms. Farrow received a letter from the camp advising her that:

> [i]t is with sadness and regret that we had to ask Soon-Yi to leave camp midway through the first camp session.... Throughout the entire orientation period and continuing during camp, Soon-Yi was constantly involved with telephone calls. Phone calls from a gentleman whose name is Mr. Simon seemed to be her primary focus and this definitely detracted from her concentration on being a counselor.

Mr. Simon was Woody Allen.

On August 4, 1992, Mr. Allen travelled to Ms. Farrow's Connecticut vacation home to spend time with his children. Earlier in the day, Casey Pascal had come for a visit with her three young children and their babysitter, Alison Stickland. Ms. Farrow and Ms. Pascal were shopping when Mr. Allen arrived. Those present were Ms. Pascal's three children; Ms. Stickland; Kristie Groteke, a babysitter employed by Ms. Farrow; Sophie Berge, a French tutor for the children; Dylan; and Satchel.

Ms. Farrow had previously instructed Ms. Groteke that Mr. Allen was not to be left alone with Dylan. For a period of fifteen or twenty minutes during the afternoon, Ms. Groteke was unable to locate Mr. Allen or Dylan. After looking for them in the house, she assumed that they were outside with the others. But neither Ms. Berge nor Ms. Stickland was with Mr. Allen or Dylan. Ms. Groteke made no mention of this to Ms. Farrow on August 4.

During a different portion of the day, Ms. Stickland went to the television room in search of one of Ms. Pascal's children. She observed Mr. Allen kneeling in front of Dylan with his head on her lap, facing her body. Dylan was sitting on the couch staring vacantly in the direction of a television set.

After Ms. Farrow returned home, Ms. Berge noticed that Dylan was not wearing anything under her sundress. She told Ms. Farrow, who asked Ms. Groteke to put underpants on Dylan.

Ms. Stickland testified that during the evening of August 4, she told Ms. Pascal, 'I had seen something at Mia's that day that was bothering me.' She revealed what she had seen in the television room. On August 5, Ms. Pascal telephoned Ms. Farrow to tell her what Ms. Stickland had observed.

Ms. Farrow testified that after she hung up the telephone, she asked Dylan, who was sitting next to her, 'whether it was true that daddy had his face in her lap yesterday.' Ms. Farrow testified:

> Dylan said yes. And then she said that she didn't like it one bit, no, he was breathing into her, into her legs, she said. And that he was holding her around the waist and I said, why didn't you get up and she said she tried to but that he put his hands underneath her and touched her. And she showed me where.... Her behind.

Because she was already uncomfortable with Mr. Allen's inappropriate behavior toward Dylan and because she believed that her concerns were not being taken seriously enough by Dr. Schultz and Dr. Coates, Ms. Farrow videotaped Dylan's statements. Over the next twenty-four hours, Dylan told Ms. Farrow that she had been with Mr. Allen in the attic and that he had touched her privates with his finger.

After Dylan's first comments, Ms. Farrow telephoned her attorney for guidance. She was advised to bring Dylan to her local pediatrician, which she did immediately. Dylan did not repeat the accusation of sexual abuse during this visit and Ms. Farrow was advised to return with Dylan on the following day. On the trip home, she explained to her mother that she did not like talking about her privates. On August 6, when Ms. Farrow went back to Dr. Kavirajan's office, Dylan repeated what she had told her mother on August 5. A medical examination conducted on August 9 showed no physical evidence of sexual abuse.

Although Dr. Schultz was vacationing in Europe, Ms. Farrow telephoned her daily for advice. Ms. Farrow also notified Dr. Coates, who was still treating Satchel. She said to Dr. Coates, 'it sounds very convincing to me, doesn't it to you? It is so specific. Let's hope it is her fantasy.' Dr. Coates immediately notified Mr. Allen of the child's accusation and then contacted the New York City Child Welfare Administration. Seven days later, during a meeting of the lawyers at which settlement discussions were taking place, Mr. Allen began this action for custody.

Dr. Schultz returned from vacation on August 16. She was transported to Connecticut in Mr. Allen's chauffered limousine on August 17, 18 and 21 for therapy sessions with Dylan. Dylan, who had become increasingly resistant to Dr. Schultz, did not want to see her. During the third session, Dylan and Satchel put glue in Dr. Schultz's hair, cut her dress and told her to go away.

On August 24 and 27, Ms. Farrow expressed to Dr. Schultz her anxiety about Dr. Schultz continuing to see Mr. Allen, who had already brought suit for custody of Dylan. She asked if Dr. Schultz would

> ... please not come for a while until all of this is settled down because ... I couldn't trust anybody. And she said she understood completely.... And soon after that ... I learned that Dr. Schultz had told [New York] child welfare that Dylan had not reported anything to her. And then a week later, either her lawyer or Dr. Schultz called [New York] child welfare and said she just remembered that Dylan had told her that Mr. Allen had put a finger in her vagina. When I heard that I certainly didn't trust Dr. Schultz.

Dr. Schultz testified that on August 19, Paul Williams of the New York Child Welfare Administration asked about her experience with Dylan. She replied that on August 17, Dylan started to tell her what had happened with Mr. Allen but she needed more time to explore this with Dylan. On August 27, she spoke more fully to Mr. Williams about her August 17 session with Dylan and speculated about the significance of what Dylan reported. Mr. Williams testified that on August 19, Dr.

Schultz told him that Dylan had not made any statements to her about sexual abuse.

Ms. Farrow did not immediately resume Dylan's therapy because the Connecticut State Police had requested that she not be in therapy during the investigation. Also, it was not clear if the negotiated settlement that the parties were continuing to pursue would include Mr. Allen's participation in the selection of Dylan's new therapist.

Dr. Coates continued to treat Satchel through the fall of 1992. Ms. Farrow expressed to Dr. Coates her unease with the doctor seeing Mr. Allen in conjunction with Satchel's therapy. On October 29, 1992, Ms. Farrow requested that Dr. Coates treat Satchel without the participation of Mr. Allen. Dr. Coates declined, explaining that she did not believe that she could treat Satchel effectively without the full participation of both parents. Satchel's therapy with Dr. Coates was discontinued on November 18, 1992. At Ms. Farrow's request, Dr. Coates recommended a therapist to continue Satchel's therapy. Because of a conflict, the therapist recommended by Dr. Coates was unable to treat Satchel. He did, however, provide the name of another therapist with whom Satchel is currently in treatment.

On December 30, 1992, Dylan was interviewed by a representative of the Connecticut State Police. She told them – at a time Ms. Farrow calculates to be the fall of 1991 – that while at Mr. Allen's apartment, she saw him and Soon-Yi having sex. Her reporting was childlike but graphic. She also told the police that Mr. Allen had pushed her face into a plate of hot spaghetti and had threatened to do it again.

Ten days before Yale–New Haven concluded its investigation, Dylan told Ms. Farrow, for the first time, that in Connecticut, while she was climbing up the ladder to a bunk bed, Mr. Allen put his hands under her shorts and touched her. Ms. Farrow testified that as Dylan said this, 'she was illustrating graphically where in the genital area.'

CONCLUSIONS
A) *Woody Allen*

Mr. Allen has demonstrated no parenting skills that would qualify him as an adequate custodian for Moses, Dylan or Satchel. His financial contributions to the children's support, his willingness to read to them, to tell them stories, to buy them presents, and to oversee their breakfasts, do not compensate for his absence as a meaningful source of guidance and caring in their lives. These contributions do not excuse his evident lack of familiarity with the most basic details of their day-to-day existences.

He did not bathe his children. He did not dress them, except from time to time, and then only to help them put on their socks and jackets. He knows little of Moses' history, except that he has cerebral palsy; he does not know if he has a doctor. He does not know the name of Dylan and Satchel's pediatrician. He does not know the names of Moses' teachers or about his academic performance. He does not know the name of the children's dentist. He does not know the names of his children's friends. He does not know the names of any of their many pets. He does not know which children shared bedrooms. He attended parent-teacher conferences only when asked to do so by Ms. Farrow.

Mr. Allen has even less knowledge about his children's siblings, with whom he seldom communicated. He apparently did not pay enough attention to his own children to learn from them about their brothers and sisters.

Mr. Allen characterized Ms. Farrow's home as a foster care compound and drew distinctions between her biological and adopted children. When asked how he felt about sleeping with his children's sister, he responded that '[s]he [Soon-Yi] was an adopted child and Dylan was an adopted child.' He showed no understanding that the bonds developed between adoptive brothers and sisters are no less worthy of respect and protection than those between biological siblings.

Mr. Allen's reliance on the affidavit which praises his parenting skills, submitted by Ms. Farrow in connection with his petition to adopt Moses and Dylan, is misplaced. Its ultimate probative value will be determined in the pending Surrogate's Court proceeding. In the context of the facts and circumstances of this action, I accord it little weight.

None of the witnesses who testified on Mr. Allen's behalf provided credible evidence that he is an appropriate custodial parent. Indeed, none would venture an opinion that he should be granted custody. When asked, even Mr. Allen could not provide an acceptable reason for a change in custody.

His counsel's last question of him on direct examination was,

'Can you tell the Court why you are seeking custody of your children?' Mr. Allen's response was a rambling *non sequitur* which consumed eleven pages of transcript. He said that he did not want to take the children away from Ms. Farrow; that Ms. Farrow maintained a non-traditional household with biological children and adopted children from all over the world; that Soon-Yi was fifteen years older than Dylan and seventeen years older than Satchel; that Mr. Farrow was too angry with Mr. Allen to resolve the problem; and that with him, the children 'will be responsibly educated' and 'their day-to-day behavior will be done in consultation with their therapist.' The most relevant portions of the response – that he is a good father and that Ms. Farrow has intentionally turned the children against him – I do not credit. Even if he were correct, under the circumstances of this case, it would be insufficient to warrant a change of custody.

Mr. Allen's deficiencies as a custodial parent are magnified by his affair with Soon-Yi. As Ms. Farrow's companion, he was a frequent visitor at Soon-Yi's home. He accompanied the Farrow-Previns on extended family vacations and he is the father of Soon-Yi's siblings, Moses, Dylan and Satchel. The fact that Mr. Allen ignored Soon-Yi for ten years cannot change the nature of the family constellation and does not create a distance sufficient to convert their affair into a benign relationship between two consenting adults.

Mr. Allen admits that he never considered the consequences of his behavior with Soon-Yi. Dr. Coates and Dr. Brodzinsky testified that Mr. Allen still failed to understand that what he did was wrong. Having isolated Soon-Yi from her family, he left her with no visible support system. He had no consideration for the consequences to her, to Ms. Farrow, to the Previn children for whom he cared little, or to his own children for whom he professes love.

Mr. Allen's response to Dylan's claim of sexual abuse was an attack upon Ms. Farrow, whose parenting ability and emotional stability he impugned without the support of any significant credible evidence. His trial strategy has been to separate his children from their brothers and sisters; to turn the children against their mother; to divide adopted children from biological children; to incite the family against their household help; and to set household employees against each

328

other. His self-absorption, his lack of judgment and his commitment to the continuation of his divisive assault, thereby impeding the healing of the injuries that he has already caused, warrant a careful monitoring of his future contact with the children.

B) *Mia Farrow*

Few relationships and fewer families can easily bear the microscopic examination to which Ms. Farrow and her children have been subjected. It is evident that she loves children and has devoted a significant portion of her emotional and material wealth to their upbringing. When she is not working she attends to her children. Her weekends and summers are spent in Connecticut with her children. She does not take extended vacations unaccompanied by her children. She is sensitive to the needs of her children, respectful of their opinions, honest with them and quick to address their problems.

Mr. Allen elicited trial testimony that Ms. Farrow favored her biological children over her adopted children; that she manipulated Dylan's sexual abuse complaint, in part through the use of leading questions and the videotape; that she discouraged Dylan and Satchel from maintaining a relationship with Mr. Allen; that she overreacted to Mr. Allen's affair with Soon-Yi; and that she inappropriately exposed Dylan and Satchel to the turmoil created by the discovery of the affair.

The evidence at trial established that Ms. Farrow is a caring and loving mother who has provided a home for both her biological and her adopted children. There is no credible evidence that she unfairly distinguished among her children or that she favored some at the expense of others.

I do not view the Valentine's Day card, the note affixed to the bathroom door in Connecticut, or the destruction of photographs as anything more than expressions of Ms. Farrow's understandable anger and her ability to communicate her distress by word and symbol rather than by action.

There is no credible evidence to support Mr. Allen's contention that Ms. Farrow coached Dylan or that Ms. Farrow acted upon a desire for revenge against him for seducing Soon-Yi. Mr. Allen's resort to the stereotypical 'woman scorned' defense is an injudicious attempt to divert attention from his failure to act as a responsible parent and adult.

Ms. Farrow's statement to Dr. Coates that she hoped that Dylan's statements were a fantasy is inconsistent with the notion of brainwashing. In this regard, I also credit the testimony of Ms. Groteke, who was charged with supervising Mr. Allen's August 4 visit with Dylan. She testified that she did not tell Ms. Farrow, until after Dylan's statement of August 5, that Dylan and Mr. Allen were unaccounted for during fifteen or twenty minutes on August 4. It is highly unlikely that Ms. Farrow would have encouraged Dylan to accuse her father of having sexually molested her during a period in which Ms. Farrow believed they were in the presence of a babysitter. Moreover, I do not believe that Ms. Farrow would have exposed her daughter and her other children to the consequences of the Connecticut investigation and this litigation if she did not believe the possible truth of Dylan's accusation.

In a society where children are too often betrayed by adults who ignore or disbelieve their complaints of abuse, Ms. Farrow's determination to protect Dylan is commendable. Her decision to videotape Dylan's statements, although inadvertently compromising the sexual abuse investigation, was understandable.

Ms. Farrow is not faultless as a parent. It seems probable, although there is no credible testimony to this effect, that prior to the affair with Mr. Allen, Soon-Yi was experiencing problems for which Ms. Farrow was unable to provide adequate support. There is also evidence that there were problems with her relationships with Dylan and Satchel. We do not, however, demand perfection as a qualification for parenting. Ironically, Ms. Farrow's principal shortcoming with respect to responsible parenting appears to have been her continued relationship with Mr. Allen.

Ms. Farrow reacted to Mr. Allen's behavior with her children with a balance of appropriate caution and flexibility. She brought her early concern with Mr. Allen's relationship with Dylan to Dr. Coates and was comforted by the doctor's assurance that Mr. Allen was working to correct his behavior with the child. Even after January 13, 1992, Ms. Farrow continued to provide Mr. Allen with access to her home and to their children, as long as the visits were supervised by a responsible adult. She did her best, although with limited success, to shield her younger children from the turmoil generated by Mr. Allen's affair with Soon-Yi.

Ms. Farrow's refusal to permit Mr. Allen to visit with Dylan after August 4, 1992 was prudent. Her willingness to allow Satchel to have regular supervised visitation with Mr. Allen reflects her understanding of the propriety of balancing Satchel's need for contact with his father against the danger of Mr. Allen's lack of parental judgment.

Ms. Farrow also recognizes that Mr. Allen and not Soon-Yi is the person responsible for their affair and its impact upon her family. She has communicated to Soon-Yi that she continues to be a welcome member of the Farrow-Previn home.

C) *Dylan Farrow*

Mr. Allen's relationship with Dylan remains unresolved. The evidence suggests that it is unlikely that he could be successfully prosecuted for sexual abuse. I am less certain, however, than is the Yale–New Haven team, that the evidence proves conclusively that there was no sexual abuse.

Both Dr. Coates and Dr. Schultz expressed their opinions that Mr. Allen did not sexually abuse Dylan. Neither Dr. Coates nor Dr. Schultz has expertise in the field of child sexual abuse. I believe that the opinions of Dr. Coates and Dr. Schultz may have been colored by their loyalty to Mr. Allen. I also believe that therapists would have a natural reluctance to accept the possibility that an act of sexual abuse occurred on their watch. I have considered their opinions, but do not find their testimony to be persuasive with respect to sexual abuse or visitation.

I have also considered the report of the Yale–New Haven team and the deposition testimony of Dr. John M. Leventhal. The YaleNew Haven investigation was conducted over a six-month period by Dr. Leventhal, a pediatrician; Dr. Julia Hamilton, who has a Ph.D. in social work; and Ms. Jennifer Sawyer, who has a master's degree in social work. Responsibility for different aspects of the investigation was divided among the team. The notes of the team members were destroyed prior to the issuance of the report, which, presumably, is an amalgamation of their independent impressions and observations. The unavailability of the notes, together with their unwillingness to testify at this trial except through the deposition of Dr. Leventhal, compromised my ability to scrutinize their findings and resulted in a report which was sanitized and, therefore, less credible.

Dr. Stephen Herman, a clinical psychiatrist who has extensive familiarity with child abuse cases, was called as a witness by Ms. Farrow to comment on the YaleNew Haven report. I share his reservations about the reliability of the report.

Dr. Herman faulted the YaleNew Haven team (1) for making visitation recommendations without seeing the parent interact with the child; (2) for failing to support adequately their conclusion that Dylan has a thought disorder; (3) for drawing any conclusions about Satchel, whom they never saw; (4) for finding that there was no abuse when the supporting data was inconclusive; and (5) for recommending that Ms. Farrow enter into therapy. In addition, I do not think that it was appropriate for YaleNew Haven, without notice to the parties or their counsel, to exceed its mandate and make observations and recommendations which might have an impact on existing litigation in another jurisdiction.

Unlike Yale–New Haven, I am not persuaded that the videotape of Dylan is the product of leading questions or of the child's fantasy.

Richard Marcus, a retired New York City police officer, called by Mr. Allen, testified that he worked with the police sex crimes unit for six years. He claimed to have an intuitive ability to know if a person is truthful or not. He concluded, 'based on my experience,' that Dylan lacked credibility. I did not find his testimony to be insightful.

I agree with Dr. Herman and Dr. Brodzinsky that we will probably never know what occurred on August 4, 1992. The credible testimony of Ms. Farrow, Dr. Coates, Dr. Leventhal and Mr. Allen does, however, prove that Mr. Allen's behavior toward Dylan was grossly inappropriate and that measures must be taken to protect her.

D) *Satchel Farrow*

Mr. Allen had a strained and difficult relationship with Satchel during the earliest years of the child's life. Dr. Coates testified, 'Satchel would push him away, would not acknowledge him.... If he would try to help Satchel getting out of bed or going into bed, he would kick him, at times had scratched his face. They were in trouble.' Dr. Coates also testified that as an infant, Satchel would cry when held by Mr. Allen and stop when given to Ms. Farrow. Mr. Allen attributes this to Ms.

Farrow's conscious effort to keep him apart from the child.

Although Ms. Farrow consumed much of Satchel's attention, and did not foster a relationship with his father, there is no credible evidence to suggest that she desired to exclude Mr. Allen. Mr. Allen's attention to Dylan left him with less time and patience for Satchel. Dr. Coates attempted to teach Mr. Allen how to interact with Satchel. She encouraged him to be more understanding of his son when Satchel ignored him or acted bored with his gifts. Apparently, success in this area was limited.

In 1991, in the presence of Ms. Farrow and Dylan, Mr. Allen stood next to Satchel's bed, as he did every morning. Satchel screamed at him to go away. When Mr. Allen refused to leave, Satchel kicked him. Mr. Allen grabbed Satchel's leg, started to twist it. Ms. Farrow testified that Mr. Allen said 'I'm going to break your fucking leg.' Ms. Farrow intervened and separated Mr. Allen from Satchel. Dylan told the Connecticut State Police about this incident.

That Mr. Allen now wants to spend more time with Satchel is commendable. If sincere, he should be encouraged to do so, but only under conditions that promote Satchel's well being.

E) *Moses Farrow*

Mr. Allen's interactions with Moses appear to have been superficial and more a response to Moses' desire for a father – in a family where Mr. Previn was the father of the other six children – than an authentic effort to develop a relationship with the child. When Moses asked, in 1984, if Mr. Allen would be his father, he said 'sure' but for years did nothing to make that a reality.

They spent time playing baseball, chess and fishing. Mr. Allen encouraged Moses to play the clarinet. There is no evidence, however, that Mr. Allen used any of their shared areas of interest as a foundation upon which to develop a deeper relationship with his son. What little he offered – a baseball catch, some games of chess, adoption papers – was enough to encourage Moses to dream of more, but insufficient to justify a claim for custody.

After learning of his father's affair with his sister, Moses handed to Mr. Allen a letter that he had written. It states:

... you can't force me to live with you.... You have done a horrible, unforgivable, needy, ugly, stupid thing ... about seeing me for lunch, you can just forget about that ... we didn't do anything wrong.... All you did is spoil the little ones, Dylan and Satchel.... Every one knows not to have an affair with your son's sister ... I don't consider you my father anymore. It was a great feeling having a father, but you smashed that feeling and dream with a single act. *I HOPE YOU ARE PROUD TO CRUSH YOUR SON'S DREAM.*

Mr. Allen responded to this letter by attempting to wrest custody of Moses from his mother. His rationale is that the letter was generated by Ms. Farrow. Moses told Dr. Brodzinsky that he wrote the letter and that he did not intend for it to be seen by his mother.

CUSTODY

Section 240(1) of the Domestic Relations Law states that in a custody dispute, the court must 'give such direction ... as ... justice requires, having regard to the circumstances of the case and of the respective parties and to the best interests of the child.'

The case law of this state has made clear that the governing consideration is the best interests of the child. *Eschbach v. Eschbach,* 56 NY2d 167 (1982); *Friederwitzer v. Friederwitzer,* 55 NY2d 89 (1982).

The initial custodial arrangement is critically important. 'Priority, not as an absolute but as a weighty factor, should, in the absence of extraordinary circumstances, be accorded to the first custody awarded in litigation or by voluntary agreement.' *Nehra v. Uhlar,* 43 NY2d 242, 251 (1977).

'[W]hen children have been living with one parent for a long period of time and the parties have previously agreed that custody shall remain in that parent, their agreement should prevail and custody should be continued unless it is demonstrated that the custodial parent is unfit or perhaps less fit (citations omitted).' *Martin v. Martin,* 74 AD2d 419, 426 (4th Dept 1980).

After considering Ms. Farrow's position as the sole caretaker of the children, the satisfactory fashion in which she has fulfilled that function, the parties' pre-litigation acceptance that she continue in that capacity, and Mr. Allen's serious parental inadequacies, it is clear that the best interests of the children will be served by their continued custody with Ms. Farrow.

VISITATION

Visitation, like custody, is governed by a consideration of the best interests of the child. *Miriam R. v. Arthur D.R.,* 85 AD2d 624 (2d Dept 1981). Absent proof to the contrary, the law presumes that visitation is in the child's best interests. *Wise v. Del Toro,* 122 AD2d 714 (1st Dept 1986). The denial of visitation to a non-custodial parent must be accompanied by compelling reasons and substantial evidence that visitation is detrimental to the child's welfare. *Matter of Farrugia Children,* 106 AD2d 293 (1st Dept 1984); *Gowan v. Menga,* 178 AD2d 1021 (4th Dept 1991). If the noncustodial parent is a fit person and there are no extraordinary circumstances, there should be reasonable visitation. *Hotze v. Hotze,* 57 AD2d 85 (4th Dept 1977), *appeal denied* 42 NY2d 805.

The overriding consideration is the child's welfare rather than any supposed right of the parent. *Weiss v. Weiss,* 52 NY2d 170, 174–5 (1981); *Hotze v. Hotze, supra* at 87. Visitation should be denied where it may be inimical to the child's welfare by producing serious emotional strain or disturbance. *Hotze v. Hotze, supra* at 88; *see also, Miriam R. v. Arthur D.R., supra; cf., State ex rel. H.K. v. M.S.,* 187 AD2d 50 (1st Dept 1993).

This trial included the observations and opinions of more mental health workers than is common to most custody litigation. The parties apparently agreed with Dr. Herman's conclusion that another battery of forensic psychological evaluations would not have been in the children's best interests and would have added little to the available information. Accordingly, none was ordered.

The common theme of the testimony by the mental health witnesses is that Mr. Allen has inflicted serious damage on the children and that healing is necessary. Because, as Dr. Brodzinsky and Dr. Herman observed, this family is in an uncharted therapeutic area, where the course is uncertain and the benefits unknown, the visitation structure that will best promote the healing process and safeguard the children is elusive. What is clear is that Mr. Allen's lack of judgment, insight and impulse control make normal noncustodial visitation with Dylan and

Satchel too risky to the children's well-being to be permitted at this time.

A) *Dylan*

Mr. Allen's request for immediate visitation with Dylan is denied. It is unclear whether Mr. Allen will ever develop the insight and judgment necessary for him to relate to Dylan appropriately. According to Dr. Brodzinsky, even if Dylan was not sexually abused, she feels victimized by her father's relationship with her sister. Dylan has recently begun treatment with a new therapist. Now that this trial is concluded, she is entitled to the time and space necessary to create a protective environment that will promote the therapeutic process. A significant goal of that therapy is to encourage her to fulfill her individual potential, including the resilience to deal with Mr. Allen in a manner which is not injurious to her.

The therapist witnesses agree that Mr. Allen may be able to serve a positive role in Dylan's therapy. Dr. Brodzinsky emphasized that because Dylan is quite fragile and more negatively affected by stress than the average child, she should visit with Mr. Allen only within a therapeutic context. This function, he said, should be undertaken by someone other than Dylan's treating therapist. Unless it interferes with Dylan's individual treatment or is inconsistent with her welfare, this process is to be initiated within six months. A further review of visitation will be considered only after we are able to evaluate the progress of Dylan's therapy.

B) *Satchel*

Mr. Allen's request for extended and unsupervised visitation with Satchel is denied. He has been visiting regularly with Satchel, under supervised conditions, with the consent of Ms. Farrow. I do not believe that Ms. Farrow has discouraged Satchel's visitation with Mr. Allen or that she has, except for restricting visitation, interfered with Satchel's relationship with his father.

Although, absent exceptional circumstances, a non-custodial parent should not be denied meaningful access to a child, 'supervised visitation is not a deprivation to meaningful access.' *Lightbourne v. Lightbourne*, 179 AD2d 562 (1st Dept 1992).

I do not condition visitation out of concern for Satchel's

physical safety. My caution is the product of Mr. Allen's demonstrated inability to understand the impact that his words and deeds have upon the emotional well being of his children.

I believe that Mr. Allen will use Satchel in an attempt to gain information about Dylan and to insinuate himself into her good graces. I believe that Mr. Allen will, if unsupervised, attempt to turn Satchel against the other members of his family. I believe Mr. Allen to be desirous of introducing Soon-Yi into the visitation arrangement without concern for the effect on Satchel, Soon-Yi or the other members of the Farrow family. In short, I believe Mr. Allen to be so self-absorbed, untrustworthy and insensitive, that he should not be permitted to see Satchel without appropriate professional supervision until Mr. Allen demonstrates that supervision is no longer necessary. The supervisor should be someone who is acceptable to both parents, who will be familiarized with the history of this family and who is willing to remain in that capacity for a reasonable period of time. Visitation shall be of two hours' duration, three times weekly, and modifiable by agreement of the parties.

C) *Moses*

Under the circumstances of this case, giving respect and credence to Ms. Farrow's appreciation of her son's sensitivity and intelligence, as confirmed by Dr. Brodzinsky, I will not require this fifteen-year-old child to visit with his father if he does not wish to do so.

If Moses can be helped by seeing Mr. Allen under conditions in which Moses will not be overwhelmed, then I believe that Ms. Farrow should and will promote such interaction. I hope that Moses will come to understand that the fear of demons often cannot be dispelled without first confronting them.

COUNSEL FEES

Ms. Farrow's application for counsel fees is granted. Mr. Allen compounded the pain that he inflicted upon the Farrow family by bringing this frivolous petition for custody of Dylan, Satchel and Moses.

Domestic Relations Law §237(b) provides that upon an application for custody or visitation, the court may direct a parent to pay the counsel fees of the other parent 'as, in the court's discretion, justice requires, having regard to the circumstances of the case and of the respective parties.'

Ms. Farrow admits to a substantial net worth, although she is not nearly as wealthy as Mr. Allen. Clearly, she is able to absorb the cost of this litigation, although it has been extraordinarily expensive. However, '[i]ndigency is not a prerequisite to an award of counsel fees (citation omitted). Rather, in exercising its discretionary power to award counsel fees, a court should review the financial circumstances of both parties together with all the other circumstances of the case, which may include the relative merit of the parties' positions.' *DeCabrera v. Cabrera-Rosete*, 70 NY2d 879, 881 (1987). Because Mr. Allen's position had no merit, he will bear the entire financial burden of this litigation. If the parties are unable to agree on Ms. Farrow's reasonable counsel fees, a hearing will be conducted for that purpose.

Settle judgment.

DATED: June 7, 1993.

J.S.C.

Source Notes

Prologue

1 Roger Ebert, *A Kiss is Still a Kiss*, Andrews, McMeel & Parker, 1984.
2. Mia Farrow, *Daily News* and *Daily Post*, 27 March 1993.
3 *People*, August 31, 1992.
4 *New York Daily News*, March 27, 1993.
5 *New York Newsday*, March 30, 1993.
6 *Time* magazine, August 31, 1992.
7 Vicky Tiel to author.

Mother Was Groucho Marx

1 Quoted, Stephen J. Spignesi, *The Woody Allen Companion*, Andrews and McMeel, 1992.
2 *New York Post*, 1963.
3 *Family Circle*, August 1974.
4 Myles Palmer, *Woody Allen: An Illustrated Biography*.
5 Graham McCann, *Woody Allen*, Polity Press, 1990.
6 *People*, October 4, 1976.
7 *New York Times* Magazine, April 22, 1979.
8 *Vanity Fair*, November 1992.
9 *New York Daily News*, March 18, 1967.
10 *Newsweek*, April 24, 1978.
11 *Moviegoer*, May 1985.
12 *Newsweek*, April 24, 1978.
13 McCalls, June 1969.
14 To Geoff Andrew, *Time Out*.
15 *Mademoiselle*, March 1986.
16 *Rolling Stone*, April 9, 1987.
17 Douglas Brode, *Woody Allen, His Films and Career*, Citadel Press, 1985.
18 *Daily News*, February 2, 1964.

19   *Rolling Stone*, April 9, 1987.
20   *Rolling Stone*, April 9, 1987.
21   *New York Daily News*, March 18, 1967.
22   *New York Daily News*, March 18, 1967.
23   Jack Victor to author.
24   *Esquire*, May 1977.

My Schoolmates Were Idiots

1   *New York Daily News*, December 14, 1987.
2   Mickey Rose to author.
3   *Esquire*, May 1977.
4   *Sunday Times* (London), October 25, 1992.
5   *New York Post*, 1963.
6   *Saturday Evening Post*, September 21, 1963.
7   Lyn Tornabene, *McCalls*, June 1969.
8   Eric Lax, *Woody Allen: A Biography*, Knopf, 1991.
9   Jack Victor to author.
10   *Newsweek*, April 24, 1978.
11   *Rolling Stone*, April 9, 1987.
12   *New York Daily News*, March 18, 1967.
13   *Newsweek*, April 24, 1978.
14   Ibid.
15   *Harpers Bazaar*, December 1971.
16   *New York Times*, October 3, 1976.
17   *Saturday Evening Post*, September 21, 1963.
18   Kathleen Carroll to author.
19   *Esquire*, May 1977.
20   Eric Lax, *Woody Allen: A Biography*, Knopf, 1991.

My Wife Was An Animal

1   Harvey Meltzer to author.
2   Eric Lax, *Woody Allen: A Biography*, Knopf, 1991.
3   Jack Victor to author.
4   *Rolling Stone*, April 9, 1987.
5   *New York Daily News*, March 18, 1967.
6   *Playboy*, May 1967.
7   *Newsweek*, August 22, 1964.
8   *Esquire*, April 1987.
9   *New York Daily News*, February 2, 1964.

Lucky I Ran Into You

1 Eric Lax, *Woody Allen: A Biography*, Knopf, 1991.
2 *ibid.*
3 *Premiere*, January 1992.
4 *ibid.*
5 Vicky Tiel to author.
6 Eric Lax, *Woody Allen: A Biography*, Knopf, 1991.
7 *Newsweek*, April 24, 1978.
8 Eric Lax, *Woody Allen: A Biography*, Knopf, 1991.
9 *Daily News*, March 18, 1967.
10 *Rolling Stone*, April 9, 1987.
11 *Esquire*, May 1977.
12 *New York Times*, July 11, 1971.
13 *New York* magazine, January 28, 1980.
14 *People*, October 24, 1976.

The Girl From Chippewa Falls

1 *Time*, September 26, 1977.
2 *New York Daily News*, December 17, 1987.
3 Quoted, Stephen J. Spignesis, *The Woody Allen Companion*, Andrews and McMeel, 1992.
4 Jonathan Moor, *Diane Keaton: The Story of the Real Annie Hall*, St Martin's Press, 1989.
5 *Sunday Times* (London), July 18, 1982.
6 Jonathan Moor, *Diane Keaton: The Story of the Real Annie Hall*, St Martin's Press, 1989.
7 *ibid.*
8 *ibid.*
9 *Time*, September 26, 1977.
10 *ibid.*
11 *ibid.*
12 Eric Lax, *Woody Allen: A Biography*, Knopf, 1991.
13 Quoted, Jonathan Moor, *Diane Keaton: The Story of the Real Annie Hall*, St Martin's Press, 1989.
14 *Look*, March 1969.
15 Jonathan Moor, *Diane Keaton: The Story of the Real Annie Hall*, St Martin's Press, 1989.
16 *Seventeen*, November 1975.
17 Jonathan Moor, *Diane Keaton: The Story of the Real Annie*

Hall, St Martin's Press, 1989.
18 Lee Guthrie, *Woody Allen: A Biography,* Drake, 1978.
19 *ibid.*
20 Jonathan Moor, *Diane Keaton: The Story of the Real Annie Hall,* St Martin's Press, 1989.
21 *G.Q.* September, 1992.
22 *Playboy*
23 *New York Times* magazine, April 22, 1979.
24 Ralph Rosenblum and Robert Karen, *When the Shooting Stops ... The Cutting Begins,* Da Capo, 1986.
25 Jonathan Moor, *Diane Keaton: The Story of the Real Annie Hall,* St Martin's Press, 1989.

I Miss Annie

1 *Redbook,* October 1976.
2 *ibid.*
3 *New York Times,* October 21, 1977.
4 *Esquire,* May 1977.
5 *Seventeen,* November 1975.
6 Ralph Rosenblum and Robert Karen, *When the Shooting Stops ... The Cutting Begins.* Da Capo, 1986.
7 *New York Post,* January 7, 1993.
8 *New York Times* Biographical Service, October 1980.
9 *ibid.*
10 Quoted, Jonathan Moor, *Diane Keaton: The Story of the Real Annie Hall* St Martin's Press, 1989.
11 *Newsweek,* April 24, 1978.
12 *ibid.*
13 *ibid.*
14 *ibid.*
15 *ibid.*
16 *New York* magazine, April 5, 1993.
17 *ibid.*
18 *Premiere,* January 1992.
19 Ralph Rosenblum and Robert Karen, *When the Shooting Stops ... The Cutting Begins,* Da Capo, 1986.
20 *Esquire,* May 1977.
21 Quoted, Douglas Brode, *Woody Allen, His Films and Career,* Citadel Press, 1985.
22 *Rolling Stone,* April 9, 1987.

23 *New York Post.*
24 *The Globe,* January 26, 1993.

Mother Mia

1 Edward Z Epstein and Joe Morella, *Mia: The Life of Mia Farrow,* Dell Publishing, 1992.
2 *ibid.*
3 *ibid.*
4 Eric Lax, *Woody Allen: A Biography,* Knopf, 1991.
5 *People* magazine, December 17, 1979.
6 *The Andy Warhol Diaries,* edited by Pat Hackett, Warner Books, 1989.
7 Sam Rubin and Richard Taylor, *Mia Farrow: Flowerchild. Madonna. Muse.,* St Martin's Press, 1989.
8 Edward Z. Epstein and Joe Morella, *Mia: The Life of Mia Farrow,* Dell Publishing, 1992.
9 *ibid.*
10 *ibid.*
11 *ibid.*
12 *ibid.*
13 *Parade,* February 9, 1986.
14 Edward Z Epstein and Joe Morella, *Mia: The Life of Mia Farrow,* Dell Publishing, 1992.
15 Kitty Kelley, *His Way: The Unauthorised Biography of Frank Sinatra,* Bantam, 1986.
16 *Parade,* February 9, 1986.
17 Kitty Kelley, *His Way: The Unauthorised Biography of Frank Sinatra,* Bantam, 1986.
18 *ibid.*
19 Sam Rubin and Richard Taylor, *Mia Farrow: Flowerchild. Madonna. Muse.,* St Martin's Press, 1989.
20 Kitty Kelley, *His Way: The Unauthorised Biography of Frank Sinatra,* Bantam, 1986.
21 *ibid.*
22 *ibid.*
23 *Vanity Fair,* November 1992.
24 Edward Z. Epstein and Joe Morella, *Mia: The Life of Mia Farrow,* Dell Publishing, 1992.
25 Roman Polanski, *Roman, by Polanski,* Willam Morrow & Co, 1984.

26 Melvyn Bragg, *Richard Burton: A Life*, Little, Brown and Company, 1988.
27 Vicky Tiel to author.
28 *Life*, May 6, 1967.
29 Roman Polanski, *Roman, by Polanski*, William Morrow & Co, 1984.
30 Edward Z Epstein and Joe Morella, *Mia: The Life of Mia Farrow*, Dell Publishing, 1992.
31 *ibid.*
32 *American Film*, March 1987.
33 Edward Z. Epstein and Joe Morella, *Mia: The Life of Mia Farrow*, Dell Publishing, 1992.
34 *ibid.*
35 *Time*, August 1992.
36 Edward Z Epstein and Joe Morella, *Mia: The Life of Mia Farrow*, Dell Publishing, 1992.
37 *New York Daily News*, December 3, 1978.
38 Heather Hale to author.
39 Sam Rubin and Richard Taylor, *Mia Farrow: Flowerchild. Madonna. Muse.*, St Martin's Press, 1989.
40 *People*, December 17, 1979.
41 Eric Lax, *Woody Allen: A Biography*, Knopf, 1991.
42 *New York* magazine, March 25, 1991.
43 *New York Times* Biographical Service, October 1980.
44 *American Film*, March 1987.
45 *New York Times* (newsclip-date?)
46 Eric Lax, *Woody Allen: A Biography*, Knopf, 1991.
47 *New York Times*, January 1986.
48 *American Film*, March 1987.
49 Eric Lax, *Woody Allen: A Biography*, Knopf, 1991.
50 *New York Times* Biographical Service, January 1986.
51 Reported Douglas Brode, *Woody Allen, His Films and Career*, Citadel Press, 1985.
52 *ibid.*
53 Eric Lax, *Woody Allen: A Biography*, Knopf, 1991.
54 Charlotte Chandler, *Hello, I Must Be Going: Groucho and His Friends*, Citadel Press, 1992.
55 *TV Guide*, April 11, 1981.
56 *Rolling Stone*, April 9, 1987.
57 *ibid.*
58 Sam Rubin and Richard Taylor, *Mia Farrow: Flowerchild.*

Madonna. Muse., St Martin's Press, 1989.
59 Quoted, Douglas Brode, *Woody Allen, His Films and Career,*
Citadel Press, 1985.
60 Harvey Meltzer to author
61 *American Film*, March 1987.
62 *ibid.*
63 *New York Times* (news clip date)
64 State Supreme Court Acting Justice Elliott Wilk. Judgement
June 7, 1993 (Findings of Fact, p 3/4).

Manhattan Movie Maestro

1 *Playboy*, May 1967.
2 State Supreme Court Acting Justice Elliott Wilk. Judgement
June 7, 1993 (Findings of Fact p. 4).
3 *New York* magazine, September 21, 1992.
4 Eric Lax, *Woody Allen: A Biography*, Knopf, 1991.
5 *Star* magazine, December 8, 1992.
6 *New York Post*, March 26, 1993.
7 *American Film*, March 1987.
8 Edward Z Epstein and Joe Morella, *Mia: The Life of Mia
Farrow*, Dell Publishing, 1992.
9 *American Film*, March 1987.
10 State Supreme Court Acting Justice Elliott Wilk. Judgement
June 7, 1993 (Findings of Fact p 4)
11 AP Wire Services, May 15, 1987
12 Eric Lax, *Woody Allen: A Biography*, Knopf, 1991.
13 To Harry Reasoner of CBS's *60 Minutes.*
14 State Supreme Court Acting Justice Elliott Wilk. Judgement
June 7 1993 (Findings of Fact p 4/5).
15 *New York Post*, March 23, 1993.
16 *Time*, August 31, 1992.
17 *New York* magazine, September 2, 1992.
18 *Vanity Fair*, November 1992.
19 *People*, August 31, 1992.
20 *Vanity Fair*, November 1992.
21 Heather Hale to author
22 *Vanity Fair*, November 1992.
23 *People*, August 31, 1992.
24 Sam Rubin and Richard Taylor, *Mia Farrow: Flowerchild.
Madonna. Muse.*, St Martin's Press, 1989.

25 *Look* magazine, August 26, 1969.
26 Quoted, Douglas Brode, *Woody Allen, His Films and Career*, Citadel Press, 1985.
27 *ibid.*
28 State Supreme Court Acting Justice Elliott Wilk. Judgement June 7 1993 (Findings of Fact, p 5)
28 *New York Post*, August 18, 1992.
29 *Daily News Magazine*, October 15, 1989.
30 Quoted, Douglas Brode, *Woody Allen, His Films and Career*, Citadel Press, 1985.
31 State Supreme Court Acting Justice Elliott Wilk. Judgement June 7 1993 (Findings of Fact p 5/6)
32 Sam Rubin and Richard Taylor, *Mia Farrow: Flowerchild. Madonna. Muse.*, St Martin's Press, 1989.
33 *Vanity Fair*, November 1992.
34 *ibid.*
35 *Time*, August 31, 1992.
36 State Supreme Court Acting Justice Wilk. Judgement June 7 1993 (Findings of Fact p 7)
37 *Time*, August 31, 1992.
38 *ibid.*
39 State Supreme Court Acting Justice Elliott Wilk. Judgement June 7, 1993 (Findings of Fact p 18/19)
40 *Vanity Fair*, November 1992.
41 *ibid.*
42 *ibid.*
43 *New York Post*, March 25, 1993.
44 *Vanity Fair*, November 1992.
45 Eric Lax, *Woody Allen: A Biography*, Knopf, 1991.
46 To author
47 *Vanity Fair*, November 1992.
48 *Vanity Fair*, November 1992.
49 State Supreme Court Acting Justice Elliott Wilk. Judgement June 10 1993 (Findings of Fact p 8/9)

Scenes From A Marriage

1 *Time* August 31, 1992.
2 *Newsweek* August 31, 1992.
3 *New York Post* December 17, 1992.
4 Court Testimony, March 26, 1993.

5 *Sunday Times* (London) June 6, 1993.
6 WNBC/Channel 4, New York.
7 Court testimony, April 9, 1993.
8 *New York Post* December 9, 1992
9 *New York Daily News*
10 *Sunday Times* (London) 28 March 1993.
11 CBS '60 Minutes', November 22, 1992.
12 Court testimony, March 26, 1993.
13 *New York Post,* November 23, 1992.
14 *New York Post,* November 24, 1992.
15 *New York Post,* November 10, 1992.
16 *New York Newsday,* August, 1992.
17 *Sunday Times* (London) June 6, 1993.
18 *New York Daily News,* March 27, 1993.
19 Court testimony, March 25 and March 26, *New York Daily News,* March 27, 1993.
20 Court testimony, March 25, 1993.
21 *New York Post,* March 25, 1993.
22 Court testimony, March 26, 1993.
23 Court testimony, March 23, 1993.
24 Court testimony, March 23, 1993.
25 Court testimony, March 23, 1993.
26 Court testimony, March 23, 1993.
27 Court testimony, March 23, 1993.
28 Court testimony, March 29, 1993.
29 Court testimony, March 26, 1993.
30 Court testimony, April 2, 1993.
31 *People,* August 31, 1993.
32 *Newsweek,* August 31, 1992.
33 *Newsweek,* August 31, 1992.
34 CBS '60 Minutes', November 22, 1993.
35 *New York Post,* December 4, 1992.
36 *New York Post,* December 4, 1992.
37 *New York Daily News,* March 25, 1993.
38 *New York Newsday,* April 3, 1993.
39 *New York Post,* March 25, 1993.
40 State Supreme Court, Acting Judge Wilk, Judgement, June 7, 1993.
41 Court testimony, March 23, 1993.
42 *Movieline,* March, 1991.

Epilogue

1   To Denis Hamill, *Hello* magazine.
2   *London Evening Standard.*
3   Author's notes.
4   Kristie Groteke with Marjorie Rosen, *Woody and Mia: The Nanny's Tale,* Hodder & Stoughton.
5   *Ibid.*
6   *Daily Express* (London), August 13, 1993.
7   *Independent on Sunday* (London), January 9, 1994.
8   *Ibid.*
9   *Ibid.*
10   Kristie Groteke with Marjorie Rosen, *Woody and Mia: The Nanny's Tale,* Hodder & Stoughton.
11   *New York Times.*
12   *Business Week,* August 23, 1993.
13   *Ibid.*
14   *Guardian* Weekend (London), September 25, 1993.
15   *Rolling Stone,* September 16, 1993.
16   Author's notes.
17   *Rolling Stone,* September 16, 1993.
18   *Ibid.*
19   *Ibid.*
20   *Ibid.*
21   *New York Post,* October 1, 1993.
22   *New York Post,* October 15, 1993.
23   To Ciaran Carty, *Wales on Sunday.*
24   *Sunday Times* (London) magazine, April 24, 1994.
25   *Ibid.*
26   *Ibid.*
27   *Ibid.*
28   *Independent on Sunday* (London), January 9, 1994.
29   To Denis Hamill, *Hello* magazine.

Bibliography

Books

The Andy Warhol Diaries, edited by Pat Hackett, Warner Books, 1989.

Charlie Chaplin, by John McCabe, Robson Books, London, 1992.

Diane Keaton: The Story of the REal Life Annie Hall, by Jonathan Moor, St Martin's Press, New York, 1989.

Everything You Always Wanted to Know About Woody Allen, by Frank Weimann, Shapolsky Publishers, Inc., New York, 1991.

Four Films of Woody Allen, by Woody Allen, Random House, New York, 1989.

Hannah and Her Sisters, by Woody Allen, Random House, New York, 1987.

Hello, I Must Be Going: Groucho and His Friends, by Charlotte Chandler, Citadel Press, (Carol Publishing, Secaucus, New Jersey), 1992.

His Way: The Unauthorised Biography of Frank Sinatra, by Kitty Kelley, Bantam Books, New York, 1986.

Loser Take All, The Comic Act of Woody Allen, by Maurice Yacowar, Frederick Ungar, New York, 1979.

Love, Sex, Death & the Meaning of Life: The Films of Woody Allen, by Foster Hirsch, Limelight Editions, New York, 1990.

Mia Farrow: Flowerchild. Madonna. Muse., by Sam Rubin and Richard Taylor, St Martin's Press, New York, 1989.

Mia: The Life of Mia Farrow, by Edward Z Epstein and Joe Morella, Dell Publishing, New York 1991.

Richard Burton: A Life, by Melvyn Bragg, Little, Brown and Company, USA, 1988.

Roman, by Polanski, by Roman Polanski, William Morrow and Company Inc., New York, 1984.

Three Films by Woody Allen, by Woody Allen, Random House, 1987.

Warren Beatty and Desert Eyes, by David Thomson, Doubleday, New York, 1987.

Without Feathers. Getting Even. Side Effects, by Woody Allen, QPB, 1989.

When the Shooting Stops … the Cutting Begins, by Ralph Rosenblum and Robert Karen, Da Capo Press Inc., New York.

Woody Allen, by Nancy Pogel, Twayne Publishers, Boston, 1988.

Woody Allen, A Biography, by Lee Guthrie, Drake, New York, 1978.

Woody Allen, A Biography, by Eric Lax, Alfred A. Knopf, New York, 1991.

Woody Allen, An Illustrated Biography, by Myles Palmer, Proteus Books, New York, 1980.

The Woody Allen Companion, by Stephen J Spignesi, Andrews and McMeel, 1992.

Woody Allen, His Films and Career, by Douglas Brode, Citadel Press, 1987.

Woody Allen: New Yorker, by Graham McCann, Polity Press, New York, 1990.

Woody Allen on Location, by Thierry de Navacelle, William Morrow & Co., 1987.

Newspaper and magazine stories

'Analyzing Husbands and Wives', by Ron Rosenbaum, Mademoiselle, December 1992.

'Auteur! Auteur!' by Caryn James, New York Times Biographical Service, January 1986.

'The Conflicting Life and Art of Woody Allen', by Tony Schwartz, New York Times Biographical Service, October 19, 1980.

'The Debacle of the Year: What Went Wrong With Saturday Night Live? Everything', by Sally Bedell, TV Guide, April 11, 1981.

'Diane Keaton: From Woody to Warren', by Suzanne Munshower, Cue New York, August 17, 1979.

'Diane Keaton Grapples With Sex and Maternity', by Leslie Bennetts, New York Times, June 26, 1988.

'Erotic Neurotic Women', by Ron Rosenbaum, Mademoiselle, March 1986.

'Everything you always wanted to know about … Sex & Woody', by Jami Bernard, New York Post, August 18, 1992.

'Everything You Always Wanted to Know About Woody and Mia (But Were Afraid to Ask)', by Phoebe Hoban, New York magazine, September 21, 1992.

'A Family Affair', People magazine, August 31, 1992.

'Funny Things Happen to Louise Lasser', by Lewis Grossberger, New York magazine, January 28, 1980.

'Hide-and-Seek With Diane Keaton', by Dominick Dunne, Vanity Fair, February 1985.

'How Bogart Made Me the Great Lover I Am', by Woody Allen, Playboy

'Inside Diane Keaton', Vanity Fair, March 1987.

'Is Woody Strictly Kosher?', by Andrew Sarris, Village Voice, February 10, 1987.

'Louise Lasser Is the Best Thing About Mary Hartman', by S.J. Diamond, Village Voice, January 19, 1976.

'Louise Lasser! Louise Lasser!', by John M Wilson.

'The Making of Annie Hall', by Ralph Rosenblum and Robert Karen, *New York* magazine, October 8, 1979.

'Manhattan's Methuselah', by Richard Zoglin.

'Mia', by Mel Gussow.

'Mia', by Glenn Plaskin, *Daily News* Magazine, October 15, 1989.

'Mia Farrow', *People* magazine, December 17, 1979.

'Mia Farrow is a Trip', by Daniel Chapman, *Look*, August 26, 1969.

'Mia's Story: The Case Against Woody Allen', by Maureen Orth, *Vanity Fair*, November 1992.

'Much Ado About Mia', Georgia A. Brown, *American Film*, March 1987.

'New Lolita Shocker in Woody Allen Child Sex Scandal', *The Globe*, January 26, 1993.

'The Night Woody Allen Turned Me On', by Judith Viorst, *Redbook*, October 1976.

'Scenes from a Breakup', Time, August 31, 1992.

'Thoroughly Modern Diane', *Newsweek*, February 15, 1982.

'Unhappily Ever After', *Newsweek*, August 31, 1992.

'Unnatural actresses', by Ron Rosenbaum.

'Walking with Woody Allen', by Lyn Tornabene, *McCall's*, 1969.

'Why Is Woody Allen Laughing', *Esquire*, July.

'Woody, by Jack Kroll', by Jack Kroll, *Newsweek*, April 24, 1978.

'Woody & Mia: "Happily Involved"', by Barbara Lovenheim, *McCall's*, May 1985.

'Woody & Mia', by Eric Lax, *New York Times* Magazine, February 24, 1991.

'Woody: The First Fifty Years', by Tom Shales, *Esquire*, April 1987.

'Woody Agonistes, or I Can't Fight the Philistines Without My Glasses', James Wolcott, *Village Voice*, June 23, 1975.

'The Woodygate Papers', by David Blum, *New York* magazine, March 25, 1991.

'Woody Allen', by William E Geist, *Rolling Stone*, April 9, 1987.

'Woody Allen's Bed of Neuroses', by John Reddy, *Reader's Digest*, July 1967.

'Woody Allen Counts the Wages of Sin', *New York Times*, October 15, 1989.

'Woody Allen: The Power of an Imperfectionist', *Harpers Bazzar*, 1971.

'Woody Allen: Schlemiel as Sex Mania', by Ross Wetzsteon, *Ms*, November 1977.

'Woody Allen: Survival of the Fittest', by Nora Ephron, *New York Daily News*, March 18, 1967.

'Woody Allen Wipes the Smile off His Face', by Frank Rich, *Esquire*, May 1977. .

'Woody's Girls: The Director Who Loves Women', by Harry Haun, *New York Daily News*, December 14–18, 1987.

Index

MICHAEL DOUGLAS

A Biography

Alan Lawson

Michael Douglas was born to be a successful film actor. The eldest son of Hollywood legend Kirk Douglas, Michael nevertheless had to earn his fame. Some of his early films are eminently forgettable, but the young Douglas persevered and learnt his craft. After four years on TV's *The Streets of San Francisco*, films like *Romancing the Stone, Fatal Attraction, Wall Street* and *Basic Instinct* established him as a major star.

Actor, producer, businessman, husband and father, Michael Douglas has not only stepped out from his father's shadow, he has surpassed him. Looking at his family life and legendary work, this revealing biography is a must for all Michael Douglas fans.

SPIKE LEE

Alex Patterson

Actor, writer and director, Spike Lee is the most influential black film maker around today. His sharp and intelligent movies have explored black issues in a new way and at the same time rubbed at some of the exposed raw nerves apparent in American white mainstream society.

The controversial *She's Gotta Have It* – with an all black cast – broke new ground in the cinema, winning wide critical acclaim, while for *Do the Right Thing* Lee was compared to Martin Scorsese. With his new film *Malcolm X* further argument and debate has been triggered.

This revealing book shines a spotlight on the innovative and popular film director, revealing the man in his context – exploring his private life and background – and examining the motivation and ideas behind his films.

[ ] MICHAEL DOUGLAS by Alan Lawson	£4.99
[ ] SPIKE LEE by Alex Patterson	£5.99
[ ] DEATH IN HOLLYWOOD by Peter Underwood	£5.99
[ ] JACK NICHOLSON by Donald Shepherd	£4.99
[ ] CHER by Lawrence J Quirk	£5.99
[ ] MARILYN'S MEN by Jane Ellen Wayne	£5.99
[ ] KEVIN COSTNER by Adrian Wright	£4.99

Warner Books now offers an exciting range of quality titles by both established and new authors which can be ordered from the following address:

Little, Brown and Company (UK),
P.O. Box 11,
Falmouth,
Cornwall TR10 9EN.

Alternatively you may fax your order to the above address. Fax No. 0326 376423.

Payments can be made as follows: cheque, postal order (payable to Little, Brown and Company) or by credit cards, Visa/Access. Do not send cash or currency. UK customers and B.F.P.O. please allow £1.00 for postage and packing for the first book, plus 50p for the second book, plus 30p for each additional book up to a maximum charge of £3.00 (7 books plus).

Overseas customers including Ireland please allow £2.00 for the first book plus £1.00 for the second book, plus 50p for each additional book.

NAME (Block Letters)

....

ADDRESS

....

....

☐ I enclose my remittance for _____

☐ I wish to pay by Access/Visa Card

Number

Card Expiry Date